UNDUE INFLUENCE AND THE FAMILY HOME

Mark Pawlowski, LLB (Hons), BCL (Oxon)
Barrister
Professor of Property Law,
Department of Law,
University of Greenwich

James Brown, LLB (Hons)
Barrister
Lecturer in Law,
Department of Law,
London Guildhall University

Cavendish
Publishing
Limited

London • Sydney

First published in Great Britain 2002 by Cavendish Publishing Limited,
The Glass House, Wharton Street, London WC1X 9PX, United Kingdom
Telephone: +44 (0)20 7278 8000   Facsimile: +44 (0)20 7278 8080
Email: info@cavendishpublishing.com
Website: www.cavendishpublishing.com

British Library Cataloguing in Publication Data

Pawlowski, Mark
Undue influence and the family home
1 Domestic relations – England 2 Undue influence – England
3 Domestic relations – Wales 4 Undue influence – Wales
I Title II Brown, James
346.4'2'015

ISBN 1 85941 720 5

Printed and bound in Great Britain

For my daughter Asia, with love
Mark

For my father Patrick, with love
James

FOREWORD

It is not surprising that the topic with which this book is concerned, undue influence and the family home, has thrown up such a plethora of cases and problems, particularly in the last few years. Much of the law of property is based on concepts and principles which go back often more than 200 years, and sometimes much further than that. On the other hand, the pace of social change has been such that familial and quasi-familial relationships are perceived and treated very differently now from how they were even 30 or 40 years ago.

However, the topic of this book is not, as it were, limited to property law and family relationships; as the title shows, it also extends to undue influence, which brings in an equitable concept which is particularly difficult to define. Furthermore, because most of the problems in the field covered by this book arise out of claims brought by third parties, notably, of course, lending institutions, there is a fourth aspect, which brings in commercial law.

A particularly striking aspect of this book is the high proportion of recent court decisions listed in the Table of Cases. I think that that illustrates as well as anything the topicality, indeed the difficulty, of the subject matter of this book. Mark Pawlowski and James Brown are to be congratulated for having produced a book on this subject, particularly a book as comprehensive and user-friendly as this volume. Not only have they considered the effect of the authorities in a clear and logical way, but they have also highlighted problems which have yet to be resolved and questions which have yet to be answered, which, to me at any rate, is one of the hallmarks of a good legal book.

The book is particularly helpful to practitioners, and in that context I applaud the inclusion of the selection of forms in the Appendix.

The Honourable Mr Justice Neuberger
Royal Courts of Justice
The Strand
London WC2A

PREFACE

This book is intended to provide the reader with a detailed exposition of the modern law of undue influence as it applies to residential mortgage transactions. It is aimed predominantly at the legal practitioner, but it is hoped it will also provide a useful source of reference for both students and academics.

Undoubtedly, this is a highly complex and technical area of law which has developed considerably over the last decade. Apart from the landmark cases of *Barclays Bank plc v O'Brien* [1993] 4 All ER 417 (HL), *CIBC Mortgages plc v Pitt* [1993] 4 All ER 433 (HL) and *Royal Bank of Scotland plc v Etridge (No 2)* [1998] 4 All ER 705 (CA), there has been a deluge of Court of Appeal cases (both reported and unreported) on the question of whether a lender will be prevented from enforcing a transaction against a person who entered into it as a result of the undue influence or misrepresentation of another. Most recently, the House of Lords in *Royal Bank of Scotland v Etridge (No 2)* [2001] UKHL 44 has sought to give authoritative guidance for both lenders and solicitors advising wives who may be at risk of being pressurised by their husbands into charging their interest in the family home as security for their partners' debts. Most of the cases have involved surety wives, but it is apparent that the governing principles are equally applicable to other non-commercial relationships (for example, cohabitees, family members, employers and employees).

The layout of the chapters reflects the four-stage process in determining whether or not a successful claim of undue influence/misrepresentation is made out (typically by a wife) against a lender under the current law. First, the wife must establish an equity to have the transaction set aside against her wrongdoing husband. This involves an examination of the two categories of undue influence – actual and presumed. In the majority of cases, the claim is based on an allegation of presumed undue influence. Both categories are discussed fully in Chapter 2. In the presumed category, a further requirement is that the transaction be manifestly disadvantageous to the wife. The meaning of this requirement and whether it should be retained as a pre-condition for relief is considered in Chapter 3. The second stage of the process involves an examination of whether or not the lender has been put on inquiry as to the wife's equity. This involves showing either that the borrower acted as the lender's agent (unlikely in most cases) or that the lender had actual or constructive notice of the wife's equity. If the lender is put on inquiry, the third stage necessitates an examination of whether the lender took reasonable steps to avoid the equity. Both these aspects are examined in Chapter 4. In most cases, the lender will be exonerated if it urges the wife to seek independent legal advice and receives confirmation that this was done. The role of the solicitor, in this context, is considered in Chapter 5. The final stage requires an examination of what remedies are available to the wife assuming that her claim against the lender is made out. The subject of remedies is explored in Chapter 6.

It has also been confirmed recently that a lender may have the means to successfully circumvent the wife's *O'Brien* defence and force a sale of the family home notwithstanding her equity arising from her husband's wrongdoing: *Alliance & Leicester plc v Slayford* [2000] EGCS 113 (CA). Chapter 7 focuses on this approach and considers the practical implications of the Court of Appeal ruling.

Apart from undue influence and misrepresentation, there is also some indication in the English case law (notably, *Credit Lyonnais Bank Nederland NV v Burch* [1997] 1 All ER 144 (CA)) that the doctrine of unconscionable dealings may be used to set aside a loan transaction which is particularly harsh and severe. This has prompted some commentators to argue for an assimilation of the related doctrines of undue influence, duress and unconscionable dealings under one common umbrella of unconscionability. Such has been the trend of the Commonwealth authorities, particularly in Canada, Australia and New Zealand. These developments and the broader question as to whether a similar approach should be adopted in this country is explored in Chapter 8. The conclusion is that such an assimilation would do much to rationalise and simplify the current law. Indeed, we propose that this whole area should become the subject of general review by the Law Commission with a view to producing a coherent statutory code replacing the existing case law.

In order to keep the book predominantly practitioner-orientated, we have consciously omitted any significant reference to the theories of restitution scholars who have suggested various alternative approaches to the now well established *O'Brien* defence based on a (strict) personal restitutionary claim subject to a defence of change of position. We therefore refer the reader elsewhere for authoritative expositions of the restitution school of thought: see, for example, Birks, P, 'The burden on the bank', Chapter 11, in *Restitution and Banking Law* (edited by Francis D Rose, 1998); O'Dell, E, 'Restitution, coercion by a third party and the proper doctrine of notice' [1997] 56 CLJ 71; and Mee, J, 'An alternative approach to third-party undue influence and misrepresentation' (1995) NILQ 46/2 147.

We would like to take this opportunity to thank our publishers, Cavendish Publishing, for their diligent efforts in bringing the manuscript to print so quickly.

We have endeavoured to state the law accurately as at 31 March 2002.

Mark Pawlowski
James Brown

CONTENTS

TABLE OF CASES

TABLE OF STATUTES

TABLE OF STATUTORY INSTRUMENTS AND OTHER LEGISLATION

TABLE OF ABBREVIATIONS

All ER . . . . All England Reports
BCLC . . . . Butterworths Company Law Cases
CLJ . . . . Cambridge Law Journal
Conv . . . . Conveyancer and Property Lawyer
EGCS . . . . Estates Gazette Case Summaries
FCR . . . . Family Court Reporter
FLR . . . . Family Law Reports
HKLJ . . . . Hong Kong Law Journal
JBL . . . . Journal of Business Law
LMCLQ . . . . Lloyd's Maritime Commercial Law Quarterly
LQR . . . . Law Quarterly Review
LS . . . . Legal Studies
MLR . . . . Modern Law Review
NILQ . . . . Northern Ireland Law Quarterly
NLJ . . . . New Law Journal
NPC . . . . New Property Cases
NZLR . . . . New Zealand Law Reports
OJLS . . . . Oxford Journal of Legal Studies
P & CR . . . . Property and Compensation Reports
RLR . . . . Restitution Law Review
SJ . . . . Solicitors Journal
VUWLR . . . . Victoria University of Wellington Law Review
WLR . . . . Weekly Law Reports

CHAPTER 1

OVERVIEW OF SUBJECT

1.1 NATURE OF THE PROBLEM

A lending institution is approached by an applicant (often a husband) who is seeking a loan/further advance (or overdraft facility) to assist in his business ventures. It is envisaged that the loan will be secured against the applicant's family home, which is co-owned by the applicant and his wife. The home has sufficient equity for the purposes of the loan and the applicant's wife seems agreeable to allow the home to be secured in this way. Despite the further loan, the husband's business does not prosper and the husband is unable to meet the mortgage repayments so the lender brings proceedings to enforce the charge and realise its security. The wife defends the lender's claim to possession of the home on the ground that the transaction was entered into by her as a result of her husband's undue influence and/or misrepresentation. In some cases, the family home will be owned by the husband alone and the wife will have an equitable interest in it which she has agreed to postpone in favour of the bank or building society. Alternatively, the wife may be asked to act as surety for her husband's debts with a charge being placed on her interest in the home to secure her guarantee.

What must the wife prove in order to have the charge set aside as against her husband? In what circumstances will the lender be affected by the husband's wrongdoing so that it will be prevented by the courts from enforcing the charge as against the wife? As we shall see, the wife has to succeed at *four* distinct stages in order to avoid liability under the guarantee or charge. First, she must establish a case of undue influence or other equitable wrong (for example, misrepresentation or duress) against her husband. Secondly, she must show that the lender is fixed with liability for this wrong either on the basis of agency (which is now likely to be rare) or actual or constructive notice on the basis that the lender was put on inquiry. Thirdly, the lender may avoid liability if it can show that it took reasonable steps to avoid the wife's equity. Thus, the inadequacy of steps taken to inform the wife forms the third stage of establishing a successful case. Finally, there is the question of what relief should be granted to the wife: see, generally, Fehlberg, B, 'The husband, the bank, the wife and her signature – the sequel' (1996) 59 MLR 675, p 677.

As was indicated by Lord Browne-Wilkinson in the landmark case of *Barclays Bank plc v O'Brien* [1993] 4 All ER 417 (HL), a high proportion of privately owned wealth is now invested in the family home, which may be owned jointly by both spouses. If either spouse therefore wishes to raise finance for some business venture, the home is the obvious source of security for any advance from the lender. In many marriages, it will be the husband who has the business experience and the wife will simply accede to her husband's wishes in relation to their financial affairs without adopting a genuinely independent mind to her decisions. The law therefore seeks to give protection to wives in these circumstances by requiring that the transaction entered into by the wife is the free exercise of her will after full and informed thought. On the other hand, the law must strike a balance and cannot ignore an equally important public interest, namely, 'the need to ensure that the wealth currently tied up in the matrimonial home does not become economically sterile'. To this end, therefore, it is important that 'a law designed to protect the vulnerable does not render the matrimonial home unacceptable as a security to financial institutions': *Barclays Bank plc v O'Brien*, p 422. As we shall see, the law on undue influence seeks to strike a fair balance between these two competing objectives. Indeed, this has been echoed recently by the House of Lords in *Royal Bank of Scotland v Etridge (No 2)* [2001] UKHL 44, where Lord Nicholls said (para 35):

> If the freedom of home-owners to make economic use of their homes is not to be frustrated, a bank must be able to have confidence that a wife's signature of the necessary guarantee and charge will be as binding upon her as is the signature of anyone else on documents which he or she may sign. Otherwise banks will not be willing to lend money on the security of a jointly owned house or flat.

In *National Westminster Bank plc v Morgan* [1985] AC 686 (HL) (p 709), Lord Scarman warned that: 'there is no precisely defined law setting limits to the equitable jurisdiction of a court to relieve against undue influence ... this is the world of doctrine, not of neat and tidy rules.' This warning was given in 1985 when the precise scope of equity's intervention in the specific context of residential mortgage transactions had not yet been fully worked out by the courts. Today, there is a mass of case law (both reported and unreported) involving claims of undue influence predominantly by a wife against her husband seeking to set aside a charge over the matrimonial home made in favour of a bank or building society. In particular, there have been numerous cases which have sought to provide guidelines as to how banks and other lending institutions are to treat, *inter alia*, wives (or husbands) who stand as surety for their partner's debts culminating, most recently, in the House of Lords decision in *Etridge (No 2)* (involving eight conjoined appeals). Undue influence, however, remains a 'flexible concept' and not one of rigid definition: *Turner v Barclays Bank plc* [1997] 2 FCR 151, p 160, *per* Neuberger J.

The principles are not, of course, limited to transactions involving wives or husbands but extend to other cases where there is an emotional relationship between the parties, for example, cohabitees, personal friends, family members and relationships between employer and employee. Indeed, most recently, in the House of Lords in *Etridge (No 2)*, Lord Nicholls confirmed that the *O'Brien* decision is not confined to sexual relationships. Logically, there was no cut-off point for the application of the *O'Brien* principle and so, according to Lord Nicholls (with whom the other Law Lords agreed), 'the only practical way forward is to regard banks as "put on inquiry" in every case where the relationship between surety and the debtor is non-commercial': *Royal Bank of Scotland v Etridge (No 2)*, para 87. So far as commercial relationships are concerned, however, his Lordship was of the view that those engaged in business 'can be regarded as capable of looking after themselves and understanding the risks involved in the giving of guarantees': para 88, and see, also, *Woodchester Equipment Leasing Co Ltd v Capital Belts Ltd* (1995) unreported, 12 April, available on Lexis. The underlying concept in all these cases is the potential risk of one party exploiting the emotional involvement or trust of the other. Where, therefore, the lending institution is aware that one party (the surety) reposes trust and confidence in the other party (the mortgagor) in relation to his (or her) financial affairs, the lender (mortgagee) will be put on inquiry and must take reasonable steps to ensure that the surety gave her (or his) free informed consent to the transaction. Otherwise, the transaction may be liable to be set aside at the option of the surety.

In some cases, this will mean that the lender will be unable to enforce the charge as a secured creditor by claiming possession of the property as against the surety if the mortgagor defaults. However, the lender may still elect to sue the mortgagor on his (or her) personal covenant (to repay the mortgage debt) and obtain a money judgment, thereby abandoning its security and acting as an unsecured creditor in any future bankruptcy proceedings. This, in turn, may lead to the bankruptcy of the mortgagor and the eventual sale of the property by the trustee in bankruptcy. How this affects the position of the surety (say, a wife who has assisted in her husband's business ventures) has been discussed recently by the Court of Appeal in *Alliance & Leicester plc v Slayford* [2000] EGCS 13: see, further, Chapter 7.

This book, therefore, seeks to provide the reader with a comprehensive survey of the law relating to undue influence in the specific context of residential mortgage transactions. The various categories of undue influence are considered in Chapter 2. The requirement of manifest disadvantage, a key concept in the presumed undue influence category, is discussed fully in Chapter 3. Chapters 4 and 5 deal with the roles of lender and solicitor, respectively. The subject of remedies is considered in Chapter 6. The question whether the lender can successfully circumvent the *O'Brien* defence so as to force a sale of the property notwithstanding the wife's equity arising from her husband's undue influence is considered in Chapter 7. Finally, the potential for subsuming the undue influence doctrine within a wider concept of unconscionability is canvassed in Chapter 8. An Appendix contains a number of useful precedents for the legal practitioner.

1.2 HISTORICAL PERSPECTIVE

The origins of the doctrine of undue influence are said to stem from Lord Hardwicke's formulation in *Morris v Burroughs* (1737) 1 Atk 398; 26 ER 253, although it can be traced to earlier case law: *Blunden & Hester v Barker* (1720) 1 P Wms 634, p 639–40; 24 ER 548, pp 549–50, *per* Lord Macclesfield.

The classic (modern) exposition of the law on undue influence is to be found in the judgments of the Court of Appeal in *Allcard v Skinner* (1887) 36 Ch D 145, involving a gift made by a novice to the mother superior of a convent. The rule of poverty within the convent required each member to give up all her property either to her relatives or to the poor, or to the convent itself for the general purposes of the sisterhood. The rule of obedience required the member to regard the voice of her superior as the voice of God and the rules also forbade any sister from seeking advice from outside the convent without the sister superior's prior approval. Within a few days of becoming a member of the convent, the claimant made a will bequeathing all her property to the mother superior, and later further substantial sums of money and railway stock were also gifted to her. Subsequently, the claimant left the sisterhood and revoked her will, but made no demand for the return of the rest of her property (including the stock) until some six years later when she brought an action against the mother superior alleging undue influence. The Court of Appeal, on the facts, accepted that the claimant's free will had been overborne, but dismissed her claim for return of the money and stock on the ground of delay and her subsequent conduct amounting to confirmation of the gift.

The importance of the decision lies primarily in the court's classification of undue influence into two broad categories. In the words of Cotton LJ (p 171):

> First, where the Court has been satisfied that the gift was the result of influence expressly used by the donee for the purpose; second where the relations between the donor and donee have at or shortly before the execution of the gift been such as to raise a presumption that the donee had influence over the donor.

In the first category, the donee has actually used some form of coercion or pressure on the donor, with whom he stands in some close and confidential relationship, in order to gain some personal advantage. In the second category, the court will automatically set aside the gift regardless of proof of unfair or improper conduct, unless the donee proves that the gift was the result of a free exercise of the donor's will. In this latter category, the donee must show that the donor had taken independent legal advice and was, thus, removed from the influence of the donee when the gift was made to him: p 181, *per* Lindley LJ. A number of cases decided prior to *Allcard*, concerning predominantly religious or spiritual influence, illustrate the development of these principles. As Lindley LJ observed (p 182), the cases fall within one or other or both (since there may be some overlap) of the two categories mentioned above.

An early case, decided in 1764, is *Norton v Relly* 2 Eden 286; 28 ER 908, a case in the first category, where a woman, suffering from a religious delusion, was persuaded by a Protestant dissenting minister to grant him an annuity of £50 (secured on her property). The minister had visited her over a two year period and induced her to become a member of his congregation. The case was the first of its kind to come before the English courts and Lord Northington LC proclaimed equity's role to be 'a guardian and protector of the weak and helpless of every denomination, and the punisher of fraud and imposition in every degree'. He ordered the annuity to be cancelled and an account to be taken of all moneys paid by the woman to the minister. Similarly, in *Nottidge v Prince* (1860) 2 Giff 246; 66 ER 103, a woman of weak intellect was induced to gift the whole of her fortune to the defendant, who had exercised a powerful dominion over her mind by making her (and other of his followers) believe that he had supernatural powers. In setting aside the transfer, Sir John Stuart VC stated the principle to be that:

> No person who stands in a relation of spiritual confidence to another so as to acquire a habitual influence over his mind can accept any gift or benefit from the person who is under the dominion of that influence, without the danger of having the gift set aside. If it can be shewn that a sufficient protection has been interposed against the exercise of the influence there may be a case to sustain the gift.

Again, in *Lyon v Home* (1868) Law Rep 6 Eq 655, a widow, aged 75, within a few days of seeing the defendant who claimed to be a spiritual medium, was induced (from her belief that she was fulfilling the wishes of her deceased husband) to adopt the defendant as her son, make her will in his favour and transfer various sums of money to him. Sir GM Giffard VC held that the relationship between the widow and the defendant implied the exercise of dominion and influence by the latter over the former's mind and, hence, in the absence of evidence that the gifts were the voluntary and understood acts of the widow, they had to be set aside: see, also, *Morley v Loughnan* [1893] 1 Ch 736 (money obtained by the actual exercise of undue influence under the guise of religion refunded).

A good example of an early case falling within the second category is *Huguenin v Baseley* (1807) 14 Ves Jun 273; 33 ER 526, involving a settlement made by a widow upon a clergyman and his family. In this case, the clergyman had not only acquired considerable spiritual influence over the widow, but was also entrusted by her with the management of her property. Although, the widow had clearly *intended* to execute the settlement, nevertheless, in the words of Lord Eldon:

> The question is, not, whether she knew what she was doing, had done, or proposed to do, but how the intention was produced: whether all that care and providence was placed round her, as against those, who advised her, which, from their situation and relation with respect to her, they were bound to exert on her behalf.

In other words, it was the duty of the donee, as agent, to advise and take care of the donor's property interests. Having failed properly to advise her of the nature and consequences of her actions, the settlement had to be set aside. The point was further addressed by Sir John Romilly MR in *Hoghton v Hoghton* (1852) 15 Beav 278; 51 ER 545, involving the relationship of father and son, where he said:

> ... wherever one person obtains, by voluntary donation, a large pecuniary benefit from another, the burden of proving that the transaction is righteous ... falls on the person taking the benefit. But this proof is given, if it be shewn that the donor knew and understood what it was that he was doing. If, however, besides the obtaining the benefit of this voluntary gift from the donor, the donor and the donee were so situated towards each other, that undue influence might have been exercised by the donee over the donor, then a new consideration is added, and the question is not, to use the words of Lord Eldon [in *Huguenin*] 'whether the donor knew what he was doing, but how the intention was produced', and though the donor was well aware of what he did, yet if his disposition to do it was produced by undue influence, the transaction would be set aside.

It was accepted, in this case, that a court would, in many cases, simply infer the probability of undue influence having been exerted from the relations existing between the parties to the transaction. Cases of guardian and ward, parent and child, solicitor and client, spiritual instructor and pupil, medical adviser and patient, all fell within this category of presumed undue influence. In such cases, the court 'watches the whole transaction with great jealousy, not merely for the purpose of ascertaining that the person likely to be so influenced fully understood the act he was performing, but also for the purpose of ascertaining that his consent to perform that act was not obtained by reason of the influence possessed by the person receiving the benefit': *Hoghton v Hoghton* above, pp 299, 553. Another early case involving parent and child is *Archer v Hudson* (1844) 7 Beav 551; 49 ER 1180, where Lord Langdale MR observed that 'if there be a pecuniary transaction between parent and child ... without any benefit moving to the child, the presumption is, that an undue influence has been exercised to procure that liability on the part of the child'. The onus then falls on the parent to rebut the presumption by showing that the child was in 'such a position ... to enable him to form an entirely free and unfettered judgment, independent altogether of any sort of control': see, also, *Hatch v Hatch* (1804) 9 Ves Jun 292; 32 ER 615 (guardian and ward); *Dent v Bennett* (1839) 4 My & Cr 269; 41 ER 105 (surgeon and patient); and *Mitchell v Homfray* (1881) 8 QBD 587 (CA) (doctor and patient). In *Wright v Vanderplank* (1856) 8 De GM & G 133; 44 ER 340, a case of father and daughter, Knight Bruce LJ stated the principle to be as follows:

> A child is presumed to be under the exercise of parental influence as long as the dominion of the parent lasts. Whilst that dominion lasts, it lies on the parent maintaining the gift to disprove the exercise of parental influence, by shewing that the child had independent advice, or in some other way.

A similar formulation of principle is to be found in *Re Holmes' Estate* (1881) 3 Giff 337; 66 ER 439, involving a solicitor and client, where Sir John Stuart VC said:

> The principle is that the relation of solicitor and client is one of such high confidence on the part of the client that the solicitor is considered to have an amount of influence over the mind and action of his client which, in the eye of this Court, while that influence remains, makes it impossible that the gift can prevail. The principle of influence vitiates the gift; but the presumption of influence may be rebutted by circumstances short of the total dissolution of the relation of solicitor and client.

Similarly, in *Rhodes v Bate* (1865) LR 1 Ch App 252, another case involving a solicitor and client, the court stated that persons standing in a confidential relation towards others could not entitle themselves to hold benefits which those others may have conferred on them, unless they could show that the latter had 'competent and independent advice' in conferring them. A limitation, however, was expressed to exist where the gift to a person standing in a confidential relation was merely trifling. In cases of trifling benefits, the court would be less likely to interfere to set them aside upon mere proof of a confidential relation and the absence of proof of competent and independent advice. In *Rhodes*, it was suggested that, in such cases, the court would require further proof of bad faith (in addition to undue influence) in order to undo the transaction.

1.3 THEORY UNDERLYING UNDUE INFLUENCE

In *National Westminster Bank plc v Morgan* [1985] 1 All ER 821, the House of Lords concluded that the principle justifying a court in setting aside a transaction for undue influence was 'the victimisation of one party by the other': pp 827–28, *per* Lord Scarman. This reflects the view taken by Lindley LJ in *Allcard v Skinner* (1887) 36 Ch D 145 (pp 182–83), where he said:

> What then is the principle? Is it that it is right and expedient to save persons from the consequences of their own folly? Or is it that it is right and expedient to save them from being victimised by other people? In my opinion the doctrine of undue influence is founded upon the second of these two principles ... to protect people from being forced, tricked or misled in any way by others into parting with their property is one of the most legitimate objects of all laws ...

On this analysis, the law of undue influence seeks to prevent 'victimisation' or improper conduct by one party that results in the victim entering into a transaction without free and informed consent. It recognises that a contract may be vitiated by a variety of different frauds committed by the wrongdoer, including, apart from undue influence, duress and misrepresentation.

Under the victimisation theory, the focus is on how the transaction was entered into rather than the substance of the transaction itself. In other words, it looks to 'procedural unfairness' (that is, the manner in which the transaction was brought into existence) and not any 'contractual imbalance' which may be manifest from the terms of the contract favouring one party to the disadvantage of the other. Because this theory looks to the misconduct of the wrongdoer, it has also been rationalised on the ground of fraud. Thus, in *Allcard*, Lindley LJ spoke of the equitable doctrine of undue influence as growing out of 'the necessity of grappling with insidious forms of spiritual tyranny and with the infinite varieties of fraud': *Allcard*, p 183. More recently, in the Court of Appeal in *Morgan* [1983] 3 All ER 85 (p 92), Slade LJ identified the public policy in applying the presumption in undue influence cases as being 'to mitigate the risk of a particular relationship existing between two parties and the influence arising therefrom from being abused'. In *CIBC Mortgages plc v Pitt* [1993] 4 All ER 433 (HL) (p 439), Lord Browne-Wilkinson stated:

> Actual undue influence is a species of fraud. Like any other victim of fraud, a person who has been induced by undue influence to carry out a transaction which he did not freely and knowingly enter into is entitled to have that transaction set aside as of right.

It has been cogently argued, however, by a New Zealand commentator that when Lord Scarman used the term 'victimisation' in *Morgan*, he had in mind something quite different from the concept of fraud as propounded in *Allcard v Skinner*. In fact, in the Scarman sense, victimisation was synonymous with the notion of 'harm' (that is, substantive unfairness), so that a claimant could not be said to be victimised (that is, harmed) unless the transaction itself was manifestly disadvantageous to him. This 'harm theory', therefore, focuses on 'nature of the exchange or the terms of the transaction' so that a party cannot claim to be victimised in a transaction which provides reasonably equal benefits to both sides: see Callaghan, C, 'Manifest disadvantage in undue influence: an analysis of its role and necessity' (1995) 25 VUWLR 289, pp 305–06. This analysis has a significant impact on the question whether the requirement of manifest disadvantage should be retained in presumed undue influence cases under English law: see, further, Chapter 3, para 3.6.

1.4 MODERN CATEGORISATION OF UNDUE INFLUENCE CASES

As we have seen, the courts have traditionally divided the cases on undue influence into two distinct categories, namely, those involving (1) actual or (2) presumed undue influence: *Allcard v Skinner* (1887) 36 Ch D 145. These two categories were further refined by the House of Lords, in *Barclays Bank plc v O'Brien* [1993] 4 All ER 417 (p 423) (adopting the twofold classification set out in *Bank of Credit and Commerce International SA v Aboody* [1992] 4 All ER 955,

CA). In class 1 cases, it is necessary for the claimant to prove affirmatively that the wrongdoer exerted undue influence on the complainant to enter into the particular transaction. In *Aboody*, for example, the Court of Appeal found evidence of actual undue influence exerted by a husband over his wife, who was 20 years his junior. Although both of them were directors and shareholders of a family company, the husband ran the company as a one man business. The wife signed company documents without question as and when they were put before her by her husband, whom she trusted to run the company for their mutual benefit. The husband borrowed various sums from the bank using a house owned by the wife as security. Although the bank had arranged for an independent solicitor to advise the wife separately on the nature of the charge she was asked to sign, the husband had burst into the room uninvited during the interview in a high state of excitement and, after a scene which reduced her to tears, she signed the legal charge. It was apparent that the husband had acted in a bullying manner and that the wife was under pressure and had signed simply because she wanted peace.

In class 2 cases (involving presumed undue influence), the presumption of undue influence arises when an appropriate relationship exists between the parties. Here, the complainant has to show, initially, that there was a relationship of 'trust and confidence' between the complainant and the wrongdoer of such a nature that it is fair to presume that the wrongdoer abused that relationship in procuring the complainant to enter into the transaction. In this category, therefore, there is no requirement to produce evidence that actual undue influence was exerted in relation to the transaction. The relationship can be established in one of two ways. First, certain types of relationship, as a matter of law, raise the presumption of undue influence automatically (class 2A). These, as we have already seen, include solicitor and client, doctor and patient, parent and child, and superior and member of a convent. Significantly, however, the relationship of husband and wife does not come within this category: *Howes v Bishop* [1909] 2 KB 390 and *Bank of Montreal v Stuart* [1911] AC 120. Secondly, even if there is no relationship falling within class 2A, the specific relationship between the particular parties may be such as to give rise to the presumption. Here, the complainant must prove the existence of a relationship under which the complainant generally 'reposed trust and confidence' in the wrongdoer (class 2B). As we shall see, the relationship of husband and wife *does* fall within this category. In this context, the dual requirement of trust and confidence leads one party (usually the wife) to rely on the other party (the husband) to act in her best interests, and not just his own. The key element, therefore, in establishing the presumption in class 2B cases is the wife's reliance on her husband's advice and judgment.

The presumption arising in class 2A and B cases can, of course, be displaced by showing that the transaction was entered into with free and informed consent. Usually, this will involve requiring the complainant to take independent legal advice, but there may be extreme cases where the transaction is so disadvantageous that the taking of independent legal advice will not rebut the presumption: *Credit Lyonnais Bank Nederland NV v Burch* [1997] 1 All ER 144, CA. Most recently, the House of Lords in *Royal Bank of Scotland v Etridge (No 2)* [2001] UKHL 44 has reiterated that the burden of proving an allegation of undue influence rests upon the person who claims to have been wronged. The evidence required to discharge that burden of proof depends on a variety of factors, including the nature of the alleged undue influence, the personality of the parties, their relationship, the extent to which the transaction cannot readily be accounted for by ordinary motives of ordinary persons in that relationship and all the circumstances of the case: *per* Lord Nicholls (para 13) and Lord Scott (para 153). Normally, proof that the complainant placed trust and confidence in the other party in relation to the management of the complainant's financial affairs, coupled with a transaction which calls for explanation, will be sufficient to discharge the burden of proof. This will then shift the evidential burden of proof onto the wrongdoer to produce evidence to counter the inference of undue influence.

It is apparent also that their Lordships were not in favour of an over-rigid classification of undue influence cases. Lord Nicholls found the usage 'a little confusing' and Lord Hobhouse went as far as to say that the class 2B presumption should not be adopted as it was not 'a useful forensic tool': para 107. Similarly, Lord Scott 'doubt[ed]' the utility' of the class 2B classification, but he considered class 2A as being 'useful in identifying particular relationships where the presumption arises': para 161. Lord Clyde considered the twofold (actual and presumed) division 'illogical' and simply 'add[ed] mystery rather than illumination': para 92. This was because the various categories confused definition with proof. At one level, the use of the term 'presumption', as we have seen, refers to a shift in the evidential burden of proof. This evidential presumption, however, falls to be distinguished from the class 2A presumption which arises upon the existence of certain types of relationship where the law presumes, irrebuttably, that one party had influence over the other.

1.5 COMPARISON WITH OTHER CONCEPTS

It is useful, at this point, to distinguish undue influence from other similar concepts.

1.5.1 Duress

Both duress and undue influence are concerned with contracts which have been obtained as a result of unwarranted oppression and persuasion. A contract depends on free consent and independent will; if one party has improperly affected the other's decision to enter into an agreement, either duress or undue influence will render the contract voidable at the option of the party oppressed. Duress has been aptly described as 'the pressure of the big stick or the bottom line' whereas undue influence 'is the pressure of the personality': Furmston, M (general editor), *The Law of Contract*, 1999, Butterworths Common Law Series, London: Butterworths, Chapter 4, p 691. In other words, duress is concerned with the exercise of pressure on the complainant which may or may not be legitimate. Some forms of coercion are viewed as legitimate and, therefore, will not render the transaction voidable. Thus, a party who simply drives a hard bargain during negotiations for a contract (for example, by stating that he will not alter his terms) will not come within the principle of duress. On the other hand, a contract made at gunpoint will be vitiated on the ground of duress.

Historically, the doctrine of duress was justified on grounds of interference with consent, whereas actual undue influence has been said to be based on the notion of constructive fraud (that is, to prevent a person from retaining the benefit of a fraud or wrongful act). Essentially, therefore, actual undue influence concerns the unconscientious use by one person of power possessed by him over another in order to induce the other person to make a gift or enter into a transaction: *Halsbury's Laws of England*, Vol 9(1), 4th edn, reissue, London: Butterworths, para 712, citing *Earl of Aylesford v Morris* (1873) 8 Ch App 484, p 490, *per* Lord Selborne LC. So far as presumed undue influence is concerned, however, in the words of Cotton LJ in *Allcard v Skinner* (1887) 36 Ch D 145 (CA) (p 171), the court interferes 'not on the ground that any wrongful act has in fact been committed by the donee, but on the ground of public policy, and to prevent the relations which existed between the parties and the influence arising therefrom being abused'.

Although originally confined to threats or acts of violence to the person or to goods, the concept of duress has now been extended to include a wide range of threats including those to a party's economic and business interests. The trigger for duress, however, is different from that used in undue influence cases. Essentially, the complainant has to prove two elements, namely: (1) that the threat or pressure was illegitimate; and (2) the lack of a reasonable or realistic alternative to making the contract: *Universe Tankships Inc of Monrovia v International Transport Workers' Federation and Laughton* [1983] AC 366 (HL). (Where, however, what is threatened is not a civil wrong (that is, a breach of contact or tort) but a crime, only the first element need be proved.) A good example of the operation of the doctrine is to be found in *B & S Contracts & Design Ltd v Victor Green Publications Ltd* [1984] ICR 419 (CA), where a builder agreed to erect stands for an exhibition at Olympia, London. Less than a week before the opening of the exhibition, the builder told the owner that he would not do it without extra payment to satisfy the demands of his workforce. Failure to erect the stands in time for the exhibition would have been disastrous for the owner, so he gave way to the demand and paid the extra amount. The court held that this was clearly illegitimate pressure and the owner had no real option but to accede to the demand. Accordingly, the extra amount was recoverable as money paid under duress.

As we have seen, the doctrine of undue influence is based on the notion of actual (or presumed) abuse of power so that the complainant is unable to form a free and informed decision to enter into the transaction. In the presumed undue influence category, the doctrine relies on establishing a relationship of trust and confidence between the parties which leads one party to place reliance on the other's impartial judgment and advice. This category also requires that the transaction be manifestly disadvantageous to the complainant. In the actual undue influence category, however, the difference with duress is less easy to discern. Here, the question is largely the same, namely, whether consent was induced by pressure which the law does not regard as legitimate. Some academic commentators have, therefore, argued strongly for the assimilation of actual undue influence cases involving pressure within the ambit of the doctrine of duress: see Birks, P and Chin, NY, 'On the nature of undue influence', in Beatson, J and Friedmann, D (eds), *Good Faith and Fault in Contract Law*, 1995, Oxford: Clarendon; and Phang, A, 'Undue influence methodology, sources and linkages' [1995] JBL 552, p 566. (See, also, *Mutual Finance Ltd v John Wetton & Sons Ltd* [1937] 2 KB 389, pp 394–95, *per* Porter J.) Most recently, in *Royal Bank of Scotland v Etridge (No 2)* [2001] UKHL 44, Lord Nicholls opined (para 8) that 'today there is much overlap with the principle of duress as this principle has subsequently developed'.

1.5.2 Abuse of confidence

In McGhee, J, *Snell's Equity*, 30th edn, 2000, London: Sweet & Maxwell, it is stated that 'the principles of undue influence and abuse of confidence overlap but do not coincide' (p 620). The essence of the principle of abuse of confidence is that, in the absence of competent independent advice, a transaction between persons in a confidential relationship is voidable, unless the person standing in such a confidential position has disclosed all material information in his possession and has shown that the transaction was a fair one, having regard to all the circumstances: *Demerara Bauxite Co Ltd v Hubbard* [1923] AC 673 (PC), involving the purchase of property by a solicitor from his former client under an option. The principle is limited in application and appears to be confined to relationships between solicitor and client, trustee and beneficiary, principal and agent, and other persons in similar positions. In relation to transactions between principal and agent, for example, the rule is strict in so far as the agent must disclose every material fact which is (or ought to be) known to him. If he fails to do this, the transaction is liable to be set aside at the option of the principal regardless of the fairness of the transaction: *Halsbury's Laws of England*, Vol 1(2), 4th edn, reissue, 1990, para 104.

The rationale behind this stringent principle is the obvious danger of an abuse of confidence on the part of the person in the confidential position. Liability and relief in these cases arises quite independently of the existence of any undue influence because a failure to disclose material information will be treated as being itself an abuse of confidence entitling the other party to equitable relief: *Moody v Cox and Hatt* [1917] 2 Ch 71, pp 79–80, *per* Lord Cozens-Hardy MR. The only way of avoiding liability is for the person in the confidential position to disclose to the other party everything that is (or may be) material prior to entering into the transaction and to prove that the transaction was fair. This duty to disclose is quite consistent with the absence of evidence of any undue influence.

Whilst it is certainly possible for a person standing in a confidential position to bring himself within both principles (that is, abuse of confidence and undue influence), this will be rare. One example given in *Snell's Equity* (see above, p 620), is that of a trustee who purchases from his beneficiary at an undervalue: *Tate v Williamson* (1866) 2 Ch App 55. But the relevant passage goes on to say:

> … a gift from the [beneficiary] raises questions of undue influence alone, while trafficking with the trust property can be attacked only as an abuse of confidence, for it is an act of the trustee and not an act of the beneficiary under the trustee's influence.

It is also pointed out that there may be undue influence in the absence of a fiduciary relationship and, conversely, not in every fiduciary relationship will undue influence be presumed. Thus, in *Re Coomber* [1911] 1 Ch 723, a son acted as agent for his mother in the running of his late father's business. Despite the existence of a fiduciary relationship between the mother and son, the Court of Appeal held that no presumption of undue influence arose so as to induce the court to set aside an assignment of the lease of the business premises by the mother in favour of her son.

Significantly, the most important distinction between the two concepts is that, whilst a transaction will not be set aside on the basis of presumed undue influence unless it is shown to be manifestly disadvantageous to the complainant, there is no such requirement in cases of abuse of confidence: *Bank of Credit and Commerce International SA v Aboody* [1992] 4 All ER 955 (CA), p 973, *per* Slade LJ. This means that a claimant relying on abuse of confidence is usually in a far stronger position than one relying on undue influence.

1.5.3 Unconscionable bargains

Alongside the doctrine of undue influence, the courts have developed a limited jurisdiction to set aside unconscionable bargains. Although originally confined to reversioners (*O'Rorke v Bolingbroke* (1877) 2 App Cas 814) and expectant heirs (*Earl of Aylesford v Morris* (1873) 8 Ch App 484), this jurisdiction was extended to other persons who were poor or ignorant and where the transaction in question was made at a considerable undervalue without the benefit of independent legal advice: *Fry v Lane* (1888) 40 Ch D 312. The circumstances of poverty and ignorance, coupled with the absence of independent advice, gave rise to a presumption of fraud which could be rebutted by proving that the transaction was fair, just and reasonable. The essential elements of the doctrine were set out by Mr Peter Millett QC (sitting as a deputy judge of the High Court) in *Alec Lobb (Garages) Ltd v Total Oil (Great Britain) Ltd* [1983] 1 WLR 87 (pp 94–95):

> First, one party has been at a serious disadvantage to the other, whether through poverty, or ignorance, or lack of advice, or otherwise, so that circumstances existed of which unfair advantage could be taken ... Second, this weakness of the one party has been exploited by the other in some morally culpable manner ... And third, the resulting transaction has been, not merely hard or improvident, but overreaching and oppressive.

A modern illustration of the jurisdiction is to be found in *Boustany v Pigott* (1995) 69 P & CR 298 (PC), involving a lease of land, where the respondent was successful in establishing all three ingredients, enabling the grant of the lease to be set aside. Similarly, in the earlier case of *Cresswell v Potter* [1978] 1 WLR 255n, a conveyance of the matrimonial home executed by a wife in favour of her husband was set aside as an unconscionable bargain. Megarry J accepted that the modern day equivalent of a poor and ignorant person was a member of a lower income group with limited education. Although the wife was employed as a telephonist requiring considerable alertness and skill, she could properly be described as 'ignorant' in the context of property transactions. There was also clearly an undervalue since she only received a release from her liability under an existing mortgage in return for giving up all her interest in the matrimonial home which had increased in value. There was also no suggestion that she had had any independent advice. The fact that she knew how to obtain such advice if she wanted it was irrelevant: see, also, *Backhouse v Backhouse* [1978] 1 All ER 1158.

In many cases, the facts may give rise to a potential defence based on either the doctrine of undue influence or equity's jurisdiction to relieve against unconscionable bargains. This has been judicially recognised, most notably in *Credit Lyonnais Bank Nederland NV v Burch* [1997] 1 All ER 144 (CA), where Nourse LJ (p 151) accepted that the legal charge in favour of the bank could have been set aside as an unconscionable bargain (as opposed to the claimant relying on undue influence), stating that such jurisdiction was still 'in good heart and capable of adaptation to different transactions entered into in changing circumstances'. Undoubtedly, there are strong similarities between the two doctrines and this has motivated a number of academic commentators to urge for a merger of the two sets of principles into one overarching notion of unconscionability or 'good faith' dealing: see, for example, Clarke (1993) 23 HKLJ 318 and *Smith v Bank of Scotland* [1997] 2 FLR 862 (HL), p 872, *per* Lord

Clyde, who suggested that Scots law could be extended in the *O'Brien* direction, but 'upon the broad principle in the field of contract law of fair dealing in good faith'. In the *Burch* case, Millett LJ also alluded to the similarities between undue influence and unconscionable dealing when he said (p 153):

> In either case it is necessary to show that the conscience of the party who seeks to uphold the transaction was affected by notice, actual or constructive, of the impropriety by which it was obtained by the intermediary, and in either case the court may in a proper case infer the presence of the impropriety from the terms of the transaction itself.

In *Burch* itself, the transaction (a second charge over the defendant's flat securing an unlimited all moneys guarantee in respect of her employer's bank overdraft) was not only manifestly disadvantageous to her, but was also one which, in the language of unconscionable bargains, 'shocked the conscience of the court'. Without knowing the extent of the liability involved, she had committed herself to a personal liability far beyond her means and risked the loss of her home and personal bankruptcy to help a company in which she had no financial interest and of which she was only a junior employee. On these facts, the presumption of undue influence on the part of her employer (who had persuaded her to provide the security) was irresistible. The bank had not taken reasonable steps to avoid being fixed with constructive notice of that undue influence since neither the potential extent of her liability had been explained to her nor had she received independent legal advice. Accordingly, the bank could not enforce the charge against her.

However, had she sought to have the transaction set aside as an unconscionable bargain, it would have been incumbent on her to show not only that the terms of the transaction were harsh or oppressive, but that 'one of the parties to it [had] imposed the objectionable terms in a morally reprehensible manner, that is to say, in a way which affects his conscience': *Multiservice Bookbinding Ltd v Marden* [1979] Ch 84, p 110, *per* Browne-Wilkinson J. It is evident, therefore, that there must be some impropriety, both in the conduct of the stronger party and in the terms of the transaction itself: *Alec Lobb (Garages) Ltd v Total Oil GB Ltd* [1983] 1 All ER 944, p 961. Moreover, as with undue influence, the lender will only be affected by the intermediary's impropriety if it has actual or constructive notice of it. Assuming such notice is present, then (as with undue influence) the complainant will have an equity to have the transaction set aside binding on the lender.

A rare opportunity to consider the interaction between the two concepts arose more recently in the case of *Portman Building Society v Dusangh* [2000] 2 All ER (Comm) 221. The defendant (and his wife) had come to England from India in 1964. His understanding of spoken English had remained poor and he was illiterate. In 1977, he bought a property which in 1989, when he was aged 72 and retired, he mortgaged to the Portman Building Society. The mortgage was guaranteed by his son, who agreed to pay it off. Most of the advance went to the son who used it to buy a supermarket business. The same solicitor acted for the building society, the defendant and the son. The son's business eventually failed and the building society began possession proceedings. The defendant argued that he was entitled to set aside the mortgage directly against the building society as an unconscionable bargain. The Court of Appeal emphasised the distinctions between this case and that of *Burch,* mentioned above. In this case, there was no undue influence because it was not manifestly disadvantageous to the defendant that he should be able to raise money by way of remortgage so as to benefit his son. There was nothing to suggest actual undue influence by the son. Moreover, the defendant was not accustomed to reposing trust and confidence in his son, so there was no question of presumed undue influence. In addition, even if there had been presumed influence, there was nothing on the facts that would put the building society on notice of the defendant's equity. On the contrary, the defendant had been advised by a solicitor throughout the transaction. So if the mortgage was to be set aside, this could only be done on the basis that it constituted an unconscionable bargain. On this issue, the defendant was clearly elderly, illiterate and on a very low income and the transaction was one which was improvident and undoubtedly placed the property at risk. However, the Court of Appeal concluded that lenders were not required to 'police' transactions to ensure that parents were wise in seeking to assist their children. The fact that it was commercially unwise for the building society to have trusted the defendant and his son did not make it morally culpable. Here, again, none of the essential elements of an unconscionable bargain were present. First, the defendant was not at a serious disadvantage to the building society. Secondly, neither the defendant nor his son had any existing indebtedness towards the society. Thirdly, there was no evidence to suggest that the society had exploited the situation or had acted in a morally reprehensible manner. Finally, the transaction was not in any sense oppressive and, therefore, the conscience of the court was not shocked.

Interestingly, the Court of Appeal took the opportunity to consider briefly the interrelationship between the two doctrines. In particular, Ward LJ adopted the approach taken by Mason J in *Commercial Bank of Australia Ltd v Amadio* (1983) 15 CLR 447 (High Court of Australia), who sought to distinguish the two concepts in the following way (p 461):

> In [undue influence] the will of the innocent party is not independent and voluntary because it is overborne. In [unconscionable conduct cases] the will of the innocent party, even if independent and voluntary, is the result of the disadvantageous position in which he is placed and of the other party unconscientiously taking advantage of that position.

In essence, therefore, undue influence is concerned with the weakness of the complainant's *consent* resulting from an over-dependence on the defendant's judgment, skill or expertise. By contrast, the doctrine of unconscionable bargains places greater emphasis on the defendant's exploitation of the complainant's weakness (that is, the wrongful conduct of the defendant): Birks, P and Chin, NY, 'On the nature of undue influence', in Beatson, J and

Friedmann, D (eds), *Good Faith and Fault in Contract Law*, 1985, Oxford: Clarendon (pp 57–97), who view undue influence cases as 'plaintiff-sided' because the essence of the doctrine is the complainant's dependency on the defendant as opposed to the defendant's wrongdoing. Thus, the learned authors point out that, in the presumed undue influence category, the defendant's conduct does not usually involve any actual coercion or abuse; the doctrine operates simply to remove from the defendant benefits which he has passively obtained under the transaction. Moreover, the defendant can rebut the presumption by establishing that the claimant entered into the transaction freely and with informed consent; the rebuttal focuses on consent and is not concerned with unconscionable conduct on the defendant's part. Indeed, the presumption will not, in certain cases, be rebutted even though the defendant's conduct does not involve any impropriety: *Cheese v Thomas* [1994] 1 WLR 129 (CA). Even in some cases involving *actual* undue influence, the evidence is merely that the defendant made the decision for the complainant and with the intention of benefiting him (or her): *Dunbar Bank plc v Nadeem* [1998] 3 All ER 876 (husband and wife). The distinction between the two doctrines was made succinctly by Deane J in the *Amadio* case (above, p 474):

> Undue influence, like common law duress, looks to the quality of the consent or assent of the weaker party ... Unconscionable dealing looks to the conduct of the stronger party in attempting to enforce, or retain the benefit of, a dealing with a person under a special disability in circumstances where it is not consistent with equity or good conscience that he should do so.

Again, in *Morrison v Coast Finance Ltd* (1965) 55 DLR (3d) 710 (p 713), Davey JA said:

> A plea of undue influence attacks the sufficiency of consent; a plea that a bargain is unconscionable invokes relief against an unfair advantage gained by an unconscientious use of power by a stronger party against a weaker.

The interrelationship between the two doctrines is discussed further in para 1.10 below, and also Chapter 8.

1.6 REQUIREMENT OF MANIFEST DISADVANTAGE

An additional element in the presumed undue influence cases (classes 2A and 2B) is the need to show that the transaction was manifestly disadvantageous to the complainant: *CIBC Mortgages plc v Pitt* [1993] 4 All ER 433 (HL). The requirement was first introduced by the House of Lords in *National Westminster Bank plc v Morgan* [1985] AC 686 and has since been criticised both academically and judicially. In the *Pitt* case, Lord Browne-Wilkinson pointed out that this requirement was at odds with the line of cases involving abuse of confidence (see, above, para 1.5.2) where the onus is on the fiduciary to show that the transaction is a fair one. Because of the obvious overlap between such relationships and those in which undue influence is presumed, a cogent argument exists for abandoning the requirement of manifest disadvantage altogether in undue influence cases. Instead, the onus would be on the person taking advantage of the claimant to show the 'righteousness' of the transaction. Unfortunately, the abuse of confidence cases were not cited to the House of Lords in *Morgan* and so the interaction between the two sets of principles was not considered.

Prior to the House of Lords' decision in *Royal Bank of Scotland v Etridge (No 2)* [2001] UKHL 44, the requirement of manifest disadvantage had a dual function. First, it assisted the complainant (usually the wife) in establishing her claim against the wrongdoer (husband). In other words, the improvident nature of the transaction will be relevant in deciding whether the presumption arises. Secondly, it was relevant to the way in which the transaction appeared to a third party (a lender) and, thus, assisted the wife in establishing that the third party had constructive notice of the impropriety. This second function is now much diminished given that, under the House of Lords' ruling, a lender will be automatically put on inquiry where a wife stands surety for her husband's debts or the debts of a company whose shares are held by her and her husband jointly: see, further, Chapter 4, para 4.2.3.

The phrase has been defined to mean 'a disadvantage which was so obvious as such to any independent and reasonable person who considered the transaction at the time with knowledge of all the relevant facts': *Bank of Credit and Commerce International SA v Aboody* [1992] 4 All ER 955 (CA). In that case, it was held that the question whether the assumption of the risk of the charge being enforced is manifestly disadvantageous to the claimant depended on the balance of two factors, namely: (1) the seriousness of the risk of enforcement to the claimant, in practical terms; and (2) the benefits gained by the claimant in accepting the risk. Thus, if the husband is already subject to potential liabilities which expose him to the risk of bankruptcy, a substantial increase of those liabilities is capable of constituting a manifest disadvantage. In *Bank of Cyprus (London) Ltd v Markou* [1999] 2 All ER 707, the wife was at the husband's mercy in respect of the conduct of the business and, in those circumstances, her shareholding in the company had little significance. She had exposed the matrimonial home to risk for the sake of the company which had little prospect of prospering. In *Goode Durrant Administration v Biddulph* [1994] 2 FLR 551, the wife had little business experience and reposed trust and confidence in her husband in financial matters and relied on him in executing the transaction. Her direct interest in the proposed development arose only from her 2.5% shareholding in the company. To make herself personally liable for a sum in excess of £300,000, in order to have a 2.5% share through the company of any profit, was held to be a transaction manifestly disadvantageous to her.

There is, however, a 'world of difference' between a case where a husband and wife are entering into a joint venture and one where it is essentially the husband's business that is being guaranteed: *Bank of Cyprus (London) Ltd v Markou*, above. In *CIBC Mortgages plc v Pitt* [1993] 4 All ER 433 (HL), the transaction consisted of a joint loan to husband and wife to finance the discharge of an existing mortgage on the matrimonial home with the balance to be applied in buying a holiday home. The loan was advanced to the parties jointly and there was nothing to indicate that it was anything other than a normal advance to a husband and wife for their joint benefit. Not surprisingly, the mere fact that there was a risk of there being undue influence because one of the borrowers was the wife was not, in itself, sufficient to put the bank on inquiry. By contrast, in *Barclays Bank v Coleman* [2000] 1 All ER 385, the husband's loan (needed to purchase a property as an investment) was secured by a legal charge over the matrimonial home, which was owned jointly by the husband and wife. The charge was an 'all moneys' charge, securing not only the funding of the property but also any future borrowings by the husband from the bank. The Court of Appeal held that manifest disadvantage did not have to be large or even medium sized. It could be small, provided that the disadvantage was clear, obvious and more than *de minimis* (trivial). In this case, the form of the charge enabled the husband, without resort to the wife, to subject their matrimonial home to much greater financial risks than she could ever have known, and that constituted a clear and obvious disadvantage to her. Interestingly, Nourse LJ alluded to the difficulties in applying the concept of manifest disadvantage to the facts of individual cases and the desirability of abandoning the requirement altogether in both categories (classes 2A and 2B) of presumed undue influence.

Although, most recently, the House of Lords in *Etridge (No 2)* recognised that the requirement of manifest disadvantage has been the subject of criticism, it declined to depart from its earlier decision, in *Morgan*, on this point. On the contrary, Lord Nicholls considered that the two prerequisites to the shift in the evidential burden of proof – namely: (1) the complainant having reposed trust and confidence in the other party; and (2) the transaction being not readily explicable by the relationship of the parties – made 'good sense', as it would be absurd for the law to presume that every transaction between say, a client and his solicitor, is brought about by undue influence unless the contrary was affirmatively proved. However, according to Lord Nicholls, the label 'manifest disadvantage' had caused difficulties in the previous cases involving wives guaranteeing payment of their husbands' debts. In a narrow sense, such a transaction would be plainly disadvantageous to the wife, in so far as she undertook a serious financial obligation in return for little or no personal gain. On a wider view, however, it is likely that the husband's business is the source of the family income and the wife has a personal interest in doing what she can to support the business. According to Lord Nicholls, therefore, the correct approach to adopt in deciding whether a transaction was disadvantageous to the wife was to abandon the label of manifest disadvantage (which gave rise to ambiguity) in favour of the test outlined by Lindley LJ in *Allcard v Skinner* (1887) 36 Ch D 145 (p 185), namely: '[is] the gift so large as not to be reasonably accounted for on the ground of friendship, relationship, charity, or other ordinary motives on which ordinary men act?' This test was applied by Lord Scarman, in *Morgan* (p 704), where his Lordship reformulated the principle in terms of a transaction which was itself wrongful in that it constituted 'an advantage taken of the person subjected to the influence which, failing proof to the contrary, was explicable only on the basis that undue influence had been exercised to procure it'. Essentially, therefore, the concept of manifest disadvantage is, as we have seen, evidential in so far as it is relevant to the question whether there is any issue of abuse which can properly be raised: *per* Lord Hobhouse (para 104) and Lord Scott (para 155).

In terms of husband and wife cases, Lord Nicholls was of the view that, in the ordinary course, a wife's guarantee of her husband's bank overdraft secured by means of a charge on her share of the family home, should *not* be regarded as a transaction which, failing proof to the contrary, was explicable only on the basis that it had been procured by the exercise of the husband's undue influence. In most cases, there will be good reasons why a wife is willing to enter into such a transaction, despite the risks involved for her and her family. His Lordship (with whom the other Law Lords concurred) did not, however, rule out the possibility that, in exceptional cases, a wife's signature of a guarantee will call for an explanation. The requirement of manifest disadvantage is discussed in detail in Chapter 3.

1.7 ROLE OF LENDING INSTITUTIONS

1.7.1 When is the lender put on inquiry?

In *Barclays Bank v O'Brien* [1993] 4 All ER 417, the House of Lords concluded that a wife's right to have a transaction set aside as against her husband on the grounds of her husband's undue influence will be enforceable against a bank (or other creditor) if either the husband was acting as the bank's *agent*, or the bank had actual or constructive *notice* of the facts giving rise to her equity. Undoubtedly, cases where the husband is acting as the bank's agent are rare, so in the majority of claims, the question has been whether the bank actually knows of the wife's equity (actual notice) or would have discovered it by taking reasonable steps (constructive notice). In most cases, of course, the bank will have only limited knowledge of the parties' circumstances and personal dealings, for example, the nature of the husband's business, the state of his accounts, the extent of his existing indebtedness (if any) and the degree of his wife's involvement in the the business. In *Banco Exterior Internacional SA v Thomas* [1997] 1 All ER 46 (CA), it was emphasised that a bank has no business inquiring into the personal relationships between those with whom it had dealings, or as to their personal motives for wanting to help one another. The bank's sole concern is to ensure that the wife knew what she was doing and wanted to do it. In any event, detailed and personal inquiries made of the claimant may be impracticable in most cases and, as suggested by the Court of Appeal in *Thomas*, an obvious intrusion and 'impertinence' on the bank's part: pp 56 and 57, *per* Sir Richard Scott VC and Roch LJ.

In *O'Brien*, Lord Browne-Wilkinson concluded that a lender will be put on inquiry when a wife offers to stand surety for her husband's debts by a combination of two factors: (1) the transaction is not, on its face, to the financial advantage of the wife; and (2) there is a substantial risk that, in procuring the wife to act as surety, the husband has committed a legal or equitable wrong that entitles her to set aside the transaction. Interestingly, the Court of Appeal, in *Royal Bank of Scotland v Etridge (No 2)* [1998] 4 All ER 705, interpreted this formulation more restrictively by stating that the lender would only be put on inquiry if, additionally, it was aware that the parties were married or were cohabitees (that is, in both instances, the bank was *prima facie* taken to be aware that the wife/cohabitee reposed trust and confidence in her partner in relation to her financial affairs). According to the House of Lords, in *Etridge (No 2)*, however, this additional restriction was inappropriate. In Lord Nicholls' view, Lord Browne-Wilkinson's formulation meant simply that a bank is put on inquiry whenever a wife offers to stand surety for her husband's debts. In other words, it is sufficient that the bank knows of the husband-wife relationship. The two factors identified in *O'Brien* were not to be read as factual conditions which must be proved in each case before a bank is put on inquiry. Whether a lender is put on inquiry did not depend on its state of knowledge of the degree of trust and confidence the wife placed in her husband. On the contrary, Lord Browne-Wilkinson's formulation was to be viewed simply as a broad explanation of the reason why a creditor is put on inquiry when a wife offers to stand surety for her husband's debts.

According to the House of Lords, therefore, the lender will *automatically* be put on inquiry where a wife stands surety for her husband's debts. Secondly, a lender will *not* be put on inquiry where money is being advanced to the husband and wife jointly, unless the bank is aware that the loan is being made for the husband's purposes as distinct from their joint purposes. Thirdly, a lender will be put on inquiry where the wife becomes surety for the debts of a company whose shares are held by her and her husband, regardless of whether she has a minority or equal shareholding with her husband. This will be so, even if the wife is a director or secretary of the company.

The foregoing principles, which are discussed fully in Chapter 4, will apply regardless of whether the land subject to the charge is registered or unregistered; *Barclays Bank v Boulter* [1997] 2 All ER 1002 (CA), p 1010; and *Royal Bank of Scotland v Etridge (No 2)* [1998] 4 All ER 705, pp 717–18. (See, also, the interesting academic debate on this issue in Chapter 4, para 4.3.)

1.7.2 What steps must be taken by the lender to avoid notice?

Once the wife establishes a *prima facie* inference of undue influence, the burden passes to the lender to show that it had taken reasonable steps to satisfy itself that the wife's consent had been properly obtained: *Barclays Bank v Boulter* [1999] 4 All ER 513 (HL) and *Royal Bank of Scotland v Etridge (No 2)* [2001] UKHL 44 (HL).

In *Barclays Bank v O'Brien* [1993] 4 All ER 417, Lord Browne-Wilkinson intimated that a bank was obliged to warn the wife at a private meeting (not attended by the husband) of the extent of her potential liability and of the risks involved, and to urge her to take independent legal advice. Although some of the cases appear to have adopted this approach, it is apparent that the trend of the decisions has been to place greater emphasis on the role of the solicitor in advising the wife of the effects of the transaction. In *Massey v Midland Bank plc* [1995] 1 All ER 929 (CA), Steyn LJ concluded that Lord Browne-Wilkinson's 'guidance ought not to be mechanically applied' (p 934). In *Banco Exterior Internacional v Mann* [1995] 1 All ER 936 (CA), Morritt LJ regarded the holding of a private meeting as the 'best practice' but not the only means of counteracting the wife's equity.

More recently, in *Royal Bank of Scotland v Etridge (No 2)* [1998] 4 All ER 705, the Court of Appeal concluded that, where the wife is not dealing with the bank through a solicitor, it is normally enough if the bank has urged her to obtain independent legal advice before entering into the transaction, especially if the solicitor provides confirmation that: (1) he has explained the transaction to the wife; and (2) she appeared to understand it. Significantly, Stuart-Smith LJ observed (without apparent criticism) that lending institutions had been unwilling to adopt the personal interview procedure laid down in *O'Brien* (even in respect of transactions post-dating *O'Brien*) and ventured to suggest that such an approach would be likely 'to expose the bank to far greater risks than those from which it wishes to be protected' (p 720). This is presumably because, if the bank conducts a private interview with the wife and does not adequately explain the nature of the transaction, it may find itself unable to enforce the charge against her.

In most of the post-*O'Brien* cases, therefore, it has been held sufficient for the lender merely to urge the wife to obtain independent legal advice. Moreover, only in exceptional circumstances was it considered necessary for the bank to *insist* that the wife actually obtained such advice. In *Credit Lyonnais Bank Nederland NV v Burch* [1997] 1 All ER 144, for example, the Court of Appeal held that the bank was required to ensure that the claimant actually received independent legal advice, because any competent solicitor would have advised her not to enter into the transaction. Here, a junior employee was persuaded to consent to a second charge over her flat in order to secure her employer's increased overdraft facility. She signed the charge in her employer's presence at the offices of the bank's solicitors. At no time was she told, either by her employer or the bank, of the former's indebtedness to the bank or the extent of the overdraft facility being granted. The bank's solicitors wrote to her pointing out that the guarantee was unlimited both in time and amount and advising her to seek independent legal advice before entering into the transaction, but she did not do so. The Court of Appeal concluded that the bank had not taken sufficient steps to avoid being fixed with constructive notice of the presumed undue influence because neither the potential extent of her liability had been adequately explained to her, nor had she received independent advice. Similarly, in *Cooke v National Westminster Bank plc* [1998] 2 FLR 783, the wife was asked to guarantee the liabilities of her husband's company by executing a charge over a jointly owned property to which she had contributed most of the purchase money. The Court of Appeal held, on the facts, that it was fairly arguable that the bank ought reasonably to have satisfied itself of the wife's consent, largely because of its knowledge of the wife's reluctance to proceed with the guarantee. This concern over her position warranted confirmation that she had actually taken separate legal advice.

The view that Lord Browne-Wilkinson's requirement of a private meeting was not intended to be prescriptive has now been endorsed by the House of Lords in *Etridge (No 2)*. As we have seen, banking practice has been to require the wife to obtain legal advice and to seek confirmation from a solicitor that he has explained the nature and effect of the documents to her. The problem, identified by the House of Lords, however, has been that such advice is usually perfunctory and does not adequately bring home to the wife the possible dangers of acting as surety for her husband's debts. According to Lord Nicholls, therefore, a lender should be expected to take reasonable steps to satisfy itself that the wife has had brought home to her, *in a meaningful way*, the practical implications of the proposed transaction. This does not mean that a bank has to attempt to discover for itself whether a wife's consent is being procured by undue influence. A personal meeting is not the only way a bank could discharge its obligation to bring home to the wife the risks she is running. It is not unreasonable for a lender to prefer that this task should be undertaken by an independent legal adviser. Normally, therefore, it will be reasonable for a bank to rely upon confirmation from a solicitor, acting for the wife, that he has advised her appropriately. If, however, the bank knows that the solicitor has not duly advised the wife, or if the bank knows facts from which it ought to have realised that the wife has not received appropriate advice, it will proceed at its own risk.

Lord Nicholls also stressed the need for banks, in the future, to take steps to check *directly with the wife* the name of the solicitor she wishes to act for her. This means that lenders should now communicate directly with the wife, informing her that, for its own protection, it will require written confirmation from a solicitor, acting for her, to the effect that he has fully explained to her the nature and effect of the loan documents and the practical implications they will have for her. She should also be told of the purpose of this requirement (that is, that thereafter she should not be able to dispute she is legally bound by the documents once she has signed them). She should also be asked to nominate a solicitor whom she is willing to instruct to advise her, separately from her husband, and act for her in giving the necessary confirmation to the bank. She should be told also that her husband's solicitor may act for her but, if she prefers, she is free to instruct a different solicitor. Ultimately, the bank should not proceed with the transaction until it has received an appropriate response directly from the wife in this regard.

1.7.3 What is the lender's position if the wife is advised by a solicitor?

In *Royal Bank of Scotland v Etridge (No 2)* [1998] 4 All ER 705, the Court of Appeal confirmed that a solicitor acts exclusively as the wife's solicitor, notwithstanding that he may also be the husband's solicitor, or has agreed to act as the bank's agent (in only a ministerial capacity) at completion. In other words, the lender is entitled to expect the solicitor to regard himself as owing a duty to the wife alone when giving her advice, regardless of who introduced the solicitor to the wife: *Barclays Bank plc v Thomson* [1997] 4 All ER 816 (CA). More importantly, the bank is under no obligation to question the sufficiency of the solicitor's advice. It is entitled to assume that a solicitor would act honestly and would give proper advice to the wife: *Bank of Baroda v Shah* [1988] 3 All ER 24 (CA). In the case of *Bank of Scotland v Bennett* [1999] Lloyd's Rep Bank 145 (CA), for example, the couple had been dealing with the bank through the husband's solicitor and the bank was entitled to assume that he would advise the wife on all relevant matters relating to the proposed mortgage, including whether it was necessary for her to obtain independent legal advice.

Although, of course, the notice of an agent is normally imputed to his principal, this rule falls to be modified in the light of the provisions of s 199(1)(ii)(b) of the Law of Property Act 1925, which makes it clear that a bank will not be affected by notice of anything which its solicitor has discovered, unless he was acting as the *bank's* solicitor at the time when he discovered it. The point was specifically addressed in *Halifax Mortgage Services Ltd (formerly BNP Mortgages Ltd) v Stepsky* [1996] 2 All ER 277, where the Court of Appeal held that, on the wording of s 199(1)(ii)(b), knowledge possessed by solicitors who were acting for both a borrower and a lender in the same transaction could not be imputed to the lender unless that knowledge was received by the solicitors in the capacity of solicitors for the lender 'as such' within the meaning of the sub-section. In that case, the information as to the true purpose of the mortgage transaction came to the knowledge of the solicitors while they were acting as the solicitors for the borrowers. That knowledge, once obtained, remained with the solicitors and could not be treated as coming to them again when they were instructed on behalf of the lender. The lender cannot, however, assume that the solicitor has discharged his duties fully and competently if it knows (or ought to know) that this is false. Thus, if the bank is in possession of material information which is not available to the solicitor, the fact that the wife had been advised by the solicitor will not prevent the bank from being fixed with constructive notice: see *Credit Lyonnais Bank Nederland NV v Burch* [1997] 1 All ER 144 (CA). In this type of situation, there is nothing that the lender can do to protect itself; it is put on inquiry but cannot discharge the imputation of constructive notice by relying on the fact that the wife has taken independent legal advice. The lender, it seems, will also have constructive notice of the husband's undue influence, if it is aware that the solicitor is acting for both lender and borrower and is the husband's company secretary involved in obtaining extra finance for the company: *National Westminster Bank plc v Breeds* [2001] Lloyd's Rep Bank 98.

The House of Lords in *Etridge (No 2)* has essentially approved much of the foregoing reasoning. Lord Nicholls, for example, accepted that in advising the wife, a solicitor is acting for her alone. He is concerned solely with her interests, despite the fact that he may also be acting for the husband and also the lender. As a corollary to this, knowledge of what passes between the solicitor and the wife cannot be imputed to the bank, since the solicitor is not acting as the bank's agent when he is advising the wife. Clearly, however, where there is a real risk of a conflict of duty, the solicitor must decline to act for the wife. The lender's position where the wife is advised by a solicitor is discussed further in Chapter 4, para 4.5.

1.8 ROLE OF THE SOLICITOR

The solicitor who is advising a wife (or other potential guarantor) will, of course, owe her a duty of care. He may also owe the lender a corresponding duty of care, notwithstanding that he is not also acting for the bank, since although in many respects the wife and the bank have conflicting interests, they do have a common interest in ensuring that the wife does not enter into the transaction without informed consent and free from any undue influence of her husband: *Royal Bank of Scotland v Etridge (No 2)* [1998] 4 All ER 705 (CA), p 722.

In *Etridge (No 2)*, the Court of Appeal set out its views of the duties of a solicitor advising a wife who may be under the influence of her husband. It was suggested that his duty was not merely to explain the documentation and ensure that his client understands the nature of the transaction and wishes to carry it out. His duty went further in ensuring that the transaction was one which she could sensibly be advised to enter into, free from undue influence. If the solicitor was not satisfied that this was the case, according to the Court of Appeal, he was obliged to advise her not to enter into it and refuse to act further in the implementation of the transaction if she persisted.

According to Lord Nicholls, however, with whom the other Law Lords agreed, in the House of Lords in *Etridge (No 2)*, this went much too far. It was not for the solicitor to veto the transaction. If he considers the transaction is not in the wife's best interests, he should give her reasoned advice to that effect. At the end of the day, however, the decision whether to proceed or not was hers, and not that of her solicitor. According to his Lordship, 'a wife is not precluded from entering into a financially unwise transaction if, for her own reasons, she wishes to do so': para 61. Lord Nicholls, however, did recognise that there may be exceptional circumstances where 'it is glaringly obvious' that the wife is being 'grievously wronged': para 62. In those circumstances, the solicitor should clearly decline to act further.

Ultimately, the responsibilities of the solicitor who is advising the wife stem from his retainer. The bank's concern is to receive confirmation from the solicitor that he has brought home to the wife the risks involved in the transaction. The content of the advice before giving such confirmation will depend very much on the circumstances of the case. A number of matters were regarded by Lord Nicholls as the 'core minimum' and these are set out fully in Chapter 5. Most importantly, the meeting with the wife should take place in the absence of the husband and the solicitor's explanations should be couched in non-technical language. Above all, the solicitor's task should not be viewed as purely a formality or a charade. He should obtain any information he needs from the lender and, if the latter fails to provide it, he should decline to provide the confirmation required. In this connection, Lord Nicholls considered that it should become 'routine practice' for lenders to send to the solicitor the necessary financial information regarding the loan. The consent of the bank's customer (that is, the husband) will be required for this purpose and, if that is not forthcoming, the transaction will not be able to proceed. If, exceptionally, the bank believes or suspects that the wife has been misled by her husband (or is not entering into the transaction of her own free will), it must inform the wife's solicitor of the relevant facts. The foregoing guidance is intended to apply to future transactions. So far as past transactions are concerned, the House of Lords reiterated that the bank will ordinarily be regarded as having discharged its obligations if a solicitor, acting for the wife, gave the bank confirmation to the effect that he had brought home to the wife the risks she was running acting as surety for her husband's debts.

It was also stressed by the House of Lords that it would obviously be unwise for the solicitor, who is already acting for the lender, to advise the wife, unless the solicitor is instructed to act for the bank only in a ministerial capacity at completion. In *National Westminster Bank plc v Breeds* [2001] Lloyd's Rep Bank 98, for example, the solicitor acted for both lender and borrower and was also the secretary of the husband's company. Significantly, the solicitor had been actively involved in raising additional funding for the company. Lawrence Collins J held that, in these circumstances, there was a strong probability of a conflict of interest and the solicitor could not possibly have given independent advice to the wife. The upshot was that the lender was deemed to have constructive notice of the husband's undue influence even though the solicitor had certified that that the wife had understood the nature of the charge. As mentioned earlier, the role of the solicitor is discussed further in Chapter 5.

1.9 REMEDIES IN RESPECT OF UNDUE INFLUENCE

Essentially, the complainant (usually the wife) has an 'equity' to have the transaction set aside against her husband, which is capable of enforcement against third parties with notice (actual, constructive or imputed) of the equity. The transaction will usually be rescinded in its entirety: see *TSB Bank plc v Camfield* [1995] 1 All ER 951 (CA), where the wife obtained no benefit for herself from the transaction. If, however, the complainant has received a benefit, the right to rescission may be conditional on making counter-restitution. In *Dunbar Bank plc v Nadeem* [1998] 3 All ER 876 (CA), for example, the wife was obliged to restore, as a condition of rescission, the beneficial interest in a lease (which was the advantage acquired by her from the transaction) and not a proportion of the debt secured by the legal charge. When the court orders restitution, the basic objective is to restore the parties, as closely as possible, to their original positions consequent upon cancelling the transaction: *Cheese v Thomas* [1994] 1 All ER 35 (CA). The right to have the transaction set aside may, of course, be barred by undue delay (laches), acquiescence, affirmation, estoppel, or ratification: *Allcard v Skinner* (1887) 36 Ch D 145 (CA).

Apart from the possibility of awarding damages in lieu of rescission under s 2(2) of the Misrepresentation Act 1967 where the wrongdoer has been guilty of a misrepresentation (see, for example, *Kingsnorth Trust Ltd v Bell* [1986] 1 All ER 423 (CA)), the court also has power to award fair compensation in equity to a claimant who has succeeded in persuading the court to set aside the transaction: *Mahoney v Purnell* [1996] 3 All ER 61. It can also order severance of distinctly separate guarantees: *Barclays Bank plc v Caplan* [1998] 1 FLR 532. The subject of remedies is discussed fully in Chapter 6.

1.10 UNCONSCIONABILITY AS AN UNDERLYING CONCEPT?

It was, of course, Lord Denning MR in the celebrated case of *Lloyds Bank Ltd v Bundy* [1974] 3 All ER 757 (CA) (p 765), who advocated the assimilation of the law on duress, unconscionable bargains and undue influence under one general notion of 'inequality of bargaining power'. Under this principle, according to his Lordship, English law would give relief to a person who:

> ... without independent advice, entered into a contract on terms which were very unfair or transferred property for a consideration which was grossly inadequate where his bargaining power was grievously impaired by reason of his own needs or desires, or by his own ignorance or infirmity, coupled with undue influence or pressure brought to bear on him by or for the benefit of the other.

Significantly, however, the other two judges (Cairns LJ and Sir Eric Sachs) based their decision on more orthodox principles relying on the existence of a relationship of trust and confidence between the assistant bank manager and his customer in order to raise a class 2 category of undue influence.

The significance, however, of Lord Denning's observations should not be underestimated. His Lordship took the bold step of seeking to bring together related doctrines under one unifying principle based on disparity of bargaining strength between the parties. This approach has had other judicial supporters, most notably Lord Diplock in *Schroeder Music Publishing Co v Macaulay* [1974] 3 All ER 616, who also invoked the broader principle of inequality of bargaining power in releasing a musician from his contract with a publishing company. It is apparent, however, that the general principle enunciated by Lord Denning MR, in *Bundy*, does not represent the modern law. Although his Lordship had occasion to repeat his principle in a number of later cases (see, for example, *Arrale v Costain Civil Engineering Ltd* [1976] Lloyd's Rep 98 (CA), p 102; *Levison v Patent Steam Carpet Cleaning Co Ltd* [1978] QB 69 (CA), pp 78–79; and *Avon Finance Co Ltd v Bridger* [1985] 2 All ER 281 (CA), p 286), it is evident that it has not found general approval.

On the contrary, there has been a universal return to orthodoxy, as is illustrated by the Privy Council decision in *Boustany v Pigott* (1995) 69 P & CR 298. Here, Lord Templeman reiterated the traditional view that it is not sufficient to attract the jurisdiction of equity to prove that a bargain is hard, unreasonable or foolish. It must be shown to be unconscionable, in the sense that 'one of the parties to it has imposed the objectionable terms in a morally reprehensible manner, that is to say, in a way which affects his conscience': *Multiservice Bookbinding Ltd v Marden* [1979] Ch 84, p 110, *per* Browne-Wilkinson J. The word 'unconscionable' in this context relates, not merely to the terms of the bargain, but also to the behaviour of the stronger party, which must be characterised by some moral culpability or impropriety. In *Alec Lobb (Garages) Ltd v Total Oil (Great Britain) Ltd* [1983] 1 WLR 87, for example, a transaction involving a lease and lease-back was held not to be harsh or unconscionable since, on the evidence, no unfair advantage had been taken by the defendants of the company's desperate financial position. Moreover, there was no element of undervalue in the price paid for the lease of the site as a tied site, nor could the mutual break clauses and the absolute prohibition on assignment in the underlease (which was in a standard form) be regarded as unconscionable or even unreasonable.

What is apparent from the *Boustany* decision is that unequal bargaining power, or objectively unreasonable terms, will not in themselves provide a basis for equitable interference in the absence of unconscientious or extortionate abuse of power where exceptionally 'it was not right that the strong should be allowed to push the weak to the wall': *Alec Lobb (Garages) Ltd v Total Oil (Great Britain) Ltd* [1985] 1 WLR 173 (CA), p 183, *per* Dillon LJ. In other words, even if the terms of the contract are unfair, in the sense that they are more favourable to one party than the other (that is, a contractual imbalance), equity will not provide relief unless the defendant is guilty of unconscionable conduct (that is, he has taken unconscientious advantage of the claimant's disabling condition or circumstances).

What then of Lord Denning's formulation of principle enunciated in *Bundy*? On a close reading of his judgment, it is apparent that his Lordship did not consider that inequality of bargaining power alone constituted a sufficient basis for equity's intervention. His statement reveals that the concepts of unconscionability and the exertion of excessive power or coercion by a stronger party over a weaker one are key elements in establishing this form of equitable relief. Unfortunately, the point seems to have been missed in *National Westminster Bank plc v Morgan* [1985] 1 All ER 821 (HL), where Lord Scarman referred to Lord Denning's formulation as being dependent simply on inequality of bargaining power. According to Lord Scarman (p 830):

> The fact of an unequal bargain will, of course, be a relevant feature in some cases of undue influence. But it can never become an appropriate basis of principle of [this] doctrine ... I question whether there is any need in the modern law to erect a general principle of relief against inequality of bargaining power. Parliament has undertaken the task (and it is essentially a legislative task) of enacting restrictions on freedom of contract as are in its judgment necessary to relieve against the mischief ... I doubt whether the courts should assume the burden of formulating further restrictions.

In this passage, Lord Scarman questions the need for a more general formulation of principle, along the lines of Lord Denning's judgment in *Bundy*, because, in his view, this is a matter for legislative intervention rather than judicial decision. But, as several commentators have noted elsewhere, there is no reason why a general principle of unconscionability could not coexist with current legislation (for example, the Unfair Contract Terms Act 1977) governing freedom of contract. Indeed, most recently, in *Credit Lyonnais Bank Nederland NV v Burch* [1997] 1 All ER 144, Nourse LJ cited (with apparent approval) the observations of Balcombe J in *Backhouse v Backhouse* [1978] 1 All ER 1158 (p 1166), suggesting that the cases involving unconscionable bargains could still come under the general heading of inequality of bargaining power.

Interestingly, moreover, Commonwealth jurisdictions, in particular Canada and Australia, have shown willingness to accept a more general doctrine of unconscionability. In the United States, such a broad doctrine is partly statutory, deriving from s 2-302 of the Uniform Commercial Code, and also common law-based in those States where the Code does not apply. Under American law, a distinction is drawn between 'procedural' and 'substantive' unconscionability. The former is invoked where some element of oppression or wrongdoing has occurred during the making of the transaction. This enables the courts to call upon the doctrines of duress and undue influence as merely examples of a broader principle requiring that undue advantage of a party should not be taken. Substantive unconscionability, on the other hand, is concerned with the actual substance of the contract (for example, excessive exclusion clauses, penalties, exorbitant prices, etc): see, further, Leff, A, 'Unconscionability and the Code – the emperor's new clause' (1967) 115 Un Pennsylvania LR 485. Although English law has moved some way to accepting substantive unconscionability in statutory form with the introduction of the Unfair Terms in Consumer Contracts Regulations 1999 (formerly 1994), it is apparent that the common law will continue to govern the majority of unconscionable bargain cases involving transactions at an undervalue.

The possible movement towards an underlying concept of unconscionability has already been canvassed by several academic commentators. In particular, Capper, in an influential article, has argued persuasively that the doctrines of undue influence and unconscionability can be merged into one by simply subsuming undue influence under the wider notion of unconscionability: Capper, D, 'Undue influence and unconscionability: a rationalisation' (1998) 114 LQR 479. He identifies several features (that is, relational inequality, transactional imbalance and unconscionable conduct) which are common to both doctrines. He also suggests, in line with Australian authority, that where a lender has actual or constructive notice of an unconscionable transaction (say, between husband and wife), it is itself acting unconscionably in relying on the transaction. Several objections have, of course, been canvassed to any such assimilation of the two doctrines: see, for example, Phang, A, 'Undue influence methodology, sources and linkages' [1995] JBL 552, pp 570–74. Most significantly, it has been suggested that the adoption of an overarching concept of unconscionability is likely to introduce considerable uncertainty into our law. This, however, is not altogether convincing since it is apparent that the courts would have little difficulty in setting out appropriate guidelines and limitations within which a new combined doctrine would operate: see, further, Chapter 8.

Until such a unified doctrine is accepted, we would venture the following definition of undue influence, namely: 'the direct or indirect exploitation of power by one person against another, which impairs the other's ability to form independent and informed judgment in relation to a transaction, agreement or gift from which the person exercising the power may benefit.'

CHAPTER 2

ACTUAL AND PRESUMED UNDUE INFLUENCE

2.1 INTRODUCTION

It has been said that 'it is impossible to define, and difficult even to describe, at what point influence becomes, in the eye of the law, undue': *Bank of Scotland v Bennett* [1997] 1 FLR 801, p 823, *per* Mr James Munby QC (sitting as a deputy judge of the High Court). This statement reflects the observation of Lindley LJ, in *Allcard v Skinner* (1887) 36 Ch D 145 (p 183), that no court has ever attempted to define undue influence. The dividing line, therefore, between permissible forms of persuasion and undue influence is a matter of public policy (*Mutual Finance Ltd v John Wetton & Sons Ltd* [1937] 2 KB 389, pp 394–95, *per* Porter J) and whether or not the conduct in question amounts to undue influence will depend, ultimately, on the particular facts of the case. In the words of Lord Nicholls, in *Royal Bank of Scotland v Etridge (No 2)* [2001] UKHL 44 (para 7):

> The circumstances in which one person acquires influence over another, and the manner in which influence may be exercised, vary too widely to permit of any more specific criterion.

Similarly, Lord Clyde opined that undue influence is 'something which can be more easily recognised when found than exhaustively analysed in the abstract': *Etridge (No 2)* (HL), para 92. As we saw in Chapter 1, cases on undue influence have traditionally been categorised under, broadly, two categories – namely, actual and presumed undue influence. In the words of Cotton LJ, in *Allcard v Skinner* (1887) 36 Ch D 145 (CA) (p 171):

> First, where the Court has been satisfied that the gift was the result of influence expressly used by the donee for the purpose; second, where the relations between the donor and donee have at or shortly before the execution of the gift been such as to raise a presumption that the donee had influence over the donor.

Further refinement of this twofold classification was made by the Court of Appeal in *Bank of Credit and Commerce International SA v Aboody* [1992] 4 All ER 955. In that case, Slade LJ (giving the judgment of the court) alluded to the 'clear distinction' between: (1) cases in which the court will uphold a plea of undue influence only if it is satisfied that such influence has been affirmatively proved on the evidence (that is, class 1 cases); and (2) cases in which the relationship between the parties will lead the court to presume that undue influence has been exerted unless evidence is adduced proving the contrary (that is, class 2 cases). This second category was capable of further sub-division into cases where the relationship between the parties will automatically give rise to the presumption (that is, class 2A cases) and those where, on the particular facts, a relationship not falling within the class 2A category may be shown to have become such as to justify the court in applying the presumption (that is, class 2B cases).

This refinement of the class 2 category was accepted by the House of Lords in *Barclays Bank plc v O'Brien* [1994] AC 180 (pp 189–90). It was stated that, in class 2 cases, the complainant only had to show initially that there was a relationship of trust and confidence between the parties of such a nature that it was fair to presume that the wrongdoer abused that relationship in procuring the complainant to enter into the transaction. Evidence of actual undue influence was unnecessary, because it was the existence of the confidential relationship itself which shifted the burden of proof onto the wrongdoer to prove that the complainant entered into the transaction with a free and independent will. In the class 2A category, certain relationships (for example, solicitor and client, doctor and patient) will raise the presumption of undue influence as a matter of law. In class 2B cases, however, the complainant has to prove the existence of a relationship under which he (or she) reposed trust and confidence in the wrongdoer in order to raise the presumption.

In both actual and presumed undue influence claims, it is not necessary to show that the person who has exerted influence has thereby derived some personal benefit from the gift or transaction: *Allcard v Skinner* (1887) 36 Ch D 145 (CA), p 181, *per* Lindley LJ. As was stated in *Bridgeman v Green* (1757) Wilm 58, 97 ER 22 (pp 65, 25):

> ... whoever receives [the gift] must take it tainted and infected with the undue influence and imposition of the person procuring the gift; his partitioning and cantoning it out amongst his relations and friends will not purify the gift, and protect it against the equity of the person imposed upon.

The point was specifically addressed in *Bullock v Lloyds Bank Ltd* [1955] Ch 317, where Vaisey J held that the doctrine of undue influence was not confined to cases in which the influence is exerted specifically to secure a benefit for the person exerting it. In this case, a young daughter (who had just reached 21), at the request of her father and his solicitor, executed a settlement whereby she assigned to the trustee of the settlement the interest she had received under her late mother's will. Under the settlement, the daughter took a life interest in the settled fund and, upon her death and in default of an appointment in favour of any children or husband who might survive her, the fund was to be held on statutory protective trusts for the benefit of her father and her brother. Notwithstanding that the father had not been prompted by any selfish motives of benefiting himself, the settlement was set aside on the ground of presumed undue influence. The point has also been addressed more recently, in *Naidoo v Naidu* (2000) *The Times*, 1 November, where Blackburne J held that the doctrine of undue influence was not confined to transactions which were in favour of, or which had been instigated by, the individual on whom reliance has been placed by the complainant. The doctrine applied equally where the wrongdoer had personal reasons for wishing the complainant to deal with the person in whose favour the transaction was made. It made no difference that the transaction originated with the third party, if it could be shown that the requisite relationship of trust and confidence between the complainant and the wrongdoer had been abused in order to induce the complainant to enter into the transaction. (See, also, *Turnbull & Co v Duval* [1902] AC 429 (PC) and *O'Sullivan v Management Agency and Music Ltd* [1985] QB 428 (CA), p 464.)

It is apparent, however, that the court will not intervene to set aside the transaction unless the claimant brings his case within one of the two categories of undue influence outlined above. The general rule, as stated by Jenkins LJ, in *Tufton v Sperni* [1952] 2 TLR 516 (CA) (p 526), is that 'a person who, in the eye of the law, is capable of managing his own affairs is bound by any disposition he chooses to make, however damaging to himself it may be'. The courts are not concerned with saving people from the consequences of their own folly. In the words of Lindley LJ, in *Allcard v Skinner* (1887) 36 Ch D 145 (pp 182–83):

> It would obviously be to encourage folly, recklessness, extravagance and vice if persons could get back property which they foolishly made away with ... On the other hand, to protect people from being forced, tricked or misled in any way by others into parting with their property is one of the most legitimate objects of all laws.

In *Lloyds Bank Ltd v Bundy* [1974] 3 All ER 757 (CA), Lord Denning MR expressed himself in this way (p 763):

> ... in the vast majority of cases a customer who signs a bank guarantee or a charge cannot get out of it. No bargain will be upset which is the result of the ordinary interplay of forces.

This sentiment was also expressed by Salmond J in the New Zealand Supreme Court, in *Brusewitz v Brown* [1923] NZLR 1106 (p 1109):

> The mere fact that a transaction is based on inadequate consideration or is otherwise improvident, unreasonable, or unjust is not in itself any ground on which this Court can set it aside as invalid ... The law in general leaves every man at liberty to make such bargains as he pleases, and to dispose of his own property as he chooses.

The court's attitude to improvident bargains has also been echoed in *Royal Bank of Scotland plc v Etridge (No 2)* [1998] 4 All ER 705 (CA), where Stuart-Smith LJ emphasised that legitimate commercial pressure, coupled with strong feelings of family and loyalty and a desire to help a husband (or son) in financial difficulty, were not sufficient to warrant equity's intervention. What was required was evidence that the complainant (usually the wife) had entered into the transaction not because she was persuaded that 'it is the right thing to do', but 'because the wrongdoer's importunity has left her with no will of her own': p 713. (See, also, *Bank of Scotland v Bennett* [1999] Lloyd's Rep Bank 145 (CA), p 157, *per* Chadwick LJ.) As one commentator has remarked, 'this essentially requires a surety to fit herself within a stereotype of the down-trodden and uninformed housewife': Fehlberg, B, 'The husband, the bank, the wife and her signature – the sequel' (1966) 59 MLR 675, p 679.

Most recently, the House of Lords, in *Etridge (No 2)*, has questioned whether an over-rigid classification of undue influence cases is appropriate. Lord Nicholls found the usage 'a little confusing' and Lord Hobhouse went as far as to say that the class 2(B) presumption should not be adopted as not being 'a useful forensic tool': *Etridge (No 2)*, para 107. Lord Scott 'doubt[ed] the utility' of the class 2(B) classification, but he considered class 2(A) as being 'useful in identifying particular relationships where the presumption arises': para 161. Lord Clyde considered the twofold (actual and presumed) division was 'illogical' and simply 'add[ed] mystery rather than illumination': para 92. This was because the various categories confused definition with proof. Lord Clyde said (para 93):

> English law has identified certain relationships where the conclusion can *prima facie* be drawn so easily as to establish a presumption of undue influence. But this is simply a matter of evidence and proof.

In the words of Lord Hobhouse (para 104):

> It is a fallacy to argue from the terminology normally used, 'presumed undue influence', to the position, not of presuming that one party reposed trust and confidence in the other, but of presuming that an abuse of that relationship has occurred; factual inference, yes, once the issue has been properly raised, but not a presumption.

Ultimately, the wife (or other person) alleging that the relevant transaction is not enforceable must prove her case. She can do this by proving an overt wrong (oppression), or simply a failure to perform an equitable duty. As his Lordship explained (para 105):

> Although the general burden of proof is, and remains, upon her, she can discharge that burden of proof by establishing a sufficient *prima facie* case to justify a decision in her favour on the balance of probabilities, the court drawing appropriate inferences from the primary facts proved. Evidentially the opposite party will then be faced with the necessity to adduce evidence sufficient to displace that conclusion.

(See, further, para 2.3.1, below, for a fuller discussion of the burden of proof.) Despite, however, their Lordships' misgivings concerning attempts at classification, it will be convenient to retain the distinction between actual and presumed undue influence cases for the purposes of this chapter.

2.2 ACTUAL UNDUE INFLUENCE

In *Royal Bank of Scotland v Etridge (No 2)* [2001] UKHL 44, Lord Hobhouse defined actual undue influence as 'an equitable wrong committed by the dominant party against the other which makes it unconscionable for the dominant party to enforce his legal rights against the other': para 103. Typically, it involves some express conduct overbearing the other party's will. Actual (or express) undue influence is, therefore, established by showing actual coercion or such control by the stronger party so as to substantially undermine the independent decision of the weaker party: *Smith v Kay* (1859) 7 HLC 750 (older man's influence over a younger man). Many of the early cases involving actual influence concerned religious and spiritual advisers: see *Morley v Loughnan* [1893] 1 Ch 736 and Chapter 1, para 1.2. There have also been cases concerning employers and employees: *Bridgeman v Green* (1755) 2 Ves Sen 627. A more recent example involved a son and his parents. In *Coldunell Ltd v Gallon* [1986] 1 All ER 429 (CA), the parents, who were elderly, had a son in his fifties who was better educated and more worldly in financial matters. The son needed money for his business and persuaded his parents to help him arrange finance from licensed moneylenders. They lent £20,000 on short term to the father, who then gave the money to the son. The loan was secured by a charge on the father's house where both parents lived. His parents' signatures to the documentation were procured by the son. The Court of Appeal had no difficulty in accepting that the son had exercised actual undue influence over his parents. Apart from the discrepancy in age and education, there was evidence that, when the father produced the land certificate in respect of his house, the son reached across and grabbed it, saying: 'That's what I want.' The mother's evidence was to the same effect. When she signed the consent to the loan giving the moneylenders priority over her interest in the house, her son had his arm over the table across the document and said: 'You sign these, mother.' She also gave evidence that he was 'in the devil of a hurry to get this thing signed'. (See, also, *Langton v Langton* [1995] 2 FLR 890, involving a gift of a bungalow by a father to his son and daughter-in-law.)

In *Allcard v Skinner* (1887) 36 Ch D 145 (p 181), Lindley LJ sought to define actual undue influence in these terms:

> ... some unfair and improper conduct, some coercion from outside, some overreaching, some form of cheating, and generally, though not always, some personal advantage obtained by a donee placed in some close and confidential relation to the donor.

The underlying rationale is that 'no one shall be allowed to retain any benefit arising from his own fraud or wrongful act': *Allcard v Skinner*, p 171, *per* Cotton LJ. But, as Mr James Munby QC (sitting as a deputy judge) said, in *Bank of Scotland v Bennett* [1997] 1 FLR 801 (p 822): 'not all influence is undue influence ... even very strong persuasion and "heavy family pressures" are not, of themselves sufficient.' In that case, the wife's evidence showed that she had been persuaded to execute the charge over the family home as a result of her husband's moral blackmail, which amounted to victimisation and coercion. In effect, she had been worn down by the husband and by the fear that, if she did not comply, her marriage would be destroyed. The plea of actual undue influence against her husband was, accordingly, made out. The decision on this point was affirmed on appeal: [1999] Lloyd's Rep Bank 145 (CA), pp 153–57.

Cases involving actual undue influence are not common. In the majority of reported cases, the claimant is able to rely successfully on a presumption of undue influence. The decision in *Bank of Credit and Commerce International SA v Aboody* [1992] 4 All ER 955 is a notable exception. In that case, the defendants were husband and wife and the directors/shareholders of a family company which was effectively run by the husband as a one man business. The wife signed company documents without question as and when they were put before her by her husband, whom she trusted to run the company for their mutual benefit. In order to secure the company's borrowing from the claimant bank, the defendants entered into a series of transactions, comprising various guarantees and charges in favour of the bank over a house owned by the wife. On the occasion of the signing of the final charge, the bank arranged for an independent solicitor to advise the wife separately on the nature of the charge but, in the course of the solicitor's interview with her, the husband burst into the room uninvited and, following an argument between the husband and solicitor, the wife signed the charge. The company subsequently collapsed and the bank sought possession of the house in order to realise its security. The wife relied on a plea of actual undue influence by way of defence.

No doubt, the facts in this case were somewhat exceptional. The wife was an Iraqi Jew, who had been born and educated in Baghdad. Both she and her family observed strictly Iraqi Jewish customs, which meant that business matters were never discussed amongst women, being considered a man's exclusive province. She had married her husband at the age of 17, and he was 20 years older than her. The marriage was arranged by the parties' parents. The husband was born and educated in British India. There was evidence from the independent solicitor (who had conducted the interview with the wife) that the husband was a bully and that the wife was under pressure and had signed because she wanted peace of mind. Indeed, during the interview, the husband had reduced the wife to tears after a distressing scene during which both the husband and solicitor had been arguing and shouting. On these facts, therefore, the wife was able to successfully prove a class 1 case of undue influence without resort to the benefit of any presumption. In the course of his judgment, Slade LJ set out the requisite ingredients for an actual undue influence claim (p 976):

(a) the other party to the transaction must have the capacity to influence the complainant;

(b) influence was actually exercised;

(c) the exercise of that influence was undue;

(d) its exercise brought about the transaction.

On the facts in *Aboody*, there was no doubt that the first three conditions had been satisfied. First, at the invitation of the husband, the wife was habitually prepared to sign documents relating to their financial affairs without considering their contents because she trusted him. He had also invited her to enter into the various transactions. Secondly, the husband, in inducing his wife to enter into the transactions, had deliberately acted so as to conceal matters from her in a way which prevented her from giving proper detached consideration to her independent interests in matters which involved substantial risks to her. Lack of any intention to injure her did not prevent the husband's conduct from being unconscionable. Nor, for that matter, was it essential to show that the husband had actually bullied or coerced her in relation to these transactions. In this connection, it is not a vital requirement that the party with the influence had taken some *positive* action, whether by way of coercion or persuasion, etc, so as to bring pressure to bear upon the mind of the complainant; mere omission or inactivity may be enough, if this has the effect of preventing the complainant from making a free, independent and informed decision: *Aboody*, pp 976–78. In the words of Slade LJ (p 977):

> If [the husband] had positively misrepresented to her the extent of the risks involved, a plea based on misrepresentation might well have been available to her. The mere fact that in order to get his own way he chose deliberately to say nothing as to the risks, rather than to misrepresent them, would not, in our judgment, save his conduct from being unconscionable or absolve him from a charge of actual undue influence bearing in mind that it was he who invited her to enter into them.

The case is significant because it appears to recognise that a husband who merely exploits his wife's trust to persuade her to enter into a transaction without proper advice will be held to be exercising actual undue influence over her, even though (as we shall see below, p 39) the transaction is not manifestly disadvantageous to her (since this is no longer a requirement in cases of actual undue influence). Despite this, the wife's claim in *Aboody* failed on the ground, *inter alia*, that her husband's undue influence did not bring about the transaction; on this point, the evidence showed, on a balance of probabilities, that the wife would have entered into the transactions *in any event*, even in the absence of undue influence. Tactically, however, it may be wiser for the wife to rely on class 2B undue influence because this will shift the burden of proof onto the husband to rebut the presumption. However, reliance on class 1 undue influence may be inevitable where, in seeking to rely on a class 2B claim, the element of manifest disadvantage is difficult to establish (or not present) on the facts.

It is apparent, therefore, that the relationship of the one party to the other need not be one of actual dominance (*Goldsworthy v Brickell* [1987] 1 All ER 853, p 865), nor must the undue influence be accompanied by a malign intent. A successful claim based on actual undue influence does not, therefore, require direct evidence of pressure being specifically brought to bear on the complainant: *Royal Bank of Scotland plc v Etridge (No 2)* [1998] 4 All ER 705, p 712, *per* Stuart-Smith LJ ('pressure is neither always necessary or sufficient'); and *Dunbar Bank plc v Nadeem* [1998] 3 All ER 876, p 883 (CA), *per* Millett LJ ('neither coercion, nor pressure, nor deliberate concealment is a necessary element in a case of actual undue influence'). In *Re Craig (decd), Meneces v Middleton* [1971] 1 Ch 95, for example, there was no evidence to the effect that 'if you do not make me this gift, I will leave you'. But there was evidence of direct pressure being exercised by the old man's secretary-companion to get her own way in other respects, which were held to be enough to establish that the gifts would not have been made unless there had been actual undue influence. Accordingly, direct evidence of pressure on other occasions and for other purposes may be sufficient to uphold a claim of actual undue influence. It was emphasised, however, that the onus of proving actual influence was a heavy one, because the more objectionable the conduct, the less likely, normally, that it would occur.

In *Bank of Montreal v Stuart* [1911] AC 120 (PC), the wife was successful in establishing that she was the victim of her husband's actual undue influence, even though no actual pressure was exerted on her by him. In this case, the wife had no will of her own and no means of forming an independent judgment because she was prepared to sign anything that her husband asked her to sign. It may be, however, that today such a case would more readily be classified as a class 2B category of undue influence. It may also be possible to characterise the husband's conduct as a misrepresentation which induced the wife to enter into the transaction. In *Bank of Cyprus (London) Ltd v Markou* [1999] 2 All ER 707, for example, the husband had persuaded his wife to go to the bank to sign some documents in connection with changing their company's bank account. He did not tell her that the papers involved an agreement to borrow money from the bank, with a second charge to be taken out on the family home. His representations to her in this regard were held to remain effective, despite the presence of the bank's assistant manager, since the latter had failed to explain the implications of the transaction to her and did not advise her to seek independent legal advice. (See, also, *Scotlife Home Loans (No 2) Ltd v Melinek* (1997) 78 P & CR 389, p 396 (CA).)

It seems also that proof of actual undue influence is not dependent on proof of a definite or direct threat; an implied threat will suffice in appropriate circumstances. In *Mutual Finance Ltd v John Wetton & Sons Ltd* [1937] 2 KB 389, a guarantee was obtained from a family company under an implied threat to prosecute a member of the family who was alleged to have forged the signature of the company to a previous guarantee. Porter J held that the guarantee was obtained by actual undue influence and, accordingly, set it aside. Similarly, in *Williams v Bayley* (1866) LR 1 HL 200, a promise was extracted by a threat to prosecute certain third parties, unless the promise was given. Lord Chelmsford, in holding that a direct threat was not necessary, said (p 216):

> ... the fears of the father were stimulated and operated on to an extent to deprive him of free agency, and to extort an agreement from him for the benefit of [others].

As intimated earlier, in cases involving actual undue influence, it is also not necessary to prove that the transaction was manifestly disadvantageous to the complainant. This is because actual undue influence is treated as 'a species of fraud': *CIBC Mortgages plc v Pitt* [1994] 1 AC 200 (HL), p 209, *per* Lord Browne-Wilkinson. In that case, the parties were husband and wife owning a matrimonial home valued at £270,000, with an outstanding mortgage of £16,700 in favour of a building society. The husband told the wife that he wished to obtain a loan on the security of the house to buy shares on the stock market, which would improve their standard of living. The wife was reluctant, but the husband exerted pressure on her and secured her consent. The lender made a written offer of a loan to the couple, secured on the home for the purpose of a remortgage, on the basis that the advance was to be used for the purchase of a second property. The couple both signed the offer, but the wife did not read the document and was not aware of the stated purpose of the loan. She also did not read the documents relating to the two legal charges which the couple executed in favour of the lender. The husband used the advance to purchase shares but later, following a stock market crash, these were sold to pay off his creditors. When the husband failed to meet the payments under the loan, the lender sought possession of the property.

The primary importance of the case has centred on the degree of knowledge required by the lender to put it on notice of the husband's actual undue influence: see, further, Chapter 4. In the present context, however, the decision is significant in so far as it overruled previous authority (notably, *Bank of Credit and Commerce International SA v Aboody* [1992] 4 All ER 955) to the effect that manifest disadvantage was a necessary prerequisite to a claim based on actual undue influence. The position since *Pitt*, therefore, is that a person who proves the exercise of actual undue influence by another in carrying out a transaction (as the wife was able to do in *Pitt*) is entitled *as of right* against the other to have the transaction set aside without proof of manifest disadvantage. A complainant in this category is to be treated like any other victim of fraud regardless of whether the transaction is advantageous or not. In the words of Lord Browne-Wilkinson (p 209):

> A man guilty of fraud is no more entitled to argue that the transaction was beneficial to the person defrauded than is a man who has procured a transaction by misrepresentation. The effect of the wrongdoer's conduct is to prevent the wronged party from bringing a free will and properly informed mind to bear on the proposed transaction which accordingly must be set aside in equity as a matter of justice.

It has been suggested, therefore, that, in the context of parties who trust the other to the extent that they sign without question, the fact that the complainant has been deprived of the opportunity to give free and informed consent in itself makes the influence undue: see *Chitty on Contracts*, Vol 1, 28th edn, 1999, London: Sweet & Maxwell, para 7-049.

It is apparent, however, that manifest disadvantage remains strong evidence that undue influence has been exercised. Thus, the more disadvantageous the transaction to the wife, the easier it will be for her to establish that it has been procured by improper means (and the more difficult for the husband to rebut the inference): *Royal Bank of Scotland plc v Etridge (No 2)* [1998] 4 All ER 705 (CA), p 713, *per* Stuart-Smith LJ.

2.3 PRESUMED UNDUE INFLUENCE

Presumed undue influence is concerned with the abuse of a relationship of trust and confidence; the influence grows naturally from the confidence reposed by the person influenced in the person exercising the influence: *Royal Bank of Scotland plc v Etridge (No 2)* [1998] 4 All ER 705 (CA), p 711, *per* Stuart-Smith LJ, who explained that, because the vice of the transaction lies in the abuse of a position of trust, the transaction must result in some unfair advantage to the person in whom trust is reposed at the expense of the person who relies upon him. Unlike actual undue influence, therefore, the court intervenes not on the ground that a wrongful act has, in fact, been committed, but on the ground of public policy and 'to prevent the relations which existed between the parties and the influence arising therefrom from being abused': *Allcard v Skinner* (1887) 36 Ch D 145 (CA), p 171, *per* Cotton LJ. In the words of Lord Nicholls, in *Royal Bank of Scotland v Etridge (No 2)* [2001] UKHL 44 (HL), (paras 9–10):

> The relationship between two individuals may be such that, without more, one of them is disposed to agree a course of action proposed by the other. Typically this occurs when one person places trust in another to look after his affairs and interests, and the latter betrays this trust by preferring his own interests. He abuses the influence he has acquired ... The law has long recognised the need to prevent abuse of influence in these 'relationship' cases despite the absence of evidence of overt acts of persuasive conduct.

It is important, therefore, to appreciate that the use of the word 'abuse' in this context does not necessarily entail any wrongful intention on the part of the person in whom confidence has been reposed. The word simply means that, once the existence of a confidential relationship has been established, any possible use of influence (irrespective of the intentions of the person possessing it) will be regarded by the courts as 'an abuse' in relation to the particular transaction under consideration. That situation will then prevail unless and until the duty of fiduciary care owed to the complainant has been properly discharged.

It will be convenient to consider the two categories of presumed undue influence (that is, classes 2A and 2B) separately, although the underlying principle governing both is the same. In the words of Nourse LJ, in *Goldsworthy v Brickell* [1987] 1 All ER 853 (p 865):

> It is that the degree of trust and confidence is such that the party in whom it is reposed, either because he is or has become an adviser of the other or because he has been entrusted with the management of his affairs or everyday needs or for some other reason, is in a position to influence him into effecting the transaction of which complaint is later made.

An earlier formulation of the same principle is to be found in the judgment of Lord Chelmsford LC, in *Tate v Williamson* (1866) 2 Ch App 55 (p 61):

> Wherever the persons stand in such a relation that, while it continues, confidence is necessarily reposed by one, and the influence which naturally grows out of that confidence is possessed by the other, and this confidence is abused, or the influence is exerted to obtain an advantage at the expense of the confiding party, the person so availing himself of his position will not be permitted to retain the advantage, although the transaction could not have been impeached if no such confidential relation had existed.

It is apparent, therefore, that where the person standing in a confidential relationship does not take unfair advantage of the other person, a claim based on presumed undue influence will not be made out: *Dunbar Bank plc v Nadeem* [1998] 3 All ER 876, p 883, where the transaction was obviously beneficial to the wife and was intended by the husband to be for her benefit.

In *Re Brocklehurst's Estate, Hall v Roberts* [1978] 1 Ch 14 (p 41), Bridge LJ identified three typical features characterising relationships within the presumed undue influence category, namely:

(a) a duty on the donee to advise the donor;

(b) a position of actual or potential dominance of the donor by the donee; and

(c) a measure of confidence and trust reposed by the donor in the donee.

A similar attempt at defining the key elements of such a relationship was made by Sir Eric Sachs, in *Lloyds Bank Ltd v Bundy* [1974] 3 All ER 757 (CA) (p 757), who said that such cases arise where A relies on the guidance (or advice) of B, where B is aware of that reliance and obtains (or may obtain) a benefit or some other interest from the transaction. He also identified 'the vital element' of confidentiality in all such cases. This last characteristic is always present, but is not necessarily synonymous with a fiduciary relation and is impossible to define other than on the facts of a particular case: see Lord Hobhouse in *Etridge (No 2)* (HL), para 104, who said that 'typically they are fiduciary or closely analogous relationships'. In *Bundy*, Sir Eric Sachs intimated that it had something in common with the words 'confiding' and 'confidant', in so far as it imported a quality which went beyond that inherent in the confidence that may exist between trustworthy men of business dealing with each other at arm's length: *Bundy*, p 767. Ultimately, however, 'there is no single touchstone for determining whether the principle is applicable': *Etridge (No 2)* (HL), *per* Lord Nicholls, para 11.

In addition to a confidential relationship, the claimant must show that the gift is so substantial that it cannot *prima facie* be reasonably accounted for 'on the ground of ordinary motives on which ordinary men act': *Re Craig (decd), Meneces v Middleton* [1971] 1 Ch 95, p 105. Thus, even where there is a relationship of trust and confidence to which the presumption is held to apply, the presumption will remain inoperative until the party who has imparted the trust and confidence makes a gift so large, or enters into such an improvident transaction, as not to be reasonably accounted for on the ground of friendship, relationship, charity or other benevolent motives. It is only then that the influence, arising from the existence of the relationship, is presumed to be undue: *Goldsworthy v Brickell* [1987] 1 All ER 853 (CA), p 865, *per* Nourse LJ, applied in *Morritt v Wonham* [1993] NPC 2 ([1994] Conv 233). This test has been held to be equivalent to that of manifest disadvantage evident in the more recent case law: *Claughton v Price* (1998) 30 HLR 396 (CA), p 405, *per* Nourse LJ, who also confirmed that the presumption is 'not perfected and remains inoperative' until the disadvantageous nature of the transaction is shown. Thus, in *Bank of Scotland v Bennett* [1997] 3 FCR 193 (p 199), it was reiterated that undue influence will not be presumed unless the complainant (usually the wife) can prove that: (1) she reposed trust and confidence in her husband in relation to their financial affairs; and (2) the transaction was manifestly disadvantageous to her. (See, further, Chapter 3.)

2.3.1 Burden of proof

It is important to appreciate that the presumption of undue influence (in either category) is merely a 'lawyer's tool' which serves to bridge a gap in evidence (where proof of the exercise of undue influence is likely to be difficult) and shifts the onus of proof from the complainant onto the wrongdoer to show that the transaction was the result of the former's free and independent exercise of his (or her) will. In other words, it is always open to the defendant to rebut the presumption by proof of the removal of any such presumed influence.

The point was addressed at some length by the House of Lords, in *Royal Bank of Scotland v Etridge (No 2)* [2001] UKHL 44. The burden of proving an allegation of undue influence (whether actual or presumed) rests upon the person who claims to have been wronged. The evidence required to discharge that burden depends on a variety of factors, including the nature of the alleged undue influence, the personality of the parties, their relationship, the extent to which the transaction cannot readily be accounted for by the ordinary motives of ordinary persons in such a relationship, and all the circumstances of the case: *per* Lord Nicholls (para 13) and Lord Scott (para 153). Normally, proof that the complainant placed trust and confidence in the other party in relation to the management of the complainant's financial affairs, coupled with a transaction which calls for explanation, will be sufficient to discharge the burden of proof. In other words, proof of these two facts is *prima facie* evidence that the defendant abused the influence he acquired in the parties' relationship: *Etridge (No 2)* (HL), para 14. This then shifts the evidential burden of proof onto the wrongdoer to produce evidence to counter the inference of undue influence. Thus, the use of the term 'presumption' in this context refers simply to a shift in the evidential burden of proof, akin to the common law principle of *res ipsa loquitur* invoked in negligence cases. This evidential presumption, however, falls to be distinguished from the class 2A presumption of undue influence (see below) which arises upon the existence of certain types of relationship where the law presumes, irrebuttably, that one party had influence over the other. It is important, therefore, not to confuse this type of legal presumption from the rebuttable evidential presumption of undue influence: *Etridge (No 2)* (HL), paras 16–18. As Lord Hobhouse observed (para 104):

> ... there is no presumption properly so called that the confidence has been abused. It is a matter of evidence. If all that has happened is that, say, a client has left a small bequest to his family solicitor or that a solicitor has made a reasonable charge for professional services rendered to the client, no inference of abuse or unfair dealing will arise.

It was also stressed by Lord Scott that the weight of the evidential presumption will vary from case to case and will depend both on the particular nature of the relationship and on the particular nature of the impugned transaction. Moreover, the type and weight of evidence needed to rebut the presumption will depend upon the weight of the presumption itself. His Lordship gave, by way of example, the case of *Allcard v Skinner* (1887) 36 Ch D 145, where the presumption was a very heavy one and, accordingly, strong evidence would have been needed to rebut it. Not even independent legal advice would necessarily have been sufficient for this purpose.

2.3.2 Types of relationship recognised as a matter of law as giving rise to the presumption

Introduction

There are several well defined relationships, as we shall see, to which the presumption of undue influence will apply automatically, as a matter of law, unless the contrary is proved. In such relationships, it is enough simply to 'look at the relative status of the parties in order to presume that the requisite degree of trust and confidence is there': *Goldsworthy v Brickell* [1987] 1 All ER 853 (CA), p 865, *per* Nourse LJ.

Spiritual adviser and disciple

The classic example of a relationship falling within the class 2A category is that between religious or spiritual adviser and follower. As we have already seen, many of the early cases involved this particular kind of relationship: see

Chapter 1, para 1.2. In one of the early leading authorities, it was recognised that 'the influence of one mind over another is very subtle, and of all influences religious influence is the most dangerous and the most powerful, and to counteract it courts of equity have gone very far': *Allcard v Skinner* (1887) 36 Ch D 145 (CA), p 183, *per* Lindley LJ. In that case, the claimant sought to recover sums of stock transferred by her to her mother superior whilst she was a member of a convent. The rule of poverty within the sisterhood required each new member to give up all her property, either to her relatives or the poor, or for the general purposes of the sisterhood itself. The rules also prohibited any sister from seeking external advice without the superior's consent. The Court of Appeal held that the case fell within the category of presumed undue influence in the absence of any evidence of actual pressure or coercion exerted by the superior over the claimant. In the words of Lindley LJ (p 184):

> She had vowed poverty and obedience, and she was not at liberty to consult externs without the leave of her superior. She was not a person who treated her vows lightly; she was deeply religious and felt bound by her promise, by her vows, and by the rules of the sisterhood. She was absolutely in the power of the lady superior ... A gift made by her under these circumstances to the lady superior cannot in my opinion be retained by the donee.

A more recent application of the doctrine to members of a religious association (*Opus Dei*) bound by vows of poverty, chastity and obedience is to be found in *Roche v Sherrington* [1982] 1 WLR 599. Here, Slade J held that a claim for rescission of a transaction on the grounds of undue influence was capable of being raised against the members of an unincorporated religious association when that claim was based on a presumption of undue influence, as opposed to actual undue influence on the part of particular members of the association. In other words, such a claim could be brought against an unincorporated body, even though the claimant could not point to any human agency within that body with whom a special relationship could be said to exist.

Doctor and patient

The relationship of doctor and patient also gives rise to an automatic presumption of undue influence. There are many early cases to this effect. In *Dent v Bennett* (1839) 4 My & Cr 269; 41 ER 105, for example, a surgeon obtained an agreement from his patient, who was 85 years old, that the latter would pay him £25,000 for his medical services completed two years before, the regular charge for which had already been paid. The agreement was set aside on the ground that it had been procured by 'some dominion exercised over [the] patient': *Dent v Bennett*, pp 277, 108. (See, also, *Billage v Southee* (1852) 9 Hare 534; 68 ER 623; *Mitchell v Homfray* (1881) 8 QBD 587 (CA); and *Radcliffe v Price* (1902) 18 TLR 466.) Similarly, the relationship of trustee and beneficiary will fall within the class 2A category: *Ellis v Barker* (1871) LR 7 Ch App 104.

Parent and child

Another relationship which gives rise to the presumption of undue influence, as a matter of law, is that of parent and child. An early case is *Wright v Vanderplank* (1856) 8 De GM & G 133; 44 ER 340, where a daughter made a gift of a life estate to her father soon after she attained the age of 21, having received no advice except that of her father's solicitor. Knight Bruce LJ stated the principle in the following terms:

> A child is presumed to be under the exercise of parental influence as long as the dominion of the parent lasts. Whilst that dominion lasts, it lies on the parent maintaining the gift to disprove the exercise of parental influence, by shewing that the child had independent advice, or in some other way.

Similarly, in *Archer v Hudson* (1844) 7 Beav 551; 49 ER 1180, a niece, two months after she came of age, entered into a voluntary security for her uncle, by whom she had been brought up. In setting the security aside, Lord Langdale MR said that 'this court does not interfere to prevent an act even of bounty between parent and child, but it will take care (under the circumstances in which the parent and child are placed before the emancipation of the child) that such child is placed in such a position as will enable him to form an entirely free and unfettered judgment, independent altogether of any sort of control' (pp 560, 1183). See, also, *Berdoe v Dawson* (1865) 34 Beav 603; 55 ER 768 (son, aged 25). It is apparent, therefore, that equity's intervention is not limited in this context to gifts made by a child to a parent, but extends to other benefits including, for example, a security executed in favour of the parent's creditor. Moreover, the presumption of parental influence may, as we have seen, continue beyond the child's majority: *Baker v Bradley* (1855) 7 De GM & G 597; 44 ER 233 ('the transaction may be one of bounty from the child to the parent, soon after the child has attained 21. In such cases, this court views the transaction with jealousy, and anxiously interposes its protection to guard the child from the exercise of parental influence') (pp 621, 242, *per* Turner LJ). The suggestion therefore made by Lord Cranworth LC, in *Smith v Kay* (1859) 7 HLC 750 (p 772), that the presumption should be taken as a period of one year after the child attained majority has not been followed.

The question is ultimately one of fact and degree, with obviously a strong presumption in the case of a child just 18 living at home, which will then diminish as the child leaves home and goes out into the world. It has been opined, however, that the presumption lasts only a 'short' time after the child has attained majority: *Lancashire Loans Ltd v Black* [1934] 1 KB 380 (CA), p 419, *per* Greer LJ. In that case, it was held that there was no rule of law that the marriage of a daughter, coupled with her departure from the parental home, necessarily puts an end to the domination of her parents. It was stressed that, whether or not parental dominion had completely ceased, was a question of fact depending on the particular circumstances of each case. Here, the daughter married at the age of 18 and left her parental home and lived with her husband. Her mother was very extravagant and frequently borrowed money from moneylenders. When the daughter came of age she, at her mother's request, raised £2,000 on her reversionary interest under her grandfather's will in order to pay off her mother's debts. The mother continued to borrow money and, a year later, she asked her daughter to sign a document so that she (the mother) might be able to borrow some more money. The mother and daughter signed a joint and several promissory note for £775 at 85% interest. The daughter also gave a second charge on her vested interest in remainder, without which the moneylenders would not lend the money. The daughter, who did not understand the transaction, signed the document at the request of her mother. The only advice which she received was that of a solicitor, who also acted for the mother and the moneylenders, and who prepared the documents. The Court of Appeal held that the daughter was under the influence of her mother and that she had no independent legal advice. Moreover, because the moneylenders had notice of the facts which constituted undue influence on the mother's part, they were in no better position than the mother and, accordingly, the transaction could not stand, so far as the daughter was concerned. In the course of his judgment, Lawrence LJ said (p 411):

> The relationship between a mother and her daughter is undoubtedly one of the greatest intimacy and confidence, and it is impossible to lay down any general rule for measuring the amount or duration of the dominion which a mother may have acquired over her daughter. I can readily imagine cases in which a husband might truthfully assert that the parental dominion of his mother-in-law over his wife had continued for a considerable time and to a considerable extent after the marriage ...

The authorities suggest that a daughter with a separate home of her own may be 'emancipated' soon after she attains majority, whereas a spinster who has never left home might be able to rely on the presumption for a much longer period. What is apparent, however, is that the presumption does not simply continue indefinitely, but until it is proved that the undue influence has ceased to exist. That would be to confuse actual with presumed undue influence.

Two other cases in this field are worthy of comment. In *London and Westminster Loan and Discount Co Ltd v Bilton* (1911) 27 TLR 184, a daughter (aged 29), who was without means of her own, continued (after coming of age) to live under her father's roof. Her father was in debt and so he borrowed money upon the security of a mortgage executed by her in respect of a reversionary legacy to which she would become entitled upon her father's death. Joyce J held that, in these circumstances, it was incumbent on the lender to satisfy himself not only that the daughter understood what she was doing, but also that she was not acting under parental pressure. In practical terms, this meant ensuring that she had competent and independent advice, which it had failed to do. In *Powell v Powell* [1900] 1 Ch 243, a voluntary settlement was executed by a daughter under the influence of her stepmother in favour of the stepmother's children. The daughter did not have the benefit of independent legal advice and the settlement was, accordingly, set aside because 'the mere existence of the fiduciary relation raises the presumption, and must be rebutted by the donee': p 246, *per* Farwell J.

Apart from showing that the child had independent advice, it must also be proved that the relevant deed or instrument was entered into with full knowledge of its contents and with a free intention of giving the parent the benefit conferred by it. It has been held that this onus extends to a volunteer claiming through the parent, and to any other person taking with notice of the circumstances which raise the equity. It will not, however, extend to a purchaser for value if a solicitor purports to act in the transaction on behalf of the child. In such circumstances, the purchaser is entitled to assume that the solicitor has given the child proper advice, even though he may also be acting as the parent's solicitor: *Bainbrigge v Browne* (1881) 18 Ch D 188; *Re Pauling's Settlement Trusts* [1964] 1 Ch 303, pp 337–38, *per* Willmer LJ.

The cases involving presumed undue influence between parent and child fall to be distinguished from those involving family arrangements, which are regarded by equity with greater favour. Here, 'even ignorance of rights, if equal on both sides, may not avail to impeach the transaction': *Baker v Bradley* (1855) 7 De GM & G 597; 44 ER 233, pp 620, 241, *per* Turner LJ. In *Hartopp v Hartopp* (1855) 21 Beav 259; 52 ER 858, for example, the son was tenant in tail, and his father the tenant for life of family estates. The son, 11 months after attaining majority, being in debt, joined his father in a resettlement of the family estates. The court, although satisfied that parental influence had been exerted to obtain the execution of the settlement (but not for the father's individual advantage), upheld the transaction. The resettlement was valid because it had not been obtained by any misrepresentation or suppression of truth, was reasonable and did not personally benefit the father: see, also, *Jenner v Jenner* (1860) 2 De GF & J 359; 45 ER 660 (resettlement reasonable and for the good of the family and not wholly for the personal benefit of the father); and *Hoblyn v Hoblyn* (1889) 41 Ch D 200. The position will be different, however, if the parent receives a disproportionate benefit arising out of the arrangement. In *Hoghton v Hoghton* (1852) 15 Beav 278; 51 ER 545, the son, who was a tenant in tail, 11 months after attaining majority, concurred with his father in barring the entail and resettling the family estates. Because the father took substantial benefits from the transaction and the son had received no professional assistance, the court held that the property had not been resettled in a reasonable manner and set aside the arrangement.

Where, of course, the transaction is characterised as a gift (as opposed to a resettlement of family estates or family property), the presumption of undue influence as between parent and child will apply with full effect, so that the onus will be on the parent to show that the child both understood the transaction and was not under parental influence: see *Turner v Collins* (1871) LR 7 Ch App 329.

Guardian and ward

Analogous to the relationship of parent and child is the relation existing between guardian and ward. A number of cases illustrate the principles at work here. In *Hylton v Hylton* (1754) 2 Ves Sen 547; 28 ER 349, a grant of an annuity of £60 by a nephew to his uncle (who acted as his guardian) soon after coming of age was set aside, the court stating that 'where a man acts as a guardian ... for an infant, the court is extremely watchful to prevent that person's taking any advantage immediately upon his ward ... coming of age, and at the time of settling account ... because an undue advantage may be taken': pp 548, 350. In *Taylor v Johnson* (1882) 19 Ch D 603, Bacon VC expressed the rule in the following terms (p 608):

> ... the relation of guardian and ward must be presumed to have conferred on the guardian such an amount of influence over the mind of the ward as to make it at least doubtful whether the act done by the ward was spontaneous, or whether it is to be referred to the influence which is necessarily to be inferred from the relative positions of the parties. It is, therefore, indispensable in all cases, that the guardian, upon whom the onus is cast, should be able to prove that the influence has ceased, or at least that it was not operative ...

In that case, however, the relationship of guardian and ward was held to be lacking between a daughter and a relation who had been entrusted by her father to stay with his daughter and look after his house. In *Hatch v Hatch* (1804) 9 Ves Jun 292; 32 ER 615, however, one of the leading cases in this area, an uncle acted as guardian to his niece who, on attaining majority, conveyed substantial property to him without the benefit of separate advice. The case is particularly strong because the ward was deaf and had no understanding of the value of the property she had conveyed. Even, therefore, where the guardianship has technically ended, the presumption of undue influence may continue to apply provided there is evidence of continuing control over the ward's property or actions. It has also been held that persons standing in *loco parentis* may be subject to the same principles: *Archer v Hudson* (1844) 7 Beav 551; 49 ER 1180 (uncle and niece); *Kempson v Ashbee* (1874) LR 10 Ch App 15 (stepfather and stepdaughter); *Powell v Powell* [1900] 1 Ch 243 (stepmother and stepdaughter); *Sercombe v Sanders* (1865) 34 Beav 382; 55 ER 682 (elder brother and younger brother); and *Grosvenor v Sherratt* (1860) 28 Beav 659; 54 ER 520 (executor and beneficiary).

Solicitor and client

The relationship of solicitor and client is another classic example of a relationship falling within the class 2A category of undue influence. As was noted in Chapter 1, a solicitor is also subject to the stricter doctrine of abuse of confidence: see para 1.5.2. So far as undue influence is concerned, the classic statement of principle is to be found in the judgment of Sir John Stuart VC, in *Re Holmes' Estate* (1881) 3 Giff 337; 66 ER 439, who said (pp 345, 443):

> ... the relation of solicitor and client is one of such high confidence on the part of the client that the solicitor is considered to have an amount of influence over the mind and action of his client which, in the eye of this Court, while that influence remains, makes it impossible that the gift can prevail.

Here again, the principle will vitiate the transaction, but the presumption may be rebutted by evidence removing all effect of the influence. This can be done by circumstances 'short of the total dissolution of the relation of solicitor and client' (*Re Holmes' Estate*, pp 346, 443) by demonstrating that the client had received 'competent and independent advice': *Rhodes v Bate* (1865) LR 1 Ch App 252, p 257, *per* Turner LJ, who also intimated that equity would not interfere so readily in the case of mere trifling gifts.

In *Wright v Carter* [1903] 1 Ch 27 (CA), the claimant, being in financial difficulty, executed a deed giving part of his property in trust after his own death in certain shares for two of his children and for his solicitor, whom he expressed a wish to benefit for services rendered but not yet paid for. The draft of the deed had been prepared in the solicitor's office, though not under his supervision, but, on his suggestion, had been submitted by the claimant to a separate solicitor to advise him in the matter. The deed was later executed by the claimant on that solicitor's advice. A year later, the claimant executed another deed whereby the whole of the his property was conveyed to the same trustees in favour of his two children and his solicitor, in consideration of a covenant by them to pay the claimant a certain annuity during his life. This deed had also been prepared by a separate solicitor, who had been called in to advise the claimant.

The Court of Appeal held that the deeds were void as against the claimant's solicitor in so far as they had both been induced by undue influence. Vaughan Williams LJ was of the view that the presumption was not sufficiently rebutted by the mere fact of the client having employed a separate and independent solicitor to advise him on the gift. In his view, the presumption would continue so long as the relation of solicitor and client continued for other purposes outside the gift (as in the present case), or at all events until it could be *clearly* inferred that the influence arising from the relationship no longer existed. That was not the case here and, hence, the deeds could not stand. It was also intimated that, if the gift was trifling in nature (or made by a wealthy individual), this was a matter which the court might consider in deciding whether the influence continued. Conversely, if the gift was one which no prudent man would make, the absence of a continuing relationship of client and solicitor would not necessarily prevent a finding that the influence of the solicitor had not ceased: p 50.

Even if the relationship of solicitor and client, in a strict sense, has been discontinued, the presumption of undue influence may still apply so long as the confidence (naturally arising from such a relationship) is proved, or may be presumed to continue: *Allison v Clayhills* (1908) 97 LT 709, pp 711–12. Thus, although no longer retained or acting in his duty, a solicitor may still owe a duty in equity to his former client in respect of the particular transaction arising out of the circumstances of the particular case: *Demerara Bauxite Co Ltd v Hubbard* [1923] AC 673 (PC) and *McMaster v Byrne* [1952] 1 All ER 1362 (PC).

The presumption has been held to apply even where the gift to the solicitor is an indirect one. In *Liles v Terry* [1895] QB 679 (CA), the client of a solicitor, without independent advice, executed a conveyance to him of leasehold premises in trust for herself for life and, after her death, in trust for his wife (who was her niece). The Court of Appeal held that the gift could not stand, unless the donor had competent and independent professional advice prior to making it. Lopes LJ set out the rationale for extending the principle to indirect benefits, namely, that a solicitor might still benefit largely by a gift to his wife, or the wife might simply make over the property to him shortly after the gift had been made to her: p 685. (See, also, *Willis v Barron* [1902] AC 271 (HL) (client executed a deed in favour of solicitor's son).)

Husband and wife

Significantly, the relationship between husband and wife does *not* give rise to an automatic presumption of undue influence. This was so held in *Bank of Montreal v Stuart* [1911] AC 120 (PC). In that case, the wife, who was an invalid, acted in passive obedience to her husband's directions relating to a series of transactions over an eight year period, resulting in her surrendering all her property to a bank, leaving her without any means. She had no means of forming an independent judgment and, in the words of Lord Macnaghten, 'she was ready to sign anything that her husband asked her to sign and do anything he told her to do' (p 136). The Privy Council, relying on the early case of *Nedby v Nedby* (1852) 5 De G & Sm 377; 64 ER 1161, held that, in the case of husband and wife, the burden of proving undue influence lies upon the person who alleges it. On the facts, it was apparent that the husband had taken unfair advantage of his wife's confidence in him and the transactions were, accordingly, set aside. This line of authority was confirmed by the House of Lords in *National Westminster Bank plc v Morgan* [1985] AC 686, where Lord Scarman (p 703) stated that 'there are plenty of confidential relationships which do not give rise to the presumption of undue influence, a notable example is that of husband and wife': see, also, *Barron v Willis* [1899] 2 Ch 578, p 585; *Howes v Bishop* [1909] 2 KB 390 (CA); *MacKenzie v Royal Bank of Canada* [1934] AC 468, p 475; *Kingsnorth Trust Ltd v Bell* [1986] 1 All ER 423 (CA), p 427; *Midland Bank plc v Shephard* [1988] 3 All ER 17 (CA), p 21; and *Bank of Credit and Commerce International SA v Aboody* [1992] 4 All ER 955 (CA), p 964. The rationale for excluding the marital relationship from the class 2A category was set out by Farwell LJ in *Howes* (p 392):

> Upon principle, it is clear that business could not go on if in every transaction by way of gift by a wife to her husband the onus were on the husband to show that the wife had had independent advice; such a position would render married life intolerable.

Engaged couple

It is arguable that the relationship of an engaged couple falls within the class 2A category in the light of the older authorities: *Page v Horne* (1848) 11 Beav 227; 50 ER 304, pp 235–36, 807; *Cobbett v Brock* (1855) 20 Beav 524; 52 ER 706 and *Lovesy v Smith* (1880) 15 Ch D 655. In *Re Lloyds Bank Ltd* [1931] 1 Ch 289, Maugham J said (p 302):

> A young woman engaged to be married is in a very different position ... In general, she reposes the greatest confidence in her future husband; otherwise she would not marry him. In many, if not most, cases she would sign almost anything he put before her ... the reasons for not extending the equitable principle to the case of husband and wife have no application.

However, by contrast, in the more recent case of *Zamet v Hyman* [1961] 1 WLR 1442, the Court of Appeal held that it was more appropriate for a transaction made between an engaged couple to give rise to a fiduciary relationship under class 2B. Lord Evershed MR considered that, in modern conditions, the existence of undue influence in such cases should not necessarily be assumed in every case. He also intimated that no necessary distinction should be drawn between a young couple and more mature parties contemplating marriage. Indeed, 'it may well be that in the case of an engagement between two elderly persons the influence liable to be exercised would be greater, in modern times, at any rate, than in the case of young people': *Zamet v Hyman*, p 1446. Donovan LJ also thought that it ought not to be presumed between engaged couples that undue influence had been exercised by one over the other and that, if the court was minded to set aside a disposition, this ought to be affirmatively proved.

The inference of a fiduciary relationship could also arise in the woman towards the man and not always in the man towards the woman: see *Barclays Bank plc v Rivett* (1997) 29 HLR 893 (married couple).

2.3.3 Specific relationships which may give rise to the presumption

Introduction

It has long been recognised that there are various other relationships lacking a recognisable status (and, therefore, not falling within the above categories) to which the presumption of undue influence may apply. Here, as we have seen, the complainant must prove the existence of a relationship under which he (or she) generally reposed 'trust and confidence' in the wrongdoer: *Griffiths v Robins* (1818) 3 Madd 191; 56 ER 480. But not all confidential relationships will necessarily give rise to the presumption (see *Re Coomber* [1911] 1 Ch 723, where Fletcher Moulton LJ recognised that 'the nature of the fiduciary relation must be such that it justifies the [court's] interference'); equally, in some cases there may be both a confidential relationship and the existence of actual (as opposed to presumed) undue influence: *Re Craig (decd), Meneces v Middleton* [1971] 1 Ch 95. It is apparent that the courts are reluctant to define the precise limits of the exercise of the doctrine in this context or to impose any unnecessary fetters on its jurisdiction: *Tate v Williamson* (1866) LR 2 Ch App 55, p 61; and *Allcard v Skinner* (1887) 36 Ch D 145, p 182. The attitude of the courts is best summed up by the following passage from the judgment of Ungoed-Thomas J, in *Re Craig (decd)* (p 104):

> Thus both undue influence and those relationships of trust and confidence which raise the presumption are left, unlimited by definition, wide open for identification on the facts and in all the circumstances of each particular case as it arises.

A similar approach was identified in the celebrated case of *Lloyds Bank Ltd v Bundy* [1974] 3 All ER 757 (CA) (p 767), where Sir Eric Sachs echoed the words of Ungoed-Thomas J by saying that:

> ... it is neither feasible nor desirable to attempt closely to define the relationship, or its characteristics, or the demarcation line showing the exact transition point where a relationship that does not entail that duty passes into one that does.

In *National Westminster Bank plc v Morgan* [1985] 1 All ER 821 (HL) (p 831), Lord Scarman also alluded to the fact that the types of relationships which may develop a dominating influence of one party over another were 'infinitely various'. In his view, therefore, there was no substitute in this branch of the law for a 'meticulous examination of the facts'. Much, therefore, will depend on the particular facts of the given case, since it is evident that the appropriate relationship may be found to exist in widely differing sets of circumstances. It is apparent, however, that the existence of a dominating influence is not an essential requirement in order to bring the relationship within the class 2B category: *Lloyds Bank Ltd v Bundy* [1974] 3 All ER 757 (CA), p 768 ('the relevant transaction does *not* depend on proof of one party being able to dominate the other as though a puppet', *per* Sir Eric Sachs).

Husband and wife

It is apparent that the relationship of husband and wife, although not falling within the class 2A category, may raise the presumption of undue influence under class 2B. In *Barclays Bank plc v O'Brien* [1994] 1 AC 180, Lord Browne-Wilkinson said (p 190):

> ... in any particular case a wife may well be able to demonstrate that *de facto* she did leave decisions on financial affairs to her husband thereby bringing herself within class 2(B), ie, that the relationship between husband and wife in the particular case was such that the wife reposed confidence and trust in her husband in relation to their financial affairs and therefore undue influence is to be presumed.

His Lordship referred to the 'invalidating tendency' which had been accepted by the courts in earlier cases involving transactions between husband and wife: *Grigby v Cox* (1750) 1 Ves Sen 517, *per* Lord Harwicke; and *Yerkey v Jones* (1939) 63 CLR 649 (High Court of Australia), p 675, *per* Dixon J. This meant that courts were more ready to find that a husband had exercised undue influence over his wife than in other cases. The main reason for this is that 'sexual and emotional ties between [husband and wife] provide a ready weapon for undue influence; a wife's true wishes can easily be overborne because of her fear of destroying or damaging the wider relationship between her and her husband if she opposes his wishes': *Barclays Bank plc v O'Brien*, pp 190–91, *per* Lord Browne-Wilkinson. Although, however, married women fall to be treated 'more tenderly' than others, this does not mean that there is any 'special equity' operating in their favour. The notion that wives should be afforded special protection in relation to mortgage transactions was firmly rejected by the House of Lords in *O'Brien* (p 195). (Contrast the position in Australia, where the 'special equity theory' continues to govern: *Yerkey v Jones* (1939) 63 CLR 649; and *Garcia v National Australia Bank Ltd* (1998) 72 ALJR 1243 (High Court of Australia).)

A number of reasons were given for this approach. First, the conferment of special protection on married women, in preference to other classes of surety, would be inconsistent with modern notions of the status of women. Secondly, there was no reason for identifying one particular class of transaction (that is, a guarantee of debts) as worthy of this special form of protection. Thirdly, the effect of recognising a special equity in favour of wives would be to impose on the lender the burden of disproving lack of free and informed consent. This would, effectively, create a presumption of undue influence between married couples which, as we have seen, would run counter to earlier authority, denying the existence of any such presumption in the marital context. Finally, in Lord Browne-Wilkinson's view, there was no need to have recourse to a special equity theory since the doctrine of notice would provide adequate protection of the legitimate interests of wives: *Barclays Bank plc v O'Brien*, p 194. (See, further, Cretney, S, 'The little woman and the big bad bank' (1992) 109 LQR 534, for a critique of the approach which treats married women as a special class requiring protection.)

Although most of the reported cases concern wives who have been influenced by their husbands, a notable exception is *Simpson v Simpson* [1992] 1 FLR 60, where the testator had made large transfers of property to his wife whilst under treatment for a malignant brain tumour. Morritt J held that testator lacked sufficient mental capacity to carry out the various transfers and, accordingly, they were void. Alternatively, he held that a presumption of undue influence arose from the evidence, *inter alia*, of the testator's reducing mental capacity and his increasing dependence on his wife. In *Barclays Bank plc v Rivett* (1997) 29 HLR 893, the Court of Appeal specifically recognised that a husband could be subject to the same fear of opposing a spouse's wishes as a wife. In that case, the parties both signed a charge on the matrimonial home to secure the borrowings of a business run by the wife, daughter and son-in-law. The business proved unsuccessful and the bank obtained a possession order.

The husband, unaware of the proceedings, later sought to have the order set aside, relying on a defence of undue influence. In his affidavit in support, he stated that he had always relied on his wife in financial matters, that he had not realised that he was signing a charge on the house and that the bank had neither explained the significance of the document to him nor advised him to obtain independent legal advice. Buckley J (who gave the leading judgment of the court), relying on *Barclays Bank plc v O'Brien* [1994] 1 AC 180 (HL) (p 198), concluded that the principles applicable to a wife also applied to all other cases were there was an emotional relationship between cohabitees. The tenderness shown by the law to married women was 'not based on the marriage ceremony but reflects the underlying risk of one cohabitee exploiting the emotional involvement and trust of the other': *Barclays Bank plc v O'Brien*, p 198, *per* Lord Browne-Wilkinson. Because cohabitation (both heterosexual and homosexual) was now widespread in society, it was accepted in *O'Brien* that the law should recognise this. In the words of Buckley J in *Rivett* (pp 733–34):

> The sexual and emotional ties between the parties which Lord Browne-Wilkinson identified as providing a ready weapon for undue influence and the fear of destroying or damaging the wider relationship between the spouses, by one opposing the other's wishes, seem to me to be capable of applying to a husband as well as to a wife.

His Lordship did, however, suggest that, as a matter of evidence (as opposed to legal principle), a wife may find it easier to persuade the court that she placed trust and confidence in her husband in relation to her financial affairs than a husband in his wife.

In many of the reported cases involving husband and wife, the parties' relationship falls short of actual pressure (see para 2.2, above) and involves, instead, what can best be described as domination by the husband over his wife so that she has no independent will of her own; in other words, her mind becomes 'a mere channel through which the wishes of the [husband] flow': *Tufton v Sperni* [1952] 2 TLR 516, p 523, *per* Morris LJ. This has been described, in a different context, as someone 'who can no longer think and decide for himself': *Re T (An Adult) (Consent to Medical Treatment)* [1992] 2 FLR 458, p 471, *per* Lord Donaldson. In *Bank of Cyprus (London) Ltd v Markou* [1999] 2 All ER 707, for example, the husband effectively ran the family business at all times. He was the dominating influence in relation to money; if his wife wanted money, she would have to ask him for it. She had no income of her own and was entirely dependent on him. In the words of Mr John Jarvis QC (sitting as a deputy judge of the High Court), '[the husband] was plainly the forceful personality in the relationship and she trusted him implicitly ... she signed any document that [he] would put in front of her because she trusted him': p 716.

In not all cases, however, will the husband's influence over his wife be such as to raise an equity in the wife's favour. In *Turner v Barclays Bank plc* [1997] 2 FCR 151, for example, although the husband was held inevitably to exercise influence over his wife 'because of their relationship, as a happily married husband and wife with four children and a matrimonial home', this did not fall to be characterised as 'undue' in the circumstances. The element of 'blind trust and confidence' was lacking since the wife applied her own judgment to her husband's assessment of the future prospects of his business. Most recently, the House of Lords, in *Royal Bank of Scotland v Etridge (No 2)* [2001] UKHL 44, has held that, *in the ordinary course*, a wife's guarantee of her husband's bank overdraft secured by means of a charge on her share of the family home, should *not* be regarded as a transaction which, failing proof to the contrary, was explicable only on the basis that it had been procured by the exercise of the husband's undue influence. In most cases, there will be good reasons why a wife is willing to enter into such a transaction, despite the risks involved for her and her family. In the words of Lord Scott (para 159):

> In cases where experience, probably bitter, had led a wife to doubt the wisdom of her husband's financial or business decisions, I still would not regard her willingness to support those decisions with her own assets as an indication that he had exerted undue influence over her to persuade her to do so. Rather I would regard her support as a natural and admirable consequence of the relationship of a mutually loyal married couple. The proposition that if a wife, who generally reposes trust and confidence in her husband, agrees to become surety to support his debts or his business enterprises a presumption of undue influence arises is one that I am unable to accept. To regard the husband in such a case as a presumed 'wrongdoer' does not seem to me consistent with the relationship of trust and confidence that is a part of every healthy marriage.

In his Lordship's view, therefore, there was no need to adduce evidence to establish the existence of trust and confidence between husband and wife. This could be assumed in most cases unless there was evidence to demonstrate the absence of reciprocal trust and confidence between the parties. He has also recognised, however, that there may be cases where a husband *does* abuse that trust and confidence. Lord Scott said (para 160):

> He may do so by expressions of quite unjustified over-optimistic enthusiasm about the prospects of success of his business enterprises. He may do so by positive misrepresentation of his business intentions, or of the nature of the security he is asking his wife to grant his creditors, or of some other material matter. He may do so by subjecting her to excessive pressure, emotional blackmail or bullying in order to persuade her to sign.

Lord Nicholls put the matter this way (para 33):

> Inaccurate explanations of a proposed transaction are a different matter. So are cases where a husband, in whom a wife has reposed trust and confidence for the management of their financial affairs, prefers his interests to hers and makes a choice for both of them on that footing. Such a husband abuses the influence he has. He fails to discharge the obligation of candour and fairness he owes a wife who is looking to him to make the major financial decisions.

None of these things, however, could be presumed merely from the fact of the relationship of general trust and confidence. The husband was not to be treated as a *prima facie* wrongdoer. Undue influence, after all, signified an element of impropriety (that is, a misuse of influence). For this reason, 'more is needed before the stage is reached at which, in the absence of any other evidence, an inference of undue influence can properly be drawn or a presumption of the existence of undue influence can be said to arise': *Etridge (No 2)* (HL), *per* Lord Scott, para 160. In particular, the husband's exaggerations should not too readily be treated as misstatements. Statements which 'do not pass beyond the bounds of what may be expressed of a reasonable husband in the circumstances would not, without more, be castigated as undue influence': para 32, *per* Lord Nicholls. What, it seems, is required is some positive misrepresentation by the husband regarding his business intentions (or of the nature of the security he is seeking), or conduct amounting to 'excessive pressure, emotional blackmail or bullying' in persuading her to sign: para 160, *per* Lord Scott. Indeed, in surety wife cases, undue influence should now be regarded as a 'relatively unlikely' explanation for the wife's agreement to become surety: *Etridge (No 2)* (HL), para 162. In *Barclays Bank plc v Harris* (one of the conjoined appeals heard by the House of Lords), for example, there was no allegation in the pleadings of any bullying of the wife or of any pressure on her by her husband to sign the loan documentation that could be characterised as excessive. Accordingly, the House of Lords held that there was nothing on the facts to raise any presumption of undue influence: para 245. In the words of Lord Scott (para 245):

> Her agreement to [sign] is consistent with a normal, trusting, relationship between a married couple.

By contrast, in *Barclays Bank plc v Coleman* (another appeal before the House of Lords), the relationship between Mr and Mrs Coleman was considered to be significant in raising a presumption of undue influence. They were Hassidic Jews and the wife's upbringing and education in a Hassidic community persuaded her to expect (and to accept) a position of subservience and obedience to the wishes of her husband. In such a case, 'the rebuttal of the presumption would have needed legal advice from someone independent of the husband who could have impressed upon her that she should not sign unless she truly wanted to do so': para 292, *per* Lord Scott.

Cohabitees

It is apparent that the principles applicable to husband and wife (see above) are equally relevant to other cases where there is an emotional relationship between cohabitees. In *O'Brien*, Lord Browne-Wilkinson said (p 198):

> The 'tenderness' shown by the law to married woman is not based on the marriage ceremony but reflects the underlying risk of one cohabitee exploiting the emotional involvement and trust of the other. Now that unmarried cohabitation, whether heterosexual or homosexual, is widespread in our society, the law should recognise this.

To date, however, there have been few cases dealing specifically with cohabitees in this context. In *Rhoden v Joseph* ((1990) unreported, 6 September, available on Lexis), Mr Roger Kaye QC (sitting as a deputy judge of the High Court) said:

> ... for the purposes of the so called presumption of undue influence, I do not think it sensible to draw any distinction any longer between a couple who are married and a couple who are cohabiting by the mere fact that one couple are married and the other cohabiting. In either case to apply the presumption would render the married or cohabiting relationship intolerable. I do not say the presumption can no longer arise or be applied between cohabiting couples from, say, the actual facts and circumstances of the case as where especial trust and confidence arises or where one is in a particularly weak or vulnerable position vis à vis the other.

In *Massey v Midland Bank plc* [1995] 1 All ER 929, the Court of Appeal applied the *O'Brien* principle to a woman who had been in a long standing sexual relationship with her male partner, although the parties had never cohabited. Although they never lived under the same roof (because her parents objected to the relationship), nevertheless they had two children together. (See, also, *Zamet v Hyman* [1961] 1 WLR 1442, CA, discussed below, and *Lloyds Bank plc v Wright-Bailey* (1995) unreported, 3 May, CA, available on Lexis.) In *Allied Irish Bank plc v Byrne* [1995] 2 FLR 325, the parties were divorced and no longer living together.

Other cases

In *O'Brien*, Lord Browne-Wilkinson alluded to the fact that other relationships, apart from husband and wife and cohabitees, could be the subject of the court's 'invalidating tendency' provided they involved the requisite element of trust and confidence: *O'Brien*, p 198. Below is a list of other cases in which the relationship between the parties has been held, on the facts, to be sufficient to raise a presumption of undue influence. Much of this case law relates to gifts, but the presumption also applies to transactions at an undervalue or excessive price: *Tufton v Sperni* [1952] 2 TLR 516 (CA), p 526, *per* Jenkins LJ.

- *Avon Finance Co Ltd v Bridger* [1985] 2 All ER 281 (CA) – an elderly couple purchased a house for their retirement, the arrangements being undertaken for them by their son. The purchase price was made up partly by way of a mortgage, their own money and a sum provided by the son. In order to raise his share of the money, the son (without informing his parents) obtained a loan from the claimant finance company on the security of his parent's property. The son obtained his parents' signatures to the legal charge by telling them that the documents they were signing were connected with their own mortgage over the house. It was held that the charge was voidable in equity because the claimants had chosen to appoint the son to procure from his parents the security which was needed to further the loan between the son and the claimants. Moreover, the relationship between the son and his parents was such that he could be expected to have some influence over them, as his elderly parents, and that was a matter of which the claimants should have been aware. In the absence, therefore, of independent advice given to the parents, the claimants could not enforce the transaction. Brandon LJ said (p 288) that 'the relationship between a son in the prime of life and parents in the evening of life is equally a relationship in which it should be appreciated that the possibility of influence exists'.

- *Langton v Langton* [1995] 2 FLR 890 – the father bought a bungalow in 1983 after serving a sentence of life imprisonment for the murder of his wife. In 1989, he was reunited with his son and daughter-in-law and they moved into the bungalow with him. In 1991, after he had spent some time in hospital, he transferred the property to them by deed of gift. In return, he was given a non-exclusive licence to occupy the bungalow. The deputy judge held that the relationship between the parties was such as to raise a presumption of undue influence. The following matters were particularly relevant: (1) the claimant was happy to have re-established relations with his only son and his family; (2) the claimant had spent a number of years in prison and this affected the parties' relationship and increased the pressure on the claimant to do what the son wanted; (3) imprisonment also resulted in the claimant having a fear of going into an old peoples' home; (4) the claimant had no other immediate family to look after him; (5) imprisonment had 'dulled' the claimant's business acumen so that he was more ready to place trust in his son; and (6) the claimant had been ill and, during his recuperation, had relied on his son and daughter-in-law to look after him in his daily needs and the management of his financial affairs. (See, also, *Mahoney v Purnell* [1996] 3 All ER 61, p 82, involving a relationship of son-in-law and father-in-law.)

- *Re Craig (decd), Meneces v Middleton* [1971] 1 Ch 95 – this case involved gifts by an older man to his secretary-companion. He was dependent on her for his comforts and emotionally for her companionship and for her participation in his business affairs. He was 84, vulnerable and failing in health. The gifts were set aside.

- *Tate v Williamson* (1866) LR 2 Ch App 55 – a young man, aged 23, who was estranged from his father, wrote to his great uncle for advice and assistance as to the payment of his debts. The uncle deputed the defendant, his nephew, to see the young man. The parties met and it was agreed that the young man would sell his interest in a freehold estate to the defendant for £7,000 payable by instalments. The defendant obtained a valuation of the property, which was in the region of £20,000. It was held that the defendant stood in a fiduciary relationship to the young man, which made it his duty to inform him of the true value of the property. Having failed to do so, the sale was set aside.

- *Tufton v Sperni* [1952] 2 TLR 516 – a house was purchased, on terms grossly unfair to the purchaser, for the purpose of a Moslem cultural centre to be promoted by a committee comprising the purchaser, the seller and a third party. Since the parties had joined together for the purpose of furthering a charitable objective, they stood in a fiduciary relationship with one another. The purchaser had reposed confidence in the seller which was abused and the purchase was, accordingly, set aside. (See, also, *Mahoney v Purnell* [1996] 3 All ER 61, father-in-law and son-in-law running hotel business in partnership.)

- *Cheese v Thomas* [1994] 1 WLR 129 – the claimant, aged 85, entered into an agreement with the defendant, his great nephew, whereby he paid the defendant the whole of his capital as his contribution to the purchase of a house, which he (the claimant) was to occupy for the rest of his life and which, thereafter, was to pass unencumbered to the defendant. The balance of the price was funded by a building society loan to the defendant, secured by a mortgage over the property. After he moved in, the claimant discovered that the defendant had failed to pay the mortgage instalments. His action to set aside the parties' agreement for undue influence was upheld. It was conceded that the relationship between the two parties was of a fiduciary character; they were close, the great nephew was considerably younger and had business experience.

- *Zamet v Hyman* [1961] 1 WLR 1442 (CA) – an engaged couple executed a deed whereby the female fiancée, in consideration of £600, agreed to give up any claim that she might have against her husband's estate on his death. It was held that a transaction made between an engaged couple which upon its face appears much more favourable to one party than the other could, in the circumstances of the case, give rise to a fiduciary relationship so as to place the onus on the party benefited of proving that the transaction was entered into by the other party after full, free and informed consent. Older cases, however, suggest that the relationship of an engaged couple falls within the class 2A category of presumed undue influence: see *Cobbett v Brock* (1855) 20 Beav 524; 52 ER ... *ovesy v Smith* (1880) 15 Ch D 655; and *Re Lloyds Bank Ltd* [1931] 1 Ch ..., p 302.

- *Horry v Tate & Lyle Refineries Ltd* [1982] 2 Lloyd's ... ep 416 – the claimant settled his claim for damages for personal ...juries sustained whilst employed with the defendants, relying he...y on the advice of h... insurers. It was held that there was a rela...ship of confidence ... the claimant and the insurers which im...ed a duty of f... ...e on them fully to advise the claimant of t... consequen... ...ng his claim.

- *O'Sullivan v Management Agency ... M... ...85*] QB 428 (CA) – the claimant was a young singer ... ...ced in business matters, who became closely acquainted w... a manager upon whose judgment he relied and who was a substantial shareholder in the defendant companies, with whom the claimant entered into various agreements. The manager was held to be in a fiduciary relationship with the claimant and, accordingly, the agreements were presumed to have been obtained by undue influence.

- *Lloyds Bank Ltd v Bundy* [1974] 3 All ER 757 (CA) – an elderly farmer, who was not versed in business affairs, was persuaded by his son to guarantee the latter's company overdraft for £1,500 and charged his house to the bank to secure that sum. The company ran into financial difficulties and the assistant bank manager suggested that the father should sign a further guarantee for £5,000 and execute a further charge for that amount. At that time, the house was worth only £10,000. The company's affairs worsened and a new assistant bank manager (together with the son) persuaded the father to increase the guarantee and charge to £11,000. The assistant manager was aware that the father relied on him implicitly to advise him about the transaction as 'bank manager'. The Court of Appeal held that the relationship between the bank and the father was one of trust and confidence and, accordingly, the father, in coming to a decision about the proposed transaction, was liable to be influenced by the bank's proposals. In these circumstances, the confidential relationship imposed on the bank a duty of fiduciary care (that is, a duty to ensure that the father formed an independent and informed judgment before committing himself). Since the bank had failed to advise the father to obtain independent advice, it was in breach of its fiduciary duty to the father and, therefore, the guarantee and charge was set aside. It should be noted, however, that the presumption of undue influence does not normally arise from the relationship of banker and customer. This is because such a relationship is not usually a confidential one: *National Westminster Bank plc v Morgan* [1985] AC 686 (HL). At what point the bank will be treated as 'crossing the line' into the area of confidentiality will depend on all the facts of the case: *Bundy*, p 772. In *Morgan*, for example, the bank manager was held not to have 'crossed the line' and, accordingly, the bank was under no duty to ensure that the wife had independent advice. The transaction was characterised as an ordinary banking transaction whereby the wife sought to save her home.

- *Credit Lyonnais Bank Nederland NV v Burch* [1997] 1 All ER 144 (CA) – a junior employee was persuaded to provide security required by a bank for an increased overdraft in favour of her employer. She executed a second charge over her flat and gave an unlimited all moneys guarantee to the bank. The Court of Appeal was able to infer the existence of a relationship of trust and confidence from the fact that the transaction was manifestly disadvantageous to her. Without knowing the extent of the liability involved, she had committed herself to a liability far beyond her means and risked the loss of her home and personal bankruptcy to help her employer's company in which she had no financial interest and of which she was only a junior employee. In these circumstances, the presumption of undue influence was 'irresistible' (p 154), *per* Millett LJ, who said that the mere fact that a transaction was improvident was not in itself sufficient to give rise to the presumption, but 'where it is obtained by a party between whom and the complainant there is a relationship like that of employer and junior employee which is easily capable of developing into a relationship of trust and confidence, the nature of the transaction may be sufficient to justify the inference that such a development has taken place; and where the transaction is so extravagantly improvident that it is virtually inexplicable on any other basis, the inference will be readily drawn'.

- *Steeples v Lea* [1998] 1 FLR 138 (CA) – a junior employee stood surety for her employer's borrowings. She was a widow, aged 51, with little assets other than her home where she lived with her son. She was a receptionist at a country club owned by her employer. Although a lady of mature years, she had a 'trusting disposition' and trusted her employer. The Court of Appeal had no difficulty in concluding that the relationship of employer and employee had 'ripened' into a relationship of trust and confidence which would put the latter in a position to exercise undue influence over her.

- *Special Trustees for Great Ormond Street Hospital for Children v Rushin, sub nom In The Estate of Morris (decd)* [2001] WTLR 1137 – a number of gifts of cash and a transfer of land by the deceased were made during her lifetime in favour of the defendants at a time when she was aged 75 and in poor physical and mental health. The defendants had befriended the deceased and acted as her housekeeper. Within a few months, she entered into an agreement with the first defendant (Mrs Rushin), which had been drawn up by solicitors, under which her house was transferred to Mrs Rushin on payment of £50, subject to an obligation on the latter's part to allow the deceased to remain in the property and to care for her during her lifetime. The deceased also made a number of gifts of over £25,000 to the defendants for the purchase of three motor cars, including a brand new BMW. Rimer J held that the relationship between the parties was one in which the presumption of undue influence arose. Since the gifts and the transfer were manifestly to the deceased's disadvantage and the defendants had failed to adduce evidence to rebut the presumption, the claim of undue influence was made out.

2.4 REBUTTING THE PRESUMPTION OF UNDUE INFLUENCE

In *Goldsworthy v Brickell* [1987] 1 All ER 853 (CA), Nourse LJ said (p 865):

... in a case where the presumption has come into operation the gift or transaction will be set aside, unless it is proved to have been the spontaneous act of the donor or grantor acting in circumstances which enable him to exercise an independent will and which justify the court in holding that the gift or transaction was the result of a free exercise of his will.

In *Royal Bank of Scotland v Etridge (No 2)* [1998] 4 All ER 705 (CA), Stuart-Smith LJ said (p 714):

As between the complainant and the alleged wrongdoer, the presumption cannot be rebutted merely by evidence that the complainant understood what he or she was doing and intended to do it, but only by showing that that she was either free from the influence of the alleged wrongdoer or had been placed by the receipt of independent legal advice in an equivalent position.

Most recently, in the House of Lords, in *Etridge (No 2)* [2001] UKHL 44, Lord Hobhouse opined (para 111) that:

... the equitable doctrine of undue influence has been created for the protection of those who are *sui juris* and competent to undertake legal obligations but are nevertheless vulnerable and liable to have their will unduly influenced. It is their weakness which is being protected not their inability to comprehend.

In deciding whether or not the donor acted spontaneously and independently or in response to undue influence, the donor's motives fall to be judged by applying a *subjective* test and not that of the ordinary man. The point arose in *Re Brocklehurst's Estate, Hall v Roberts* [1978] 1 Ch 14 (CA), where the deceased, an independently minded man, aged 87, granted a 99 year lease of shooting rights over his estate to the defendant, a small garage proprietor who had for some years enjoyed limited shooting over the estate as a friend and practical helper during the latter years of the deceased's life. The effect of the lease was drastically to reduce the value of the estate in the hands of any owner. The trial judge set aside the lease largely on the ground that the size and nature of the gift were such as not to be accounted for on the objective test of the ordinary motives of ordinary men. The majority of the Court of Appeal rejected this approach, holding that an objective test of motivation was inappropriate given that the question is always whether the donor acted spontaneously and independently (or in response to undue influence); that being the case, it would be wholly artificial to exclude his own personal character and attributes: *Brocklehurst*, p 40, *per* Bridge LJ. Proof of independent advice will not, therefore, be necessary if the party presumed to have been influenced is clearly able to form his (or her) own judgment. In *Brocklehurst*, it was apparent that the deceased had a strong and eccentric character and would have made the same gift however much he had been independently advised against it. Similarly, a gift made by Baroness Thatcher would presumably be upheld, notwithstanding the non-receipt of independent advice, on the basis that the gift came about by the free and independent exercise of her will!

In most cases, however, the presumption of undue influence will be rebutted by showing that the donor had 'competent and independent' legal advice before making the gift or entering into the transaction: *Re Coomber*

[1911] 1 Ch 723, p 730, *per* Fletcher Moulton LJ. The duty of the donor is to ensure that the donee has formed 'an independent and informed judgment' or, in the words of Lord Evershed MR, in *Zamet v Hyman* [1961] 3 All ER 933 (p 938), 'after full, free and informed thought'. The reference to an 'informed' judgment suggests that, in some cases, independent legal advice may not be sufficient if some important factor capable of affecting the donor's judgment is not disclosed: *Lloyds Bank Ltd v Bundy* [1974] 3 All ER 757 (CA), p 768, *per* Sir Eric Sachs. Conversely, it has been suggested that, if the transaction is for full consideration, competent advice will not be necessary: *Wright v Carter* [1903] 1 Ch 27, pp 54–55, *per* Vaughan Williams J.

In some of the cases, it has been suggested that it is not enough that the donor has an independent adviser unless he actually acts on that advice. If this were not so, 'the same influence that produced the desire to make the [transaction] would produce disregard of the advice to refrain from executing it, and so defeat the rule': *Powell v Powell* [1900] 1 Ch 243, p 246, *per* Farwell J; and see, also, *Bruty v Edmundson* (1915) 113 LT 1197, p 1202, *per* Eve J; and *Credit Lyonnais Nederland NV v Burch* [1997] 1 All ER 144 (CA), p 156, *per* Millett LJ. In *Inche Noriah v Shaik Allie Bin Omar* [1929] AC 127, however, the Privy Council considered that the receipt of independent legal advice may rebut the presumption, although it is *not* acted upon, if it is given with a knowledge of all the relevant circumstances and be such as a competent and honest adviser would give if acting solely in the interests of the donor. Similarly, in *Re Coomber*, referred to above, it was stressed that 'it is for adult persons of competent mind to decide whether they will do an act, and I do not think that independent and competent advice means independent and competent approval': pp 729–30, *per* Fletcher Moulton LJ. The view that the decision whether or not to proceed with the transaction is ultimately a matter for the donor has been confirmed most recently by the House of Lords, in *Royal Bank of Scotland v Etridge (No 2)* [2001] UKHL 44. Lord Nicholls, for example, stressed that 'a wife is not precluded from entering into a financially unwise transaction if, for her own reasons, she wishes to do so': *Etridge (No 2)* (HL), para 61. This, of course, mirrors the approach taken by Fletcher Moulton LJ, in *Re Coomber*, which was expressly cited with approval by Lord Nicholls.

In *Inche*, referred to above, the deed of gift executed by the widow was set aside despite the fact that she had received independent legal advice because the adviser did not have knowledge of all the material facts (that is, that the gift in question comprised a large part of the widow's property). It is apparent, therefore, that the receipt of independent advice will not always operate so as to rebut the presumption of undue influence: see, also, *Tate v Williamson* (1866) LR 2 Ch App 55, p 65, where Lord Chelmsford LC stated that any advice given was 'of no consequence, when once it is established that there was a concealment of a material fact'.

The Privy Council in *Inche* also held that independent advice was only one of the methods by which the presumption can be rebutted. In the words of Lord Hailsham LC (p 135):

It is necessary for the donee to prove that the gift was the result of the free exercise of independent will. The most obvious way to prove this is by establishing that the gift was made after the nature and effect of the transaction had been fully explained to the donor by some independent and qualified person so completely as to satisfy the Court that the donor was acting independently of any influence from the donee and with the full appreciation of what he was doing; and in cases where there are no other circumstances this may be the only means by which the donee can rebut the presumption. But ... if evidence is given of circumstances sufficient to establish [these facts], their Lordships see no reason for disregarding them merely because they do not include independent advice from a lawyer.

The above-cited passage was approved by Lawton LJ, in *Re Brocklehurst's Estate* (p 36), where the presumption was held to be rebutted, not by proof that the deceased had been independently advised, but by showing that the gift came about by the free, informed and independent exercise of the deceased's will for motives of ordinary friendship. Significantly, the case of *Shears & Sons Ltd v Jones* (1922) 128 LT 218, where Russell J held that the wife did understand the nature of the documentation but, nevertheless, concluded that the absence of independent advice was fatal to the lender's claim to enforce the security, was doubted by Scott LJ in the Court of Appeal, in *O'Brien*: [1992] 3 WLR 593 (p 605). In cases involving parent and child, it has also been held that independent legal advice is 'desirable' (but not essential), greater importance being placed on whether the gift was the spontaneous act of the child and whether he knew what his rights were at the time: *Re Pauling's Settlement Trusts* [1964] 1 Ch 303, p 336 (CA), *per* Willmer LJ. For this reason, it is not essential that the advice be necessarily from a lawyer; in some situations it may be more appropriate that the advice comes from an accountant or other financial adviser: *Inche*, p 135, *per* Lord Hailsham, who suggested that advice from a non-lawyer may be sufficient depending on the circumstances. What, however, is important is that the adviser is an independent person who is technically qualified to explain the nature of the transaction. As we shall see in Chapter 5, the adviser must have not only the necessary professional qualifications as a lawyer (or financial adviser), but sufficient knowledge of the relevant circumstances to be able to advise properly on the full significance of the transaction: *Inche*, pp 135–36, *per* Lord Hailsham.

Indeed, strictly speaking, in all cases falling within the class 2A or 2B categories, the primary function of the rebutting evidence is to show that the donee's duty of confidence has been fulfilled. This will usually involve demonstrating that the donor had come to a free and informed judgment, but, ultimately, discharge of the duty will depend on the particular circumstances of each case. As was intimated in *Bundy*, referred to earlier, in some cases the question will centre round whether or not other material information had been disclosed to the donor prior to the transaction. In the words of Lord Eldon LC, in *Huguenin v Baseley* (1807) 14 Ves Jun 273; 33 ER 526 (pp 300, 536):

> The question is, not, whether she knew what she was doing ... but how the intention was produced; whether all that care ... was placed round her, as against those, who advised her, which, from their situation and relation with respect to her, they were bound to exert on her behalf.

A good illustration of this approach is to be found in the recent case of *Claughton v Price* (1998) HLR 396 (CA), where the claimant was a patient of the defendant, a consultant psychiatrist. They became personal friends and (in 1981) the claimant purchased several properties in Florida from a group of developers subject to short term mortgages in their favour. When he was unable to repay the monies due on the mortgages, he approached the defendant who suggested that he (the psychiatrist) should purchase the properties in order to provide the claimant with the money required to discharge the mortgages. He wrote to the claimant's lawyer (who had been representing him in negotiations with the developers), suggesting that he should prepare the necessary deeds for the claimant to repurchase the properties from him in due course. The lawyer agreed to this course of action, but stipulated that his client should employ a solicitor on his own behalf and supply him with various documentation, including a repurchase agreement. This documentation, however, was never provided, despite correspondence between the defendant's solicitors and the claimant, asking him to provide them with the required documents. Subsequently, the claimant sought to repay the loan to the defendant and requested transfer of the properties back into his name. When the defendant refused, the claimant sought to have the transactions set aside for undue influence.

The Court of Appeal held that there was a relationship of undue influence between the parties, thus placing the onus on the defendant to show that the claimant's participation in the transactions was his spontaneous act under circumstances which enabled him to exercise an independent will. On this point, the defendant knew that the claimant suffered from an unstable personality; he also could not reasonably have believed that a solicitor acting for the claimant would have advised him to enter into the transactions without the protection of a repurchase agreement which the defendant had originally offered and to which he would have been willing to agree, if requested. It was, clearly, irrational for the claimant to go ahead without that protection, and so mere confirmation that he had taken independent legal advice was held not to be sufficient to rebut the presumption. The defendant had a duty to take care of the claimant in the transaction, which he had failed to discharge and, accordingly, the presumption was not rebutted. It should be stressed, therefore, that legal advice 'is neither always necessary nor always sufficient' to rebut the presumption of undue influence: *Credit Lyonnais Bank Nederland NV v Burch* [1997] 1 All ER 144 (CA), p 156, *per* Millett LJ.

Where advice has, in fact, been given, the court will examine what was said to see if it was sufficient. In the so called 'two party' cases (that is, between complainant and wrongdoer where there is no third party involvement), the requirement of *independent* advice appears to be strict in so far as the legal adviser must act solely in the interests of the person he is advising: *Inche*, p 135, *per* Lord Hailsham. In other words, the solicitor must have 'an absolutely independent outlook' (*Bullock v Lloyds Bank Ltd* [1955] Ch 317, p 326), which means that he must be independent of the other party to the transaction: *Powell v Powell* [1900] 1 Ch 243, p 246, *per* Farwell J who stated that: 'this cannot be if he is solicitor for both'. It seems, also, in this connection, that the solicitor will not be independent if he receives instructions from the donee or the latter is present during the meeting when the advice is given: *Cavendish v Strutt* (1903) 19 TLR 483. Where, however, the question of independent advice is raised in the context of a 'three party' scenario (that is, involving the surety, borrower and lender), the solicitor may, as we shall see in Chapter 5, act for the other parties (including the borrower and/or lender) since the lender will be entitled to assume that the solicitor, when acting for the surety, will be doing so honestly and will give proper advice: see O'Hagan, P, 'Legal advice and undue influence: advice for lawyers' (1996) 47 NILQ 74.

The presumption may also be displaced if the donor was no longer under the influence of the donee at the time of the making of the gift. The point is alluded to by Farwell J in *Powell v Powell* [1900] 1 Ch 243 (pp 245–46), who suggested that the presumption can be rebutted if the fiduciary relation had ceased at the material time so that the donor was 'emancipated' from the wrongdoer's further control or dominion. The same point is made by Vaughan Williams LJ in *Wright v Carter* [1903] 1 Ch 27 (CA), who stated that the presumption arising from the relationship of solicitor and client would continue as long as that relation continued 'or at all events until it can be clearly inferred that the influence had come to an end' (p 50). In the same case, it was suggested that, although the presumption of undue influence arising from the relationship of solicitor and client is not 'entirely irrebuttable', nevertheless, 'it is one which is extremely difficult to be rebutted' at least in the context of a substantial gift: *Wright v Carter*, p 57, *per* Stirling LJ. Since the capacity of one person to influence the other will vary with the degree of trust and confidence reposed by that other in him, it is apparent that, in some relationships (notably, between solicitor and client), the onus of rebutting the presumption may be very heavy indeed. This mirrors the approach taken most recently in *Etridge (No 2)*, where the House of Lords stressed that the type and weight of evidence needed to rebut the presumption will depend upon the weight of the presumption itself.

CHAPTER 3

MANIFEST DISADVANTAGE

3.1 INTRODUCTION

A transaction falling within the class 2 category of undue influence will not be set aside unless it is shown to be to the manifest disadvantage of the person subjected to the dominating influence. The House of Lords so held in *National Westminster Bank plc v Morgan* [1985] 1 All ER 821, one of the leading cases in this field.

In that case, the husband, who was in difficulties with his business, was unable to meet the repayments under a mortgage secured over the home, which he owned jointly with his wife. In order to avoid the mortgagee taking proceedings for possession, the husband made refinancing arrangements with a bank to be secured by a legal charge over the home. When the bank manager visited the wife in order to obtain her signature to the charge, he incorrectly told her that the charge only secured the amount advanced to refinance the existing mortgage. In fact, the charge was, by its terms, unlimited in extent and, therefore, could extend to all the husband's liabilities to the bank. The wife did not receive independent legal advice before signing the charge. The bank subsequently obtained an order for possession of the home after the husband and wife fell into arrears with the payments. Soon afterwards, the husband died without owing any indebtedness to the bank for business advances. The bank argued that the wife's defence of undue influence could only be raised if she could show that the charge was manifestly disadvantageous to her and, since her husband had died without business debts owing to the bank, she was not manifestly disadvantaged but, in fact, had benefited from the transaction because it had averted the proceedings for possession by the prior mortgagee. The House of Lords agreed, holding that the principle justifying the court setting aside a transaction by reason of undue influence was 'the victimisation of one party by the other' and, accordingly, the transaction 'must constitute a disadvantage sufficiently serious to require evidence to rebut the presumption that in the circumstances of the relationship between the parties it was procured by the exercise of undue influence': pp 827–28, *per* Lord Scarman.

This approach mirrors the view taken in the earlier cases, namely, that the presumption of undue influence will remain inoperative (despite the existence of an appropriate relationship of trust and confidence) until the party who has relied on that trust and confidence makes a gift so large, or enters into such an improvident transaction as not to be reasonably accounted for on the ground of friendship, relationship, charity or benevolent motives: *Allcard v Skinner*

(1887) 36 Ch D 145, p 185, *per* Lindley LJ; and *Goldsworthy v Brickell* [1987] 1 All ER 853 (CA), p 865, *per* Nourse LJ. As we saw in Chapter 2 (para 2.3), this test has been held to be synonymous with that of manifest disadvantage enunciated in *Morgan*: see *Claughton v Price* (1998) 30 HLR 396 (CA), p 405, *per* Nourse LJ. Various other formulations of the same principle appear in several pre-*Morgan* cases. In the early case of *Ormes v Beadel* (1860) 2 Giff 166; 66 ER 70 (pp 174, 74), Sir John Stuart VC said that where an agreement 'hard and inequitable in itself' is exacted under circumstances of pressure, a court of equity will set it aside. Similarly, in *Bank of Montreal v Stuart* [1911] AC 120 (PC) (p 137), Lord Macnaghten spoke of the transaction having to be 'immoderate and irrational' and, in *Poosathurai v Kannappa Chettiar* (1919) LR 47 Ind App 1 (PC) (p 4), Lord Shaw indicated that the bargain '[must be] with the influencer and in itself unconscionable', relying on the provisions of s 16(3) of the Indian Contract Act 1872, which his Lordship stated was no different on the subject of undue influence than English law. Again, in *Wright v Carter* [1903] 1 Ch 27 (CA) (p 55), Vaughan Williams LJ described the transaction in that case as being one which 'no prudent person would for one moment have entertained'. In *Morgan*, Lord Scarman summed up this earlier case law by saying (p 829):

> The wrongfulness of the transaction must, therefore, be shown: it must be one in which an unfair advantage has been taken of another.

The requirement of manifest disadvantage in class 2 cases has been re-affirmed most recently by the House of Lords in *Royal Bank of Scotland v Etridge (No 2)* [2001] UKHL 44. Lord Nicholls, for example, considered that the two prerequisites to the shift in the evidential burden of proof – namely: (1) the complainant having reposed trust and confidence in the other party; and (2) the transaction being not readily explicable by the relationship of the parties – made 'good sense' as it would be absurd for the law to presume that every transaction between, say, a client and his solicitor, was brought about by undue influence unless the contrary was affirmatively proved: *Etridge (No 2)* (HL), para 24. In the words of Lord Scott (para 156):

> Some transactions will be obviously innocuous and innocent. A moderate gift as a Christmas or birthday present would be an example. A solicitor who is appointed by a client as his executor and given a legacy of a moderate amount if he consents to act, is not put to proof of the absence of undue influence before he can take the legacy. If the nun/postulant/novice in *Allcard v Skinner* had given moderate Christmas presents to the Mother Superior, or to the sisterhood, no inference that the gifts had been procured by undue influence could be drawn and no presumption of undue influence would have arisen.

It is apparent, therefore, that the nature of the transaction (in terms of its inexplicability with reference to the normal motives by which people act) constitutes important evidential material in cases involving a class 2 presumption of undue influence. Ultimately, however, it is the combination of the relationship and the nature of the transaction which gives rise to the presumption of undue influence and shifts (as we saw in Chapter 2) the onus of proof to the other party. However, according to Lord Nicholls, the label 'manifest disadvantage' had caused difficulties in the previous cases involving wives guaranteeing payment of their husbands' business debts: see para 3.3, below. In his view, therefore, the label was apt only when applied to straightforward transactions, such as a substantial gift or a sale at an undervalue.

It was not made clear in *Morgan* whether the concept of manifest disadvantage applies equally to class 1 (actual undue influence) cases as it does to cases falling with the presumed undue influence category (that is, classes 2A and 2B). To this we now turn before embarking upon a detailed examination of the meaning of manifest disadvantage.

3.2 DOES MANIFEST DISADVANTAGE APPLY TO ACTUAL UNDUE INFLUENCE CASES?

A number of cases, decided after *Morgan*, accepted that the House of Lords had established a general principle in respect of manifest disadvantage applicable to all cases (both actual and presumed) involving undue influence.

In *Coldunell Ltd v Gallon* [1986] 1 All ER 429 (CA), for example, Oliver LJ said (p 435):

> ... whether the relationship between the parties is one from which undue influence is to be presumed *or whether there is evidence of actual influence*, it has to be shown that the transaction constituted a manifest disadvantage to the party seeking to avoid it, explicable only on the basis that undue influence has been used to procure it. (Emphasis added.)

Similarly, in *Bank of Credit and Commerce International SA v Kanamia* ((1986) unreported, 6 March, available on Lexis), Hoffman J concluded that, in the context of an allegation of actual undue influence by a wife against her husband, the transaction had to be shown to have been manifestly disadvantageous to the person (in this case, the wife) who entered into it. Again, in *Goldsworthy v Brickell* [1987] 1 All ER 853 (p 868), Nourse LJ was clearly of the view that, since the House of Lords' decision in *Morgan*, before any transaction could be set aside for undue influence, whether actual or presumed, it had to be shown that the transaction was wrongful in the sense that it had constituted a 'manifest and unfair disadvantage' to the person seeking to avoid it. (See, also, *Midland Bank plc v Shepherd* [1988] 3 All ER 17, p 22, *per* Neill LJ; *Midland Bank plc v Johns* [1987] CA transcript 824, unreported, where Nourse LJ rejected an allegation of actual undue influence by a wife against her husband on the ground, *inter alia*, that she had 'also failed to establish that the transaction was one which was to her manifest disadvantage'; and *Bank of Baroda v Shah* [1988] 3 All ER 24 (CA), p 30, *per* Neill LJ.)

The point also arose for consideration in *Bank of Credit and Commerce International SA v Aboody* [1992] 4 All ER 955 (CA). In this case, the husband

and wife were directors and shareholders of a family company, which was effectively run by the husband alone. The wife signed company documents without question as and when they were put before her by her husband, whom she trusted to run the company for their mutual benefit. In order to secure the company's borrowing from the bank, the couple entered into six transactions, comprising three joint and several guarantees and three charges in favour of the bank over a house owned by the wife. In relation to the last charge, the bank sought to give the wife independent legal advice, but the husband, during the course of the interview, burst into the room and, after an argument between the husband and the solicitor, the wife signed the charge. When the bank later sought to enforce its securities, the wife challenged the validity of the transactions on the ground that they had been obtained by the actual undue influence of her husband: see Chapter 2, para 2.2. Although the trial judge found that the husband had used actual undue influence over the wife, he refused to set aside the transactions on the ground that there was no proof that they were to the manifest disadvantage of the wife. The Court of Appeal agreed, holding that, in this respect, there was no distinction between a plea based on actual or presumed undue influence. Both categories required the additional element of manifest disadvantage, unless the claim involved actual undue influence and the claimant could also show that there had been an abuse of confidence by the other party, in which case the onus was then on that other party to establish the fairness of the transaction: see Chapter 1, para 1.5.2.

The view taken in *Aboody*, that there was no distinction in this respect between class 1 and class 2 cases, was prompted to some extent by the following passage in the judgment of Lord Scarman in *Morgan* (p 828):

> The need to show that the transaction is wrongful ... before the court will set aside a transaction *whether relying on evidence or the presumption of the exercise of undue influence* has been asserted in ... cases. (Emphasis added.)

Quite apart from the fact that his Lordship was not specifically addressing the question of manifest disadvantage in this passage, it is apparent that there are vital conceptual differences between the two categories of undue influence. In a class 2 case, where the presumption of undue influence alone is relied on, the claimant is not in a position affirmatively to prove the wrongfulness of the transaction. In such a case, therefore, it seems appropriate that the court, before applying the presumption, should be satisfied of the *prima facie* wrongfulness of the transaction by being shown that it was manifestly disadvantageous to the complainant. In a class 1 case, however (where the complainant is able affirmatively to prove undue influence), the court focuses on the conduct of the wrongdoer. If, as we saw in Chapter 2 (see para 2.2), coercion or some form of other improper conduct is established, this by itself will demonstrate the wrongfulness of the transaction so that it becomes unnecessary (and, indeed, irrelevant) to establish the additional requirement of manifest disadvantage. In short, proof of actual undue influence itself proves the wrongfulness of a transaction. In the course of argument in *Aboody*, the Court of Appeal was presented with a forceful submission on behalf of the claimant that, if manifest disadvantage had to be shown in all cases, an old lady who had been the subject of actual undue influence by her solicitor to sell him her family home, but had been paid the full market price for it, would be unable to have the sale set aside. Although initially impressed with this argument, the court rejected it on the basis that, in such a case, the old lady would have a remedy under the alternative doctrine of abuse of confidence: see Chapter 1, para 1.5.2. (Interestingly, the *Aboody* decision has been followed in New Zealand (*Contractors Bonding Ltd v Snee* [1992] 2 NZLR 157, p 166, New Zealand Court of Appeal), but not universally in Australia (*Baburin v Baburin* [1990] 2 Qd R 101, Queensland Supreme Court).)

The question whether manifest disadvantage is a necessary ingredient in class 1 undue influence cases was re-examined by the House of Lords in *CIBC Mortgages plc v Pitt* [1993] 4 All ER 433. In that case, the husband and wife jointly owned the matrimonial home, which was valued at £270,000 in 1986. The only encumbrance on it was a mortgage in favour of a building society for £16,700. In the same year, the husband told the wife that he wanted to borrow some money on the security of the house in order to buy shares on the stock market. The wife was not happy with this suggestion, but was persuaded by her husband to agree. They signed an application form for a loan from the lender of £150,000 for a period of 20 years, the purpose of the loan being expressed to be to pay off the existing mortgage and purchase a holiday home. The parties duly signed the mortgage offer and also a legal charge prepared by the lender's solicitor. The wife did not read the documents before signing them or receive separate advice. The husband's speculation on the stock market ended when it crashed in 1987. The husband was then unable to meet the payments on the loan and the lender sought possession of the matrimonial home. The wife defended on the grounds, *inter alia*, that her consent to the mortgage transaction had been obtained as a result of her husband's actual undue influence.

In both the High Court and Court of Appeal, the case proceeded on the basis that manifest disadvantage was a necessary element in both actual and presumed undue influence cases. This view, however, was emphatically rejected by the House of Lords, who held that a claimant relying on actual undue influence was entitled, as of right, to have the transaction set aside regardless of manifest disadvantage since actual undue influence was a species of fraud and a person guilty of fraud was no more entitled to argue that the transaction was beneficial to the person defrauded than was a person who had procured a transaction by misrepresentation. Lord Browne-Wilkinson (who gave the leading speech, with whom all the other Law Lords concurred) had no doubt that the decision in *Morgan* did not extend to cases of actual undue influence. In his view, Lord Scarman's speech in that case was primarily concerned 'to establish that disadvantage had to be shown, not as a constituent element of the cause of action of undue influence, but in order to raise a presumption of undue influence within class 2': *Pitt*, p 439. Moreover, *Morgan* itself was a case involving presumed undue influence and, with the exception of one case (namely, *Ormes v Beadel* (1860) 2 Giff 166; 66 ER 70), all the cases cited by Lord Scarman were cases of presumed undue influence. That being so, the inescapable conclusion was that the decision in *Morgan* was not laying down any general principle applicable to all claims of undue influence.

It is also apparent that the requirement of manifest disadvantage has no application to cases where the wife is seeking to set aside the transaction on the ground of her husband's misrepresentations: *Bank of Cyprus (London) Ltd v Markou* [1999] 2 All ER 707, p 713, where Mr John Jarvis QC (sitting as a deputy judge of the High Court) said that 'in equity, misrepresentation is akin to and really a form of undue influence …'.

3.3 MEANING OF MANIFEST DISADVANTAGE

3.3.1 Introduction

In *Bank of Credit and Commerce International SA v Aboody* [1992] 4 All ER 955, the Court of Appeal defined manifest disadvantage as meaning a disadvantage which was 'obvious as such to any independent and reasonable person who considered the transaction at the time with knowledge of all the relevant facts' (p 974). It was stressed, however, that the mere fact that the complainant had been deprived of the power of choice (for example, because his will had been overborne through the failure to draw his attention to the risks involved) was not of itself a manifest disadvantage rendering the transaction voidable.

More recently, Nourse LJ, giving the leading judgment of the Court of Appeal, in *Barclays Bank plc v Coleman* [2000] 1 All ER 385, held that manifest disadvantage did not have to be large or even medium sized. It could be small, provided that the disadvantage was clear, obvious and more than *de minimis*. In this case, the husband's loan (needed to purchase a property as an investment) was secured by a legal charge over the matrimonial home, which was owned jointly by the husband and wife. The charge was an 'all moneys' charge securing not only the funding of the property, but also any future borrowings by the husband from the bank. The form of the charge, therefore, enabled the husband, without resort to the wife, to subject the family home to much greater financial risks than she could ever have known and that was held to constitute a clear and obvious disadvantage to her. (The interpretation of the word 'manifest' as meaning 'clear and obvious' is also reflected in the judgment of Nicholls VC in *Cheese v Thomas* [1994] 1 All ER 35, p 39.) Essentially, the requirement of manifest disadvantage has involved a balancing process, since the giving of a guarantee or charge always (by its very nature) involves some risk that the guarantee might be called in or the charge enforced. The question, therefore, whether the assumption of the risk is manifestly disadvantageous to the giver of the guarantee (or charge) has depended on balancing the seriousness of the risk of enforcement to the giver, in practical terms, and the benefits gained by the giver in accepting the risk. The overall disadvantageous nature of a transaction will not, therefore, be said to be manifest 'if it only emerges after a fine and close evaluation of its various beneficial and detrimental features': *Aboody*, p 974, *per* Slade LJ. In other words, the disadvantage must be 'obvious' to the reasonable person. The test is an objective one, looking at the financial and practical implications of the particular transaction existing at the date of the transaction, although 'subsequent events may conceivably throw light on what could reasonably have been foreseen as at that date': *Aboody*, p 974. Thus, even if the claimant was already subject to potential liabilities, the substantial increase of those liabilities would be capable of constituting a manifest disadvantage. Ultimately, however, this would depend on the particular circumstances of the case. The spectrum is wide, ranging, at one extreme, from where the transaction is 'not on its face to the financial advantage of the complainant' to cases where the transaction 'shocks the conscience of the court': *Credit Lyonnais Bank Nederland NV v Burch* [1997] 1 All ER 144 (CA), p 152, *per* Millett LJ.

3.3.2 Wives' surety cases

Latest guidance from the House of Lords, in *Royal Bank of Scotland v Etridge (No 2)* [2001] UKHL 44, suggests abandoning the label of 'manifest disadvantage', in the specific context of wives guaranteeing payment of their husband's business debts, in favour of the test outlined by Lindley LJ, in *Allcard v Skinner* (1887) 36 Ch D 145 (p 185), namely: 'is the gift so large as not to be reasonably accounted for on the ground of friendship, relationship, charity, or other ordinary motives on which ordinary men act?' Or, in the words of Lord Nicholls in *Etridge (No 2)*, the transaction must 'constitute a disadvantage sufficiently serious to require evidence to rebut the presumption' of undue influence: para 25. Lindley LJ's test was applied by Lord Scarman, in *Morgan*, where his Lordship reformulated the principle in terms of a transaction which was itself wrongful in that it constituted 'an advantage taken of the person subjected to the influence which, failing proof to the contrary, was explicable only on the basis that undue influence had been exercised to procure it' (p 827). The concept of manifest disadvantage, according to the House of Lords, is, therefore, evidential in so far as it is relevant to the question of whether there is any issue of abuse which can properly be raised. In the words of Lord Hobhouse, 'it is relevant to the determination whether in fact abuse did or did not occur': *Etridge (No 2)* (HL), para 104 and Lord Scott (para 155).

In several previous cases, the wife was held to have acquired a substantial counterbalancing right or benefit from the transaction so as to outweigh any possible disadvantages. A good illustration is to be found in the case of *Dunbar Bank plc v Nadeem* [1998] 3 All ER 876 (CA). Here, the husband was heavily indebted to the bank and, in order to improve his financial position, he applied to the bank for further funds to purchase, jointly with his wife, a new lease of the family home of which he was at that time the sole lessee. The bank made an advance of £260,000 to the parties, which was secured by an 'all moneys' charge against the property under which the wife became liable, not only for her joint debts with the husband, but also for his personal debts to the bank. Despite this obvious disadvantage to the wife, the Court of Appeal held that the transaction, viewed as a whole, was not manifestly disadvantageous to her since she had, for the first time, obtained a beneficial joint interest in an equity of redemption in the property: see, further, Chandler, A, 'Manifest disadvantage: limits of application' (1999) 115 LQR 213.

In other cases, the courts have taken into account the *potential* benefits to the wife of the husband's business continuing in trade by virtue of the additional loan facilities secured over the family home. In *Aboody*, for example, although the wife had taken on substantial (potential) liabilities and her family home was at risk as a result of the various transactions, these were counterbalanced by the fact that the loans gave the family company a 'reasonably good chance' of surviving. If the company had, in fact, survived, then undoubtedly the potential benefits to the wife would have been very substantial. In the words of Slade LJ (p 975):

> [The company] was the family business and the sole or principal means of support of Mr and Mrs Aboody. [It] might still have collapsed with or without the facilities covered by the six transactions. But at least these facilities gave it some hope of survival.

On this basis, therefore, the Court of Appeal concluded that the transactions were not manifestly disadvantageous to the wife and, accordingly, dismissed her claim. The same conclusion was reached in *Leggatt v National Westminster Bank plc* [2000] All ER (D) 1458, where the Court of Appeal held that a new charge over the family home was not, on its face, manifestly disadvantageous to the wife because the partnership business (run by the husband) would have collapsed, but for the execution of the charge. Significantly, the partnership profits were the sole income of the husband and wife. (See, also, *Bank of Scotland v Kustow* (1998) unreported, 22 January, available on Lexis, where Chadwick LJ said: 'it is perfectly legitimate to take into account that a wife may consider that the indirect advantage to her of saving her husband from bankruptcy is a sufficient benefit to outweigh the risk that her house may be possessed by the bank.')

The acceptance by the courts of the essentially speculative benefit to the wife that her husband's business might recover has made it potentially difficult for wives who are not financially independent of their husbands to prove manifest disadvantage. In this connection, it is apparent that, if the marriage is secure and the husband's indebtedness has been incurred by a family business which provides not only the husband's livelihood but also prosperity for his wife and family, it may be impossible for the wife to argue manifest disadvantage in the absence of any real conflict between the interests of husband and wife: *Royal Bank of Scotland v Etridge (No 2)* [1998] 4 All ER 705 (CA), p 716, *per* Stuart-Smith LJ. In these circumstances, it will not matter whether the business is carried on by the husband personally or by means of a small family company. It will also be largely immaterial whether the wife holds a substantial or virtually no shareholding in the company. In the words of Stuart-Smith LJ (p 716):

> It may be a very difficult question in any particular case whether it is worth putting the roof over their heads at risk in order to continue to carry on the business. But if it is, then the transaction may be as much in the interest of the wife as of the husband; and if it is not, it may be as much against his interest as against hers.

Curiously, however, in most of the cases, the potential gain does not actually materialise and the wife is left in a financially worse position at the end of the day. The justification for such an approach is that the courts view the question of manifest disadvantage at the time of the transaction and not from the standpoint of its eventual outcome. This is apparent in the judgment of Slade LJ in *Aboody* (p 974), where he states that manifest disadvantage 'has to be judged in the circumstances subsisting at the date of the transaction, though ... subsequent events may conceivably throw light on what could reasonably have been foreseen as at that date'. Ultimately, it seems that the weaker the wife is financially in relation to her husband, the less likely she will be in a position to challenge the validity of the transaction. This has led one commentator to remark that: 'there is a real risk here of the law developing into a "no win" situation for wives, since those wives who *are* financially independent are *ipso facto* more likely to be found able to bring "a truly independent mind and will to bear on financial decisions" and therefore not to have been influenced by anyone' (Oldham, M, 'Neither a borrower nor a lender be – the life of O'Brien' (1995) 7 Child and Family LQ 104, p 110). (See, also, the approach of the New Zealand Court of Appeal in *Contractors Bonding Ltd v Snee* [1992] 2 NZLR 157, p 174, where it was held that, in the context of unconscionability, there was no 'contractual imbalance' because the claimant had gained a benefit from the ability to help the debtor, her son.)

Not all the cases, however, have been consistent in accepting speculative benefit as a counterbalancing factor in assessing manifest disadvantage. In *Turner v Barclays Bank plc* [1997] 2 FCR 151, for example, the benefit to the wife (and the family as a whole) of a further loan from the bank was to enable the husband's business to continue trading. If the charge had not been executed, the bank would not have continued an existing overdraft facility and the business would have ceased or, at least, run into serious difficulties. Significantly, also, the family was benefiting to the extent of about £1,000 per month from payments made out of the business account at the bank. Nevertheless, Neuberger J held that the loan transaction was not to the financial advantage of the wife since it involved charging her interest in the family home to secure her husband's debts to the bank. The substantial benefits to the wife (outlined above) did not contradict this view since 'the wife will almost always benefit indirectly, and could normally be presumed by the bank to benefit indirectly, from the provision of lending facilities to her husband' (p 165).

A similar approach was taken in *Bank of Cyprus (London) Ltd v Markou* [1999] 2 All ER 707. Here, the husband and wife each held an equal share in a company which operated the family business. The husband, however, controlled the business and the wife had no practical involvement. She never had any drawings out of the business; on the contrary, he had control of the account and would draw out such moneys as he saw fit towards her housekeeping. The husband decided to move the company's account to the claimant bank and apply for loan facilities. At that time, the company was running at a loss, had no real assets and had little prospect of making profits. The bank, nevertheless, agreed to provide the loan facilities on the strength of the security of the family home. Subsequently, the wife attended the bank and executed an unlimited guarantee over the company's liabilities and a legal charge over the home. The company later failed and the bank sought possession of the house. In response to the wife's allegation that she had signed the documents under her husband's undue influence, the bank denied that the transaction was manifestly disadvantageous to her because of her equal shareholding in the family company. Mr John Jarvis QC (sitting as a deputy judge of the High Court) held that, as between the husband and wife, the matter had to be viewed from the perspective of the parties to the transaction and not from the point of view of the creditor (that is, the bank). Thus, where a wife charged the family home to secure loans made to her husband's business, the knowledge of the husband and wife was relevant in deciding whether the transaction was manifestly disadvantageous to the wife. In this case, the wife was effectively at the husband's mercy in respect of the conduct of the business and, in those circumstances, her shareholding in the company had very little significance. She had clearly exposed the home (her only asset) to risk for the sake of a company which had little prospect of success and the transaction, therefore, was to her manifest disadvantage. The deputy judge said (p 716):

> ... there is a world of difference between a case where a husband and wife are entering into a joint venture together and one where it is essentially the husband's business that is being guaranteed.

Manifest disadvantage was also shown in *Barclays Bank plc v O'Brien* [1993] 4 All ER 417 (HL), where the husband was a shareholder in a company which had a substantial unsecured overdraft. He arranged with the bank that the company would be allowed an overdraft facility of £135,000, reducing to £120,000 after three weeks, secured by a second charge over the matrimonial home owned jointly by him and his wife. The necessary documentation was signed by both the husband and wife. It was apparent that the wife simply executed the charge in order to guarantee her husband's liabilities, whereas he was the sole director of the company of which she had no financial interest. The House of Lords held that the charge was not to her financial advantage because she had no direct pecuniary interest in her husband's business. Again, in *Goode Durrant Administration v Biddulph* [1994] 2 FLR 551, the bank lent £316,750 to a property company, of which the husband and wife were directors. The husband, however, held 90% of the shares with the remaining 10% being divided between his wife, their two children and their son-in-law. The husband alone dealt with the bank on the company's behalf. The wife had little business experience and relied on her husband in executing the loan, the purpose of which was to carry out a development project. This project, however, proved unsuccessful and the company went into liquidation. Mr Judge Rich QC (sitting as a deputy judge of the High Court) held that a transaction involving a risk of personal liability for a large sum (that is, in excess of £300,000) in order to have a 2.5% share of any profit made was manifestly disadvantageous to the wife. Accordingly, she was entitled to have the transaction as against her husband set aside. In contrast to the case of *Aboody*, referred to above, manifest disadvantage was not precluded here because the wife was financially dependent on her husband's business for support. The following further cases are also worthy of comment:

- *Davies v Norwich Union Life Insurance Society* (1999) 78 P & CR 119 (CA) – the parties were husband and wife and owned the matrimonial home as beneficial joint tenants. Their prospective liability under an existing charge over the house was limited to £150,000 and the burden would fall primarily on the husband's share in the property. However, once the subject charge had been executed, the position changed to the wife's detriment from one in which there was a minimal risk that her share in the property would be affected to one in which, if her guarantee was called in, she would now lose 50% of her share in the property. Moreover, under this later charge, the amount secured by the guarantee could be increased without reference to the wife. Accordingly, the transaction was held to be to her manifest disadvantage.

- *Barclays Bank plc v Caplan* [1998] 1 FLR 532 – the bank agreed to grant an overdraft facility of £300,000 to the husband's company. The facility was secured by the husband's personal guarantee supported by a charge over the jointly owned family home of the husband and wife. A year later, the husband's borrowing was increased significantly and the debts of other companies were guaranteed at the same time. Whilst the initial facility was not disadvantageous to the wife (as it simply replaced an existing mortgage), the subsequent transaction was held to be plainly disadvantageous as it substantially burdened her interest in the home with her husband's business debts. Although she had an indirect interest in her husband incurring those debts (because they enabled him to pursue a business career which financed a comfortable lifestyle), this was ignored by the court on the basis that 'a husband is bound to maintain his wife in accordance with his means' and 'such indirect advantages as these are a feature of virtually every case of this kind' (p 542). Significantly, the wife had no direct financial interest of her own in her husband's business, since she was neither a shareholder nor director. (See, also, *Midland Bank plc v Greene* [1994] 2 FLR 827, where HH Judge Rich held that a mortgage charging the wife's home as security for the husband's present and future debts was manifestly to her disadvantage.)

- *Midland Bank plc v Shephard* [1988] 3 All ER 17 (CA) – the husband's bank account became overdrawn and he made arrangements with the bank to transfer the overdraft to a new joint account held by him and his wife. The mandate for the new joint account was signed by both the husband and the wife. The husband subsequently required a loan for business purposes and the bank agreed to an overdraft of £10,000 on the joint account. The wife took no part in the arrangements and, although she was aware of the husband's intention to borrow the money, she did not know and was not told that it would be a liability on the joint account. The Court of Appeal held that the signing of the mandate was potentially disadvantageous to the wife.

The House of Lords in *Etridge (No 2)*, as mentioned earlier, has now sought to give authoritative guidance on the meaning of manifest disadvantage in the context of wives' suretyship transactions. According to Lord Nicholls, a transaction whereby a wife guaranteed payment of her husband's debts would, in a narrow sense, be plainly disadvantageous to her in so far as she undertook a serious financial obligation in return for no personal return. On a wider view, however, it is likely that the husband's business is the source of the family income and the wife has a personal interest in doing what she can to support the business. Such a transaction may well be, therefore, for her benefit since 'ordinarily, the fortunes of husband and wife are bound up together' (para 28). In the words of Lord Scott (para 159):

> In the fairly common circumstances that the financial and business decisions of the family are primarily taken by the husband, I would assume that the wife would have trust and confidence in his ability to do so and would support his decisions.

According to Lord Nicholls, the correct approach lay in discarding the label (that is, manifest disadvantage) which gave rise to this sort of ambiguity. Instead, the formulation applied by Lord Scarman, in *Morgan* (see above), should be applied. In terms of husband and wife cases, therefore, he was of the view that, *in the ordinary course*, a wife's guarantee of her husband's bank overdraft secured by means of a charge on her share of the family home, should *not* be regarded as a transaction which, failing proof to the contrary, was explicable only on the basis that it had been procured by the exercise of the husband's undue influence. In the words of Lord Scott (para 162):

> In the surety wife cases it should, in my opinion, be recognised that undue influence, although a possible explanation for the wife's agreement to become surety, is a relatively unlikely one.

In most cases, as we have seen, there will be good reasons why a wife is willing to enter into such a transaction, despite the risks involved for her and the family. His Lordship did not, however, rule out the possibility that, in exceptional cases, a wife's signature of a guarantee and charge will call for an explanation. In this connection, however, Lord Nicholls emphasised that 'statements or conduct by a husband which do not pass beyond the bounds of what may be expected of a reasonable husband in the circumstances should not, without more, be castigated as undue influence': *Etridge (No 2)* (HL), para 32. Similarly, when a husband is forecasting the future of his business, the courts should not be too ready to characterise his exaggerations as misrepresentations or misstatements. His Lordship also noted, however (para 33), that:

> Inaccurate explanations of a proposed transaction are a different matter. So are cases where a husband, in whom a wife has reposed trust and confidence for the management of their financial affairs, prefers his interests to hers and makes a choice for both of them on that footing. Such a husband abuses the influence he has. He fails to discharge the obligation of candour and fairness he owes a wife who is looking to him to make the major financial decisions.

What is likely to be perceived as abuse, on the one hand, and legitimate exaggerations, on the other, is not easy to discern from their Lordships' speeches.

3.3.3 Other cases

Significantly, Lord Nicholls, in *Etridge (No 2)*, considered that the label of 'manifest disadvantage' was 'apt enough' when applied to straightforward transactions (that is, other than those involving a wife guaranteeing payment of her husband's debts), such as gift or a sale at an undervalue. What follows is a list of other cases in which the requirement of manifest disadvantage has been established on the facts:

- *Coldunell Ltd v Gallon* [1986] 1 All ER 429 (CA) – elderly parents were persuaded by their son (in his fifties and better educated) to arrange a loan from licensed moneylenders to further his business. The son arranged a short term loan of £20,000 from the lenders to his father, secured by a charge on the house were his parents lived and which was owned by the father. The rate of interest on the loan was 20%. The Court of Appeal held that the transaction was manifestly disadvantageous to the parents since they derived nothing at all from it except some onerous obligations which they were incapable of fulfilling.

- *Claughton v Price* (1998) 30 HLR 396 (CA) – the claimant needed funds in order to meet the repayments on various mortgages in respect of properties he had purchased in Florida. He approached the defendant, a personal friend, who suggested that he would purchase the properties in order to provide the claimant with the money to discharge the mortgages. It was understood that the claimant should have an option to repurchase the properties, but the requisite documentation to this effect was never executed. When the claimant later sought to repurchase the properties back into his own name, the defendant refused. The claimant then sought to have the sale transactions set aside on the ground of undue influence. The valuation evidence showed that the properties were purchased by the defendant at a gross undervalue. In fact, the price was based simply on the amount required to redeem the mortgages and was never properly negotiated. Such a price, therefore, could only be rational if it was supplemented by an option to repurchase the properties. Since no such option had been entered into, the transactions were held to be manifestly disadvantageous to the claimant.

- *Credit Lyonnais Bank Nederland NV v Burch* [1997] 1 All ER 144 (CA) – a junior employee was persuaded to provide security required by a bank for an increased overdraft required by her employer. She agreed to a second charge over her flat and an unlimited all moneys guarantee. The flat was valued at £100,000 and her equity was £70,000. The Court of Appeal concluded that the transaction was manifestly disadvantageous to her in so far as she had committed herself to a liability far beyond her limited means and risked the loss of her home and personal bankruptcy to help her employer's company in which she had no financial interest and of which she was only a junior employee. In fact, she received nothing in return except a relatively small increase in her employer's overdraft facility. The case was characterised as 'extreme' and 'crying out for an explanation' (p 152, *per* Millett LJ).

- *Steeples v Lea* [1998] 1 FLR 138 (CA) – a junior employee was persuaded to offer her house as security for a loan obtained by her employer. The employer made no payments on the mortgage and the lender sought to enforce the security. The transaction was held to be one from which the employee derived no advantage at all and was, accordingly, held to be manifestly disadvantageous to her. She stood to risk her home, which was virtually her only asset, with no counter-security. In the words of Millett LJ, the transaction was 'extravagantly improvident' and cried out for an explanation (p 148).

- *Cheese v Thomas* [1994] 1 All ER 35 (CA) – the claimant (an elderly man) and the defendant (his great nephew) agreed to buy a house for £83,000 for the purpose of providing accommodation for the claimant for the remainder of his life. The claimant contributed £43,000 towards the purchase price and the defendant contributed £40,000 by means of a building society mortgage. The house was purchased in the defendant's sole name and it was agreed that the claimant would live there until his death and it would thereafter belong to the defendant. The defendant failed to keep up the mortgage payments and the claimant brought proceedings against him claiming that the transaction should be set aside on the ground of undue influence. The Court of Appeal held that the arrangement was clearly disadvantageous to the claimant as he had used all his money to purchase the right to live in a house for the remainder of his life and that right was insecure and tied him to a particular property. The benefit of the right to live rent-free in the house for life (which he could not afford to buy) was outweighed by the obvious risks involved. For example, if he needed or wished to live elsewhere, there was no way he could compel the defendant to sell the house or return his money. Moreover, he was 85 years old and, at some point, might need to live in sheltered accommodation. In addition and most importantly, he would have no security if the defendant failed to keep up the mortgage payments to the building society. Since he had no money of his own, he would be evicted by the lender and would have to remain content with a claim for damages for breach of contract against the defendant. (See, further, Chen-Wishart, M, 'Loss sharing, undue influence and manifest disadvantage' (1994) 110 LQR 173, pp 174–75, who views the case as a judicial relaxation of the requirement of manifest disadvantage because, although the court identified the very considerable benefits which the claimant stood to gain under the transaction (that is, rent-free accommodation for the rest of his life), nevertheless, these were found to be 'clearly and obviously' outweighed by the drawbacks in the arrangement.)

- *Mahoney v Purnell* [1996] 3 All ER 61 – the claimant operated a hotel business in partnership with his son-in-law. The business was incorporated as a company and each party held approximately 50% of the shares. The son-in-law indicated that he wanted to run the hotel on his own and negotiations began with the claimant with a view to buying out his shares in the company. The parties agreed a price of £200,000, calculated on the basis of an assessment of the company's assets and liabilities. The company accountant later proposed a scheme of annual payments to the claimant of £20,000 over 10 years, which effectively valued his shares at only £64,000. This was later accepted by the claimant. The son-in-law subsequently sold the hotel for £3.27 m. May J held that the transaction was materially disadvantageous to the claimant. The sum of £200,000, payable over 10 years without interest, did not fairly represent the value of the claimant's shareholding (and his loan account) since the value of his shares at the relevant time was in the region of £267,000.

- *Nightingale Finance Ltd v Scott* [1997] EGCS 161 – manifest disadvantage was held to exist in this case, despite the fact that the wife had a stake in the business activities financed by the loan, because the lender's agent deliberately attempted to defraud both the husband and wife. In other words, the loan was always going to be disadvantageous to the wife as the agent's plan was that she would lose everything. Carnwath J held that manifest disadvantage had to be examined against the circumstances in which the mortgage was made (that is, with the agent's intention to defraud the wife).

- *Langton v Langton* [1995] 2 FLR 890 – a father gifted his bungalow to the defendants, his son and daughter-in-law. The gift was coupled with the grant of a non-exclusive licence to occupy the property in favour of the father. Mr AWH Charles (sitting as a deputy High Court judge) held that the gift was manifestly disadvantageous to the father because he had given away the bulk of his capital and committed himself to living with the defendants. The deputy judge said: 'he thereby deprived himself of the opportunity to sell his property to finance such nursing care as he might need in the last years of his life and effectively placed his future in the hands of the defendants.' This abdication of control over his destiny and lack of choice rendered the transaction manifestly improvident.

- *Wright v Cherrytree Finance Ltd* [2001] 2 All ER (Comm) 877 (CA) – the claimant had entered into a loan agreement with the lender secured by her house as a result of undue influence exerted by the defendants, her daughter and son-in-law. Within two months of the claimant's husband's death, the defendants had asked to borrow money against the security of the claimant's house to enable the son-in-law to purchase shares in a company. The claimant eventually agreed and applied jointly with her daughter to the lender for a loan with the claimant's house as security. The lender granted a loan at a rate of 18% or, if the payments were received on time, at a rate of 12.9%. Later, the claimant sought to rescind the loan agreement on the grounds of undue influence and misrepresentation by the defendants. At first instance, Neuberger J found that the claimant had relied on her husband to take care of financial affairs and had failed to appreciate the consequences of non-payment of the mortgage instalments. Moreover, her insight into commercial and financial affairs was minimal. In particular, she did not know what shares were and she had placed confidence and trust in her daughter and son-in-law and had no one else to turn to for advice. She had signed the application documents without reading or fully understanding them. On this basis, his Lordship found actual undue influence on the part of the defendants, of which the lender had constructive knowledge, but who failed to dispel the effects of such influence. The Court of Appeal, agreeing with these conclusions, held that for a recently widowed lady to mortgage the house in which she lived which was her only asset, for no sensible reason, put her at a manifest disadvantage in the transaction. This, coupled with the fact that the loan was at an extravagant rate of interest, was sufficient to put the lender on inquiry. The fact that the lender had stated in documents that the claimant should seek independent advice was not sufficient to dispel the effects of the undue influence.

In some cases, the transaction is so improvident and one-sided as to qualify also as a harsh and unconscionable bargain: *Royal Bank of Scotland v Etridge (No 2)* [1998] 4 All ER 705 (CA), p 713, *per* Stuart-Smith LJ. This was the position in *Burch*, mentioned above, where the Millett LJ characterised the transaction as one which 'shocks the conscience of the court' (p 152).

3.4 DUAL FUNCTION OF MANIFEST DISADVANTAGE

Prior to the House of Lords' ruling in *Etridge (No 2)*, the requirement of manifest disadvantage had a dual function. This was recognised in *Royal Bank of Scotland v Etridge (No 2)* [1998] 4 All ER 705 (CA) (p 714), where Stuart-Smith LJ stated that:

(i) it assists the complainant in establishing her claim against the wrongdoer in a case of presumed undue influence; and (ii) it is relevant to the way in which the transaction appears to a third party and thus assists [the complainant] in establishing that the third party had constructive notice of the impropriety.

As we have seen, so far as the claim against the wrongdoer is concerned, the presence of manifest disadvantage is a 'powerful evidential factor', because the more disadvantageous the transaction to the complainant, the easier it is for the complainant to prove that it had been procured by improper means and the more difficult for the wrongdoer to rebut the presumption: *Etridge (No 2)* (CA), p 713, *per* Stuart-Smith LJ. This was most evident in *Credit Lyonnais Bank Nederland NV v Burch* [1997] 1 All ER 144 (CA), p 154, where Millett LJ said that 'where the transaction is so extravagantly improvident that it is virtually inexplicable on any other basis, the inference [of a relationship of trust and confidence] may be drawn'. As we have already seen, the issue of manifest disadvantage as between complainant and wrongdoer will depend on two factors, namely: (1) the seriousness of the risk of enforcement to the giver, in practical terms and (2) the benefits gained by the giver in accepting the risk: *Bank of Credit and Commerce International SA v Aboody* [1992] 4 All ER 955, p 974, *per* Slade LJ.

The relevance of manifest disadvantage vis à vis third parties was considered in *Britannia Building Society v Pugh* [1997] 2 FLR 7 (CA). Here, the parties (husband and wife) were property developers based in Devon. They obtained from the building society an advance of £970,000 secured against two development sites and the family home. The loan was repayable within a year, with interest payments of £12,500 payable each month. The construction works were delayed and further monies were needed. So the building society lent a further sum of £160,000. The developments did not proceed to a sale and the monthly interest payments were not made. The building society sought to foreclose on the mortgage and the wife defended possession proceedings in respect of the family home on the ground that she had been under the undue influence of her husband in agreeing to the mortgage. She also argued that the building society had actual or constructive notice of such influence.

On this latter point, she argued that the loan was unusual in so far as it was for a sum twice the actual value of the matrimonial home (three times the insurance value of the buildings) and repayable within only a year. Moreover, it must have been apparent to the building society that the husband was orchestrating the transaction so that there was a clear risk that the wife was being subjected to undue influence. The Court of Appeal, however, rejected the wife's attempt to categorise the loan as abnormal. The true test, in line with *Barclays Bank plc v O'Brien* [1993] 4 All ER 417, was whether the building society knew of certain facts which ought to have put it on inquiry as to the possible existence of the wife's equity. On the facts, the court held that there was nothing in the nature of the transaction which alerted the building society to the possibility that the mortgage was not to the financial advantage of the wife. The application for funds had been made in joint names, the development properties and the family home were jointly owned and the inference could fairly be made that the proceeds of sale would be jointly held. Although the husband had taken the lead in the management of the family finances, that, in the court's view, did not of itself suggest the risk of improper pressure being exerted on a subservient wife. Most importantly, in the court's analysis, was the fact that the parties' accountants had stated the development business as being carried on jointly by the husband and wife. Accordingly, the wife's claim failed.

Similarly, in *CIBC Mortgages plc v Pitt* [1993] 4 All ER 433 (CA), the money was advanced, so far as the bank was concerned, for the purchase of a second property for the husband and wife. The loan was advanced to the parties jointly and there was nothing to suggest that it was anything other than a normal advance to a husband and wife for their joint benefit. Here again, the mere fact that there was a risk of there being undue influence because one of the borrowers was the wife was not, in itself, sufficient to put the bank on inquiry. In the course of his judgment, Lord Browne-Wilkinson referred to the distinction between 'joint advance' and 'surety' cases in the following terms (p 441):

> ... in the latter, there is not only the possibility of undue influence having been exercised but also the increased risk of it having in fact been exercised because, at least on its face, the guarantee by a wife of her husband's debts is not for her financial benefit. It is the combination of these two factors that puts the creditor on inquiry.

The combination of these two factors was, however, noticeably absent in the *Pugh* case, referred to above. Although the sum borrowed far exceeded the value of the matrimonial home (or its insurance value), that had to be set against the added value of the development properties which were also offered as security. Moreover, the term of the loan requiring repayment within a year was not unusual given the commercial character of the loan and the commercial enterprise it was intended to finance. In addition, there was every reason to suppose that the property development would be successful and both husband and wife would benefit from it.

As noted earlier, where the question of manifest disadvantage is being considered in the context of an allegation of undue influence brought by one party against another, it is appropriate to view the matter from the position of the two parties who are involved in the initial transaction. The position of the creditor is, at this stage, irrelevant since it is only the knowledge of the husband and wife which is material. Where, however, the issue of manifest disadvantage is linked to the question whether the lender is put on inquiry, wider factors have been held to come into play. Here, the issue prior to the House of Lords' ruling in *Etridge (No 2)* depended largely on what facts were made known to the lender at the time of the transaction: *Bank of Cyprus (London) Ltd v Markou* [1999] 2 All ER 707, p 717; and *National Westminster Bank plc v Breeds* [2001] Lloyd's Rep Bank 98.

In *Bank of Scotland v Bennett* [1999] Lloyd's Rep Bank 145, for example, the wife had a small (10%) shareholding in her husband's business. The matrimonial home was in her sole name. The husband persuaded her to second mortgage the home to finance his business expansion. When the bank claimed possession of the home, she argued that her signature to the guarantee and charge had been obtained by undue influence on the part of the husband in circumstances which had put the bank on inquiry. The Court of Appeal rejected this argument on the ground that, on the facts known to it, the bank could take the view that there was no real risk of the wife's apparent consent having been improperly obtained. It was held that, in the absence of other facts known to the lender, a transaction by which a wife is asked to provide a guarantee for the debts of a business from which the family derived its income could not be said to be extravagantly or even necessarily improvident. Moreover, the bank was not aware, at the time of the making of the advance, of the parties' respective shareholdings in the business or of the wife's sole beneficial ownership of the house. Finally, this was not a case of a bank seeking security in the face of impending disaster; on the contrary, the bank was satisfied at the time that the husband's venture had a real prospect of success.

By contrast, in *Barclays Bank plc v Sumner* [1996] EGCS 65, the husband and wife each held one-half of the shareholding in a company of which they were the only directors. They approached the bank saying that they wanted to expand the company's activities into property development. The bank duly provided the finance for this and other projects, its security for the advances being an unlimited guarantee signed by both the husband and wife. Mr James Munby QC (sitting as a deputy judge of the High Court) held that, when the question of manifest disadvantage arose in the context of a family company, it had to be answered by reference to the wife's direct financial interest in the company. He said that the question was whether potential direct financial benefit to the wife through the company was so small compared with her potential liability as to put a reasonable lender on notice of a possibility that the wife had been induced to enter into a manifestly disadvantageous transaction. On the facts, the guarantee was not to the wife's manifest disadvantage because she had a direct financial interest in the company which was, for all practical purposes, of the same size as that of her husband.

The decision may be compared with *Goode Durrant Administration v Biddulph* [1994] 2 FLR 551, where the wife's direct interest in the family company was only a 2.5% shareholding. To make herself personally liable, therefore, for a sum in excess of £300,000 in order to have a 2.5% share (through the company) of any profit arising from the proposed development was held to be a transaction manifestly disadvantageous to her. Looking at the matter from the point of view of the lender, the existence of the possibility of undue influence being exercised by reason of the relationship of husband and wife, coupled with the increased risk of its having, in fact, been exercised because the transaction was not on its face for the financial benefit of the wife, put the bank on inquiry as to the wife's equity against her husband. Although accepting that the distinction between joint loan and surety cases was useful, HH Judge Rich also considered that it was 'not a final and determinative categorisation': p 554. If there is a joint advance which, on its face, appears to be for the financial benefit of both husband and wife, there will be nothing to put the lender on inquiry. Equally, where the wife acts as surety for the debts of her husband (or for the debts of the husband's company in which she has no direct financial interest), the lender will be put on inquiry. In the instant case, the transaction fell to be characterised as a joint loan to the company in which both the husband and wife had a direct interest. So far as the lender was concerned, however, it knew that the wife had only a limited financial share in the company, that she was a director of it, but had only limited involvement in its affairs. Although she clearly had an indirect interest in her husband's prosperity, this was not something which was strictly material since the question was 'what the bank might, on the face of the transaction, reasonably assume about the benefit directly or through the company to [the wife]': p 555. The reality was that the outstanding debt amounted to £160,000 whereas the most the wife could expect to profit from the venture was only £5,000.

Much of this reasoning has now been encapsulated in the House of Lords' ruling in *Etridge (No 2)*. In particular, Lord Nicholls identified three distinct scenarios which called for comment in answering the question of when a lender will be put on inquiry. First, the lender will *automatically* be put on inquiry where a wife becomes surety for her husband's debts. Secondly, a lender will *not* be put on inquiry where money is being advanced to the husband and wife jointly, unless the bank is aware that the loan is being made for the husband's purposes, as distinct from their joint purposes. This accords with the reasoning of the above cases: see, especially, *CIBC Mortgages plc v Pitt*. Thirdly, a lender will be put on inquiry where the wife becomes a surety for the debts of a company whose shares are held by her and her husband, regardless of whether she has a minority or equal shareholding with her husband. This will be so, even if the wife is a director or secretary of the company (see, further, Chapter 4, para 4.2.3).

3.5 CAUSATION

It seems that, regardless of whether or not the transaction is manifestly disadvantageous to the complainant, a plea of actual or presumed undue influence will fail if the evidence shows that, on the balance of probabilities, the complainant would have entered into the transaction in any event. The point was addressed in *Aboody*, where the wife's claim failed, *inter alia*, because the husband's conduct (which, on the facts, constituted actual undue influence) was not operative on his wife's mind; it did not cause her to enter into the relevant transactions since she would have done so regardless of the undue influence (pp 978–79).

Similarly, in *Leggatt v National Westminster Bank plc* [2000] All ER (D) 1458 (CA), the bank wrote to the wife's solicitors indicating the nature of the proposed transaction, but the letter mistakenly referred to the charge as securing an advance to her husband's partnership, whereas the charge was in replacement of an existing mortgage over the matrimonial home. The Court of Appeal held that this inaccuracy in the bank's letter was immaterial in so far as the wife would have signed the charge, even if the true position had been disclosed to her by her solicitors. Again, in *Midland Bank plc v Kidwai* [1995] 4 Bank LR 227 (CA), the Recorder held that the wife would have been prepared to sign the form postponing her equitable interest in the home in favour of the bank in any event. He said:

> Put shortly, I am satisfied on the balance of probability that had she been given full information, either by her husband or the bank, she would have acted in exactly the same way that she did ... Accordingly, I hold that [she] is bound by the terms of the letter of consent signed by her and that the same takes effect.

Unfortunately, the point was not addressed on appeal to the Court of Appeal, who decided against the wife on different grounds. It is apparent, however, that the onus is clearly on the wrongdoer to show that the undue influence did not induce the transaction (that is, that it made no difference to the complainant's decision).

3.6 SHOULD MANIFEST DISADVANTAGE BE A NECESSARY REQUIREMENT?

In *CIBC Mortgages plc v Pitt* [1993] 4 All ER 433, Lord Browne-Wilkinson pointed out that the requirement of manifest disadvantage was at odds with the line of cases involving abuse of confidence where the onus is clearly on the fiduciary to show that the transaction is a fair one. Because of the obvious overlap between such relationships (see Chapter 1, para 1.5.2) and those in which undue influence is presumed, there is certainly a strong argument for abandoning the requirement of manifest disadvantage altogether in undue influence cases. Instead, the onus would be on the person taking advantage of the complainant to show the 'righteousness' of the transaction. But, as Lord Browne-Wilkinson observed in *Pitt* (p 440):

> The abuse of confidence principle is founded on considerations of general public policy, viz, that in order to protect those to whom fiduciaries owe duties *as a class* from exploitation by fiduciaries *as a class*, the law imposes a heavy duty on fiduciaries to show the righteousness of the transactions they enter into with those to whom they owe such duties. This principle is in sharp contrast with the view of this House in *Morgan* that in cases of presumed undue influence (a) the law is not based on considerations of public policy and (b) that it is for the claimant to prove that the transaction was disadvantageous rather than for the fiduciary to prove that it was not disadvantageous.

Unfortunately, the abuse of confidence cases were not cited to the House of Lords in *National Westminster Bank plc v Morgan* [1985] 1 All ER 821, and so the interaction between the two sets of principles was not considered. More recently, however, Nourse LJ in *Barclays Bank plc v Coleman* [2000] 1 All ER 385 (CA), alluded to the difficulties in applying the 'elusive' concept of manifest disadvantage to the facts of individual cases and the desirability of abandoning the requirement altogether in cases of presumed undue influence. According to his Lordship, the remarks of Lord Browne-Wilkinson in *Pitt* (cited above) 'have put a serious question mark over the future of the requirement of manifest disadvantage' (p 399). He identified the introduction of the requirement as stemming from the House of Lords' decision in *Morgan* and a misinterpretation by Lord Scarman in that case of the Privy Council decision in *Poosathurai v Kannappa Chettiar* (1919) LR 47 Ind App 1. That was a case decided under s 16(1) of the Indian Contract Act 1872 which provides that a contract is induced by undue influence 'where the relations existing between the parties are such that one of the parties is in a position to dominate the will of the other, and uses that position to obtain *an unfair advantage* over the other' (emphasis added). As Nourse LJ explains, the first requirement (that is, domination of the will) is not part of English law: *Goldsworthy v Brickell* [1987] 1 All ER 853, p 865. The second requirement (that is, unfair advantage) does reflect English law but 'it does not at all follow that every transaction in which one party uses his position to obtain an unfair advantage over the other is, as Lord Scarman appears to have thought, manifestly disadvantageous to that other': *Coleman*, pp 399–400. The two things were not necessarily synonymous. In any event, it has been noted that the requirement of manifest disadvantage was statutorily imposed in *Poosathurai* by virtue of the very wording of s 16(1) of the 1872 Act. In *Morgan*, on the other hand, the House was not constrained by any such statutory provision but was free to consider the matter from general principles: Phang, A, 'Undue influence methodology, sources and linkages' [1995] JBL 552, p 559.

As Nourse LJ indicated in *Coleman*, the House of Lords in *Pitt* 'signalled' that the requirement of manifest disadvantage may need to be reviewed in the future: see, also, *National Westminster Bank plc v Breeds* [2001] Lloyd's Rep Bank 98, where Lawrence Collins J described the role of manifest disadvantage as being 'controversial' in cases of presumed undue influence. Several academic commentators have also questioned the need for it. Capper, for example, indicates that no decision, prior to *Morgan*, appears to have treated what he describes as 'transactional imbalance' as a prerequisite to relief, although he does concede that such imbalance is, in fact, an 'invariable feature' of the pre-*Morgan* cases: see Capper, D, 'Undue influence and unconscionability: a rationalisation' (1998) 114 LQR 479, p 487.

One solution to the problem, suggested by Oldham, is to accept that the doctrine of presumed undue influence is founded upon public policy considerations, like the abuse of confidence cases (that is, the protection of a class of people who are potentially at risk by requiring those who take advantage of them to establish the probity of their transactions) and that, therefore, the requirement of manifest disadvantage should be removed in cases of presumed undue influence in order to bring the two lines of authority together: Oldham, M, 'Neither a borrower nor a lender be – the life of O'Brien' (1995) 7 Child and Family LQ 104, pp 108–09. He cites the judgment of Cotton LJ, in *Allcard v Skinner* (1887) 36 Ch D 145 (CA), p 171, in support of his argument. Such rationalisation, he says, would also bring the rationale of undue influence into line with that of other vitiating factors in the law of contract (that is, duress and misrepresentation) where the fairness or unfairness of the contract is treated as irrelevant. He also argues that the requirement of manifest disadvantage runs counter to older authority where the adequacy of consideration was not treated as conclusive of whether undue influence had been exerted. In *Allcard v Skinner* (1887) 36 Ch D 145, p 181, for example, Lindley LJ said that class 1 undue influence cases involve 'generally, *though not always*, some personal advantage obtained by a donee' (emphasis added). This suggests that a court would be prepared to grant relief even where the gift in question was small and, therefore, of no great disadvantage to the donor. Indeed, the older authorities appear to have regarded the size of the gift as no more than an *evidential factor* to be taken into account in determining whether undue influence had been exercised and, crucially, whether the victim acted with free and fully informed judgment: see, for example, *Wright v Carter* [1903] 1 Ch 27, p 50. A similar approach was taken in cases of undue influence involving contractual transactions: *Tate v Williamson* (1866) LR 1 HL 200, p 213, where Lord Chelmsford LC stated that '[e]ven if the defendant could have shown the price he gave was a fair one, this would not alter the case against him'; see Tiplady, D, 'The limits of undue influence' (1985) 48 MLR 579, p 583, who emphasises that it cannot be assumed that a person who receives a commercially fair price must, as a result, have acted of his own free will.

The point was also made by the Court of Appeal in *Morgan* [1983] 3 All ER 85, subsequently reversed by the House of Lords, in which Slade LJ said (p 92):

> [It] is still possible that the relationship and influence therefrom has been abused, even though the transaction is, on the face of it, one which, in commercial terms, provides reasonably equal benefits for both parties.

Similarly, Dunn LJ alluded to the case of a solicitor who bought his client's house at a full and fair valuation, where the requisite relationship of confidence would exist and where there would be a presumption of undue influence so that the transaction could only be upheld if the solicitor could show that the client had formed an independent and informed judgment. In his view, the mere fact that the price was fair would not be enough to discharge the presumption since 'there might be all sorts of reasons, apart from the price, why the client did not want to sell his house': *Morgan*, p 90. Oldham, in his article, argues that this analysis must also apply to surety cases, which involve placing the family home at risk: Oldham, p 109.

There is no doubt that the approach of the Court of Appeal in *Morgan* has much to recommend it. According to Dunn LJ, it was a matter of public policy which required that, once the relationship of trust and confidence was established, any possible use of the influence fell to be regarded as an abuse, unless the presumption could be displaced by showing that the party liable to be influenced had formed an independent judgment. Slade LJ also alluded to the purpose of the court in applying the presumption as being essentially one of public policy, namely, 'to mitigate the risk of a particular relationship existing between two parties and the influence arising therefrom from being abused': *Morgan*, p 92. The view taken here is that if the transaction has been obtained by improper pressure, it ought not to be upheld regardless whether there has been manifest disadvantage.

One New Zealand commentator, Catherine Callaghan, who has entered into this debate, has identified two competing theories underlying undue influence cases. Under the victimisation theory, the law attempts to prevent improper conduct by the wrongdoer that results in the victim entering into a transaction without free and informed consent. The focus is on 'procedural unfairness' (that is, the unfair manner in which the transaction is entered into) rather than 'contractual imbalance' (that is, unfair by reason of the terms of the contract itself). Under the 'harm theory', on the other hand, exemplified by Lord Scarman's opinion in the House of Lords in *Morgan*, a transaction cannot be set aside unless it is 'wrongful' in the sense that it results 'in a substantive imbalance or detriment to one party': Callaghan, C, 'Manifest disadvantage in undue influence: an analysis of its role and necessity' (1995) 25 VUWLR 289. Giving effect to the 'victimisation' theory as explained above, Callaghan argues, has 'significant ramifications' for the requirement of manifest disadvantage (p 304):

> Put simply, if the courts are concerned to ensure that there has been procedural unfairness or that a complainant acted of his or her own free will, then once it is shown that a transaction was brought about in an unfair manner through the exercise of undue influence, the transaction should be set aside. The inequality of exchange or the presence of manifest disadvantage is irrelevant. After all, a person can take part in a commercially fair exchange, yet still have been coerced into the transaction or have failed to form an independent and free judgment on the matter.

So long as the 'harm theory' dominates English law, the requirement of manifest disadvantage would seem, logically, to be applicable to *both* actual and presumed undue influence cases. The fact that, since *Pitt*, the requirement has been confined to cases of presumed influence, only highlights the current inconsistencies in the law. As Lehane comments, 'if "manifest disadvantage" is an inappropriate requirement in class 1, where the equivalent of fraud is proved to have happened, why (it may be asked) it is appropriate in class 2, where it is presumed to have happened': Lehane, JRF, 'Undue influence, misrepresentation and third parties' (1994) 110 LQR 167, p 172. In terms of doctrinal consistency, it is apparent that duress (closely linked with undue influence) does not require proof of substantive unfairness. Here, what triggers the law's response is the illegitimacy of the wrongdoer's conduct coupled with its effect on the free will of the victim: see Goff, R and Jones, G, *Law of Restitution*, 8th edn, 1988, London: Sweet & Maxwell, p 362, who also do not see why undue influence should be treated differently from other vitiating factors.

Assuming, however, the element of manifest disadvantage is to remain within the law of undue influence, it is submitted that this should take the form of a purely evidential consideration when the wrongdoer is seeking to rebut the presumption of undue influence. This is the view taken by the High Court of Australia in *Johnson v Buttress* (1936) 56 CLR 113, where Sir Owen Dixon concluded that the presumption arises upon proof of the special relationship and that the sufficiency of the consideration only becomes relevant in deciding whether the presumption is rebutted. Similarly, in *Commercial Bank of Australia v Amadio* (1983) 57 ALJR 358 (High Court of Australia), p 369, Deane J said: 'Notwithstanding that adequate consideration may have moved from the stronger party, a transaction may be unfair, unreasonable and unjust from the viewpoint of the party under the disability.' (See, also, Cope, M, 'Undue influence and alleged manifestly disadvantageous transactions: *National Westminster Bank plc v Morgan*' (1986) 60 Aust LJ 87, pp 96–97; and Bigwood, R, 'Undue influence: "impaired consent" or "wicked exploitation"?' (1996) 16 OJLS 503, p 513.) Alternatively, the requirement of manifest disadvantage should be viewed as one only of a variety of *evidential factors* relevant to *raising* the presumption by a claimant: *O'Connor v Hart* [1985] 1 NZLR 159

(PC), p 166. Interestingly, in Canada, the requirement has not been favoured: *Geffen v Goodman* [1991] 2 SCR 353.

Most recently, in *Royal Bank of Scotland v Etridge (No 2)* [2001] UKHL 44, the House of Lords has openly recognised that the requirement of manifest disadvantage leads to considerable uncertainty and unpredictability in claims based on presumed undue influence. As Goff and Jones point out, 'what is manifestly disadvantageous for one court may not be [so] for another'. This uncertainty is viewed by the learned authors as 'most regrettable' since it may force the complainant to rely on actual (as opposed to presumed) undue influence with consequent difficulties of proof: Goff and Jones, *Law of Restitution* (8th edn), 1988, p 362. As we have seen, the House of Lords has retained the concept for presumed undue influence cases, albeit recognising that its primary function is evidentiary in deciding whether there is any issue of abuse which can properly be raised by the complainant. As such, it is only one of the factors determining whether a successful plea of undue influence has been made out.

CHAPTER 4

ROLE OF THE LENDER

4.1 INTRODUCTION

We saw in Chapters 2 and 3 that a presumption of undue influence can only be rebutted by proof that the charge/guarantee was executed as a result of the free and informed exercise of the complainant's will, usually as a result of the wife having received independent legal advice. In other words, the burden passes to the husband or, in the *O'Brien*-type situation, to the lender to show that it had taken reasonable steps to satisfy itself that the wife's consent to the transaction had been properly obtained: *Barclays Bank plc v Boulter* [1999] 4 All ER 513 (HL); and *Royal Bank of Scotland v Etridge (No 2)* [2001] UKHL 44 (HL).

In this chapter, we examine the circumstances in which a lender will be put on inquiry as to the wife's right to have the transaction set aside as against her husband and what steps the lender must take to avoid having notice of her equity so as to enforce the charge/guarantee against her: see the approach taken by Mr James Munby QC in *Bank of Scotland v Bennett* [1997] 1 FLR 801, p 807. It was emphasised by the House of Lords, in *Etridge (No 2)*, that the steps to be taken by the lender are not concerned to discover whether the wife has been wronged by her husband, but to minimise the *risk* that such a wrong may have been committed: *Etridge (No 2)*, para 41, *per* Lord Nicholls.

4.2 WHEN IS THE LENDER PUT ON INQUIRY?

4.2.1 Introduction

The starting point in answering this question is the House of Lords' ruling in *Barclays Bank plc v O'Brien* [1993] 4 All ER 417. In that case, it was held that a wife's equity to have a mortgage transaction set aside as against her husband on the ground of his undue influence (or misrepresentation) will be enforceable against a lender if either the husband was acting as the lender's *agent*, or the lender has actual or constructive *notice* of the facts giving rise to her equity. It should be stressed, however, that the so called 'agency theory' underlying several of the pre-*O'Brien* cases was rejected by the House of Lords in *O'Brien* in favour of a more general doctrine of notice. It is likely, therefore, that, in future, there will be few cases decided on the basis that the husband acted as agent for the lender. It will be convenient to consider: (1) agency; and (2) notice, separately.

4.2.2 Husband acts as agent for the lender

In *Barclays Bank plc v O'Brien* [1993] 4 All ER 417 (HL), p 425, Lord Browne-Wilkinson said that if a husband is acting as agent for a lender in obtaining security from his wife, the lender will be fixed with the wrongdoing of the husband, regardless of actual or constructive notice. The position is the same regardless of whether the wife was induced to enter into the transaction as a result of her husband's undue influence or misrepresentations. His Lordship, however, stated that cases where the husband acts as agent for the lender 'without artificiality ... will be of very rare occurrence': *O'Brien*, p 428. The same point was made by Stuart-Smith LJ, in *Royal Bank of Scotland v Etridge (No 2)* [1998] 4 All ER 705 (CA) (p 717):

> In most cases the reality of the relationship is that the creditor stipulates for security, and in order to raise the necessary finance the principal debtor seeks to procure the support of the surety. In doing so he is acting on his own account and not as agent for the creditor.

Indeed, his Lordship doubted whether 'it will ever be possible to treat [the husband] as the creditor's agent where he or his company is the principal debtor': *Etridge* (CA), p 717. There are, however, several pre-*O'Brien* cases where the husband was held to have acted as agent for the lender. In *Kingsnorth Trust Ltd v Bell* [1986] 1 All ER 423 (CA), the husband wished to expand his partnership activities with his son by buying another business. He arranged to borrow £18,000 from the claimant bank on the security of two charges on the partnership premises and also the matrimonial home, in which his wife had a beneficial interest. The bank's solicitors requested the husband's solicitors to arrange for the execution of the mortgage deeds and to act as their agents on completion. The husband's solicitors, in turn, entrusted the husband to obtain his wife's signature. The bank had, however, no knowledge of this arrangement. The wife executed the mortgage deed in the belief, induced by a fraudulent misrepresentation made by the husband, that the loan was being sought by him for the benefit of his own business. She did not instruct solicitors of her own, nor did she receive any independent legal advice before signing. The Court of Appeal held, relying on *Turnbull & Co v Duval* [1902] AC 429 (PC) and *Chaplin & Co Ltd v Brammall* [1908] 1 KB 233 (CA), that, under the general law of principal and agent, a lender who as principal (irrespective of how personally innocent he was) instructed a husband as agent to obtain the signing of a document by his wife, was liable for any misrepresentation made by the husband to obtain his wife's signature. The same principle applied where the wife's consent to the transaction was obtained by the husband's undue influence. Accordingly, the bank was bound by the husband's impropriety and could not enforce the mortgage against his wife. Dillon LJ said (p 427):

> ... if a creditor, or potential creditor, of a husband desires to obtain, by way of security for the husband's indebtedness, a guarantee from his wife or a charge on property of his wife, and if the creditor entrusts to the husband himself the

task of obtaining the execution of the relevant document by the wife, then the creditor can be in no better position than the husband himself, and the creditor cannot enforce the guarantee or the security against the wife if it is established that the execution of the document by the wife was procured by undue influence by the husband and the wife had no independent advice.

The case is, on any view, quite remarkable, given that the lender had no knowledge of how the wife's signature was actually obtained or who was going to obtain it. The basis of the decision is that the lender was bound by the husband's acts either because the husband's solicitor, as the lender's agent, had left it to the husband to obtain the wife's signature or because, through their own solicitors, they had chosen to leave it to the husband's solicitors (and, thus, to the husband) to obtain her signature. It seems that the only way of avoiding such a result would have been for the lender to insist that the wife had independent legal advice: *Kingsnorth Trust Ltd v Bell*, p 428.

In *Bank of Credit and Commerce International SA v Aboody* [1992] 4 All ER 955 (CA), the husband was also held to have acted as agent of the bank to procure his wife's consent to and execution of the relevant documents. Slade LJ said (pp 979–80):

> ... it would be inconsistent with the equitable nature of the relief for the bank not to be affected by the undue influence exerted by its agent when the transaction would not exist but for the wrongful acts of its agent.

It was highlighted in this case that agency alone was sufficient to render the bank liable for the misconduct of the husband. There was no need, therefore, to show also notice on the part of the bank that undue influence would or might have been exercised. Agency and notice are, clearly, alternative grounds for founding liability as against the lender. Similarly, in *Midland Bank plc v Shephard* [1988] 3 All ER 17 (CA), Neill LJ said (p 22):

> The court will not enforce a transaction at the suit of a creditor if it can be shown that the creditor entrusted the task of obtaining the alleged debtor's signature to the relevant documents to someone who was, to the knowledge of the creditor, in a position to influence the debtor and who procured the signature of the debtor by means of undue influence or by means of fraudulent misrepresentation.

In that case, however, the wife's allegation that the bank was disentitled to enforce a mandate for a new joint account because they sent the document to the husband (and did not themselves obtain the wife's signature) was rejected. This was simply an ordinary document which was signed, as a matter of routine, whenever a joint account was opened. Moreover, there was nothing to suggest that the bank had used the husband in order that he should exert pressure on his wife. Similarly, in *Bradford & Bingley Building Society v Chandock* (1996) 72 P & CR D28 (CA), Nourse LJ accepted that the agency principle might succeed on certain facts but felt that, in the light of *O'Brien*, the outcome of a case would now depend more on a finding of constructive notice. His Lordship dismissed the agency argument because the lender could not, on any footing, be said to have constituted the husband as its agent.

The building society had merely requested that the husband take his wife to an independent solicitor to have the relevant forms completed. (See, also, *Midland Bank plc v Perry* [1988] 1 FLR 161 (CA) where there was no evidence that the bank had engaged the husband as agent to procure the wife's signature to the charge; *Lloyds Bank plc v Egremont* [1990] 2 FLR 351 (CA) where the agency argument failed because the bank had merely sent the documents for signature, not to the husband, but to his solicitors; and *Barclays Bank plc v Khaira* [1992] 1 WLR 623 where the bank simply asked the husband to request his wife to attend the bank's offices.)

In *Barclays Bank plc v Kennedy* [1989] 1 FLR 356 (CA), on the other hand, the allegation of agency was made out. In this case, the husband wished to guarantee the overdraft of a business associate. In support of the guarantee, the bank required a charge over the family home and the husband's wife signed the charge at his request. The Court of Appeal concluded that the bank manager was content to leave the husband to obtain her signature and a retrial was ordered, limited to the issues of undue influence and misrepresentation. It was emphasised that the proper test in deciding whether the husband was acting as the bank's agent was not whether actual or ostensible authority had been given to the husband to act on the bank's behalf (the test propounded by the trial judge), but whether the bank had been content to leave it to the husband to obtain the wife's signature. In this case, that test had been satisfied because: (1) the execution of the charge was of crucial importance to the bank; (2) the terms of the charge had been fully agreed between the husband and the bank manager; and (3) the bank manager had left it to the husband to persuade the wife to add her signature as a mere formality to accord with the bank's policy. In other words, an agency relationship was inferred simply because the bank had left it to the husband to procure the necessary signature from the wife. The decision, therefore, represents the high water mark of the 'agency theory' which, as mentioned earlier, has now been largely discarded and replaced by the doctrine of notice, following the House of Lords' decision in *O'Brien*, where Lord Browne-Wilkinson said (p 427):

> ... in the majority of cases the reality of the relationship is that, the creditor having required of the principal debtor that there must be a surety, the principal debtor on his own account in order to raise the necessary finance seeks to procure the support of the surety. In so doing he is acting for himself not for the creditor.

The agency principle has also been held to apply outside the field of husband and wife. In *Avon Finance Co Ltd v Bridger* [1985] 2 All ER 281, the defendants, an elderly couple, purchased a house for their retirement with the help of their son. In accordance with the terms of the son's loan agreement with a finance company (necessary to finance his contribution to the purchase price of the house), the son undertook to procure the execution by the defendants of a legal charge on their property. The son obtained their signatures to the legal charge by telling them that the documents were connected with their own mortgage over the house to a building society. The Court of Appeal (see the judgments of Brandon and Brightman LJJ) held that the legal charge was voidable because the finance company had chosen to appoint the son to procure from his parents the security which was needed to further the son's loan with them. From the lender's standpoint, the son could be expected to have some influence over his elderly parents, especially since they were both old aged pensioners and much less well educated than he was. The case is particularly strong since there was, in fact, a specific agreement between the lender and the son that the latter would obtain his parents' execution of the charge to secure the money lent to him. In that respect, it was indistinguishable from the *Chaplin* case (mentioned above), where the claimants also left everything to the son to arrange for their benefit.

In *Coldunell Ltd v Gallon* [1986] 1 All ER 429 (CA), on the other hand, also involving elderly parents and a son, an agency between the lender and the son was not established on the facts. In that case, the solicitors acting for the lender dealt solely with the son and communicated with the parents by messages carried by the son. However, they sent the loan documentation directly to the parents but, either before or after delivery at his parents' house, the son intercepted the papers and procured their signatures before returning the documentation to the lender's solicitors. The lender then handed the son a cheque in favour of his father for the amount of the loan. The Court of Appeal held that the lender was not affected by the son's undue influence over his parents because they had never constituted him as their agent in the transaction. His unilateral assumption of the conduct of the transaction (which had been unauthorised) was not sufficient for this purpose. What was required was a conscious act of, or consent to, delegation by the lender: *Gallon*, p 446. Subsequent adoption of the third party's conduct could also be sufficient. (See, also, *Contractors Bonding Ltd v Snee* [1992] 2 NZLR 157 (New Zealand Court of Appeal), p 183, where it was held, applying the English authorities, that where a creditor has entrusted a third party with the task of obtaining execution of the loan documents, that may be sufficient to make that person the agent of the creditor, but ultimately it was a question of fact. The mere fact, however, that the loan documentation was sent to the debtor for execution by himself and his guarantor was not in itself sufficient: see, further, Watts, P, 'The undue influence of others' (1992) 108 LQR 384.)

One example of a post-*O'Brien* case where an argument based on agency was successful is *Shams v United Bank* ((1994) unreported, 24 May, available on Lexis). The facts, however, were somewhat unusual. The bank leaked confidential information about the finances of Mrs Shams to a Mr Ahmed, who (with the aid of two employees of the bank) persuaded Mrs Shams to stand surety for Mr Ahmed's debts. The court held that both Mr Ahmed and the two employees had acted as the bank's agents and, consequently, had imputed notice of the latter's undue influence and misrepresentations.

(Contrast *Hill Samuel Bank v Medway* ((1994) unreported, 10 November, available on Lexis) where the agency argument failed on the facts.)

4.2.3 Lender having actual or constructive notice

General principles

Apart from the (now) rare case where agency is made out, if the lender has actual or constructive notice of the husband's undue influence (or misrepresentation), it will take subject to the wife's equity to have the transaction set aside. This is the position even though the lender is, technically, a purchaser for value: *Barclays Bank plc v O'Brien* [1993] 4 All ER 417 (HL), p 425; and *Bainbrigge v Browne* (1881) 18 Ch D 188, p 197, where Fry J held that the onus of rebutting the presumption of undue influence extended, not only to a volunteer claiming through the wrongdoer, but to any person taking with notice of the circumstances giving rise to the equity. As Lord Browne-Wilkinson explained in *O'Brien*, 'the doctrine of notice lies at the heart of equity' (p 429). Thus, according to his Lordship, as between the separate rights of wife and lender, the former will prevail against the latter, only if the lender knows of the wife's right (actual notice), or would have discovered it upon making reasonable inquiry (constructive notice). Strictly speaking, however, contrary to Lord Browne-Wilkinson's analysis, the situation is not that the lender is a third party taking subject to the wife's prior right, but that the lender is an original party to the loan transaction (that is, the mortgage) who cannot enforce it because it has notice of the circumstances in which the wife executed the mortgage: see, further, below, para 4.3 and, in particular, Battersby, G, 'Equitable fraud committed by third parties' [1995] 15 LS 35, p 43. In this connection, s 199(1)(ii)(a) of the Law of Property Act (LPA) 1925 provides that:

> A purchaser shall not be prejudicially affected by notice of – (ii) any other instrument or matter or any fact or thing unless – (a) it is within his own knowledge, or would have come to his knowledge if such inquiries and inspections had been made as ought reasonably to have been made by him ...

The burden, therefore, lies on the purchaser (lender) to establish that it took without notice. More particularly, in the constructive notice category, the lender must show:

(a) that there were no inquiries that it ought reasonably to have made (that is, the facts which it knew were not such as to put it on inquiry); or

(b) that it did make such inquiries as it ought reasonably to have made, but that no further relevant facts came to its knowledge; or

(c) that no further relevant facts would have come to its knowledge if it had made such inquiries as it ought reasonably to have made.

It has been held, in this context, that a lender does not have to act as a suspicious bank would act, but only as a 'reasonably prudent' bank would act, having regard to its state of knowledge at any particular time: *Woolwich plc v Gomm* (2000) 79 P & CR 61 (CA). The standard, in other words, is an *objective* one in determining whether the lender should be fixed with notice under s 199(1)(ii)(a). It does not depend on the particular instructions given to its solicitors, which were only relevant as evidence of what the reasonably prudent bank would expect its solicitor to do: *Woolwich plc v Gomm*, p 74. In *Abbey National v Tufts* [1999] 2 FLR 399 (CA), a bankrupt mortgage broker fraudulently obtained a mortgage in his wife's name in order to purchase a joint home for them. He falsely declared that they were separated and that his wife was employed. The lender sought possession of the property because of the mortgage arrears and the wife resisted on the ground that the lender could not enforce the charge as they had constructive or imputed knowledge of the husband's fraud under s 199(1)(ii)(a) of the LPA 1925. The Court of Appeal rejected this contention, holding that the lender had no requisite knowledge under the sub-section because it had made such enquiries as were reasonable in the circumstances as to the wife's purported employment, given that those enquiries only went to her credit rating and not to whether it would obtain good legal title to the security on the loan (which is the purpose to which s 199 was addressed).

How much notice?

What degree of notice is sufficient in a given case will depend upon the nature of the undue influence alleged. Thus, in cases involving actual undue influence (class 1), the lender must have notice of either: (1) the type of relationship which is irrebuttably presumed to be a relationship of trust and confidence; or (2) the circumstances alleged to constitute the actual exercise of the undue influence: *Royal Bank of Scotland v Etridge (No 2)* [1998] 4 All ER 705 (CA), p 719. In class 2 cases (that is, presumed undue influence), the lender must have notice of the circumstances from which the presumption of undue influence is alleged to arise: *Bank of Credit and Commerce International SA v Aboody* [1992] 4 All ER 955 (CA), pp 980–81. More specifically, in *O'Brien*, Lord Browne-Wilkinson concluded that a lender will be put on inquiry when a wife offers to stand surety for her husband's debts by the combination of two factors:

(a) the transaction is not, on its face, to the financial advantage of the wife; and

(b) there is a substantial risk that, in procuring the wife to act as surety, the husband has committed a legal or equitable wrong that entitles her to set aside the transaction.

As we have already seen, this second requirement stems from the fact that, in informal business dealings between spouses, there may be 'a substantial risk that the husband has not accurately stated to the wife the nature of the liability she is undertaking, that is, he has misrepresented the position, albeit negligently': *O'Brien*, p 429, *per* Lord Browne-Wilkinson. In other words, the risk is that the husband has exploited the emotional pressure and trust which derive from the parties' relationship with one another. These principles enunciated by the House of Lords in *O'Brien* reflect the so called 'invalidating tendency' or 'tender treatment' afforded to wives under English law: see Chapter 2, para 2.3.2. Interestingly, however, the Court of Appeal, in *Etridge (No 2)*, interpreted Lord Browne-Wilkinson's formulation more restrictively by stating that the lender would only be put on inquiry if, additionally, it was aware that the parties were married or were cohabitees (because, in both instances, the bank was *prima facie* taken to be aware that the wife/cohabitee reposed trust and confidence in her partner in relation to their financial affairs): *Etridge (No 2)* (CA), p 719. According to Lord Nicholls, however, in the House of Lords (*Royal Bank of Scotland v Etridge (No 2)* [2001] UKHL 44), this additional restriction was inappropriate. In his view, Lord Browne-Wilkinson's formulation meant simply that a bank is put on inquiry whenever a wife offers to stand surety for her husband's debts. In other words, it is sufficient that the bank knows of the husband-wife relationship. According to his Lordship, 'that bare fact is enough' (para 84). Normally, whether the wife is standing surety for her husband's debts should be an easy question for the bank to answer: para 109, *per* Lord Hobhouse. This is because the bank should know who the principal debtor is and what is the purpose of the facility.

According to the House of Lords, the two factors identified in *O'Brien* were not to be read as factual conditions, which must be proved in each case before a bank is put on inquiry. Whether a lender is put on inquiry, in husband and wife cases, did not depend on its state of knowledge of the parties' marriage, or of the degree of trust and confidence the wife placed in her husband. On the contrary, Lord Browne-Wilkinson's formulation was to be viewed simply as a broad explanation of the *reason* why a creditor is put on inquiry when a wife offers to stand surety for her husband's debts. It merely formed an underlying rationale, which was equally applicable to cases where a husband stands surety for his wife's debts, and also where the parties are unmarried (whether in a heterosexual or homosexual relationship), where the bank is aware of the relationship. In this connection, a husband can be subject to the same fear of opposing a spouse's wishes as a wife: *Barclays Bank v Rivett* [1999] 1 FLR 730 (CA), where it was held that the transaction was not on the face of it to the husband's financial advantage and, accordingly, the bank had been put on inquiry as to any undue influence by his wife. Outside the marriage context, it has also been held that a lender will be put on inquiry where the transaction is so extravagantly improvident that it is difficult to explain in the absence of some impropriety: see *Credit Lyonnais Bank Nederland NV v Burch* [1997] 1 All ER 144 (CA); and *Royal Bank of Scotland v Etridge (No 2)* [1998] 4 All ER 705 (CA), p 719. In *Burch*, it was suggested that the lender's knowledge could be inferred from the lender knowing that there was a relationship of trust and confidence (arising between a junior employee and employer in a small business) and that the transaction was entirely for the employer's benefit: *Burch*, p 154, *per* Millett LJ.

According to Lord Nicholls, in *Etridge (No 2)* (HL), the test as to what puts the lender on inquiry should be 'simple and clear and easy to apply in a wide range of circumstances' (para 46). Three distinct scenarios called for comment. First, as we have already seen, the lender will be put on inquiry where a wife becomes *surety* for her husband's debts. Secondly, a lender will *not* be put on inquiry where money is being advanced to the husband and wife *jointly*, unless the bank is aware that the loan is being made for the husband's purposes as distinct from their joint purposes: see *CIBC Mortgages plc v Pitt* [1993] 4 All ER 433 (HL) (discussed below). Thirdly, a lender will be put on inquiry where the wife becomes *surety* for the debts of a company whose shares are held by her and her husband, regardless of whether she has a minority or equal shareholding with her husband. This will be so, even if the wife is a director or secretary of the company. In this category of case, 'the shareholding interests, and the identity of the directors, are not a reliable guide to the identity of the persons who actually have the conduct of the company's business': para 49, *per* Lord Nicholls.

It is enough, therefore, that the lender knows the primary facts which indicate the mere possibility (or risk) of undue influence being exerted: *O'Brien*, p 430. In *O'Brien* itself, the bank had actual knowledge that Mr and Mrs O'Brien were husband and wife. It was also aware that the proposed security was over the family home to secure the debts of the husband's company in respect of which she had no direct interest. This was enough, therefore, to put the bank on inquiry as to the circumstances in which she had agreed to stand as surety for her husband's debts.

In most cases, of course, the bank will have only limited knowledge of the parties' circumstances and personal affairs. It may know of the nature of the husband's dealings, the state of his accounts, the extent of his existing indebtedness (if any) and the degree of his wife's involvement in the running of the business, but it should be emphasised that there is no obligation on a bank to inquire into the personal relationships between those with whom it has business dealings, or as to their personal motives for wanting to assist one another: *Banco Exterior International SA v Thomas* [1997] 1 All ER 46 (CA); and *Royal Bank of Scotland v Etridge (No 2)* [2001] UKHL 44 (HL).

In *Bank of Cyprus (London) Ltd v Markou* [1999] 2 All ER 707, Mr John Jarvis QC (sitting as a deputy judge of the High Court) said (p 720):

A bank, who knows that a business is run by the husband and the wife has really no involvement, it seems to me, is put on inquiry that things may not be right – that this is the kind of class 2(B) situation where the bank needs in these circumstances to ask a few more questions.

In that case, the bank was held to have constructive notice of the wife's equity because it had failed to make further inquiries since it had been aware the husband controlled the family business and the wife had no practical involvement.

In *Bank of Scotland v Bennett* [1999] Lloyd's Rep Bank 145, however, the Court of Appeal concluded that the bank was entitled, on the facts known to it, to take the view that there was no real risk of the wife's apparent consent having been improperly obtained by her husband. A transaction by which a wife was asked to provide a guarantee for the debts of a business from which the family as a whole derived its income could not be said to be necessarily improvident so as to warrant further inquiry. Moreover, the bank was unaware that the wife held only a small (11.8%) shareholding in the family company (as compared to the husband's 47.1%). Looking at the matter from the eyes of the bank, there was nothing to suggest that the company was in financial difficulty, or about to become insolvent. Importantly also, the bank knew that the wife would be receiving legal advice in relation to the execution of the charge and could rely on this fact (in the absence of any special features from which a lender would conclude that the transaction was such that no legal adviser could possibly advise its client to enter). Presumably, following the House of Lords' ruling in *Etridge (No 2)*, the bank would now be automatically put on inquiry where the wife stands surety for the debts of her husband's company.

In *Britannia Building Society v Pugh* [1997] 2 FLR 7 (CA), it was argued on behalf of the wife that the loan was unusual in terms (being twice the actual value of the family home and repayable within a year) and that the husband was orchestrating the transaction so that there was a clear risk, known to the lender, that she was being subjected to undue influence. This approach was, however, rejected by the Court of Appeal. It was not relevant to consider whether the loan was 'abnormal' (despite being for the joint benefit of husband and wife). The correct test was simply whether the lender knew of facts which ought to have put it on inquiry as to the possible existence of the wife's equity. Here, there was nothing to suggest that the transaction was manifestly disadvantageous to the wife. The loan was made in joint names and the wife stood to benefit jointly from the success of the development business. Significantly, the lender was aware that the business was being carried on jointly by the husband and wife. The mere fact, therefore, that the husband had taken the lead in the management of the finances was held not to be sufficient to raise a suspicion of improper pressure. The case, therefore, accords with the reasoning of the House of Lords in *Etridge (No 2)*.

Joint loan and surety cases

As highlighted by the House of Lords in *Etridge (No 2)*, a distinction exists between joint advance cases (where the bank is ordinarily not put on inquiry) and cases where it is essentially the husband's business that is being guaranteed by the wife (where the bank is put on notice that all may not be right). In *CIBC Mortgages plc v Pitt* [1993] 4 All ER 433 (HL), the transaction consisted of a joint loan to the husband and wife to finance the discharge of an existing mortgage on the family home, with the balance to be applied in buying a holiday home. The loan was advanced to the couple jointly and there was nothing to indicate that it was anything other than a normal (routine) remortgaging transaction for the benefit of both husband and wife. The mere fact that there was a risk of there being undue influence because one of the borrowers was the wife was not, in itself, sufficient to put the bank on inquiry. Although the borrowing on the house was greatly increased, the valuation indicated that there would still be a substantial net equity after the loan. Lord Browne-Wilkinson said (p 441):

> If third parties were to be fixed with constructive notice of undue influence in relation to every transaction between husband and wife, such transactions would become almost impossible.

What usually distinguishes the 'joint advance' from the 'surety' case is that, in regard to the latter, there is not only the *possibility* of undue influence being exercised, but the '*increased risk*' of it having been in fact exercised because, on its face, the transaction is not for the wife's financial benefit: *Pitt*, p 441. As we have seen, the 'combination of these two factors' puts the lender on inquiry. It is important, however, not to take the distinction between joint advance and surety cases too far. In the Court of Appeal proceedings in *Pitt*, Peter Gibson LJ observed that:

> ... if there is a secured loan to a husband and wife but the creditor is aware that the purposes of the loan are to pay the husband's debts or otherwise for his (as distinct from their joint) purposes, the creditor, without taking precautionary steps, may be affected by the husband's misconduct.

Similarly, in *Dunbar Bank plc v Nadeem* [1997] 2 All ER 253 ([1998] 3 All ER 876 (CA)), Mr Robert Englehart QC (sitting as a deputy judge of the High Court) said (p 270) that:

> ... merely because a lending institution makes a joint loan it does not follow that constructive notice of any undue influence is excluded.

In *Goode Durrant Administration v Biddulph* [1994] 2 FLR 551, HH Judge Rich QC also opined that the categorisation of cases into joint loan or surety was not 'final and determinative' of the issue of whether the lender is put on inquiry. In his view, there could well be cases where a joint loan transaction was not to the financial benefit of the wife and, thus, liable to put the lender on inquiry. In this case, for example, despite a joint loan to the husband and wife, the bank was held to be put on inquiry because of the manifestly disadvantageous nature of the transaction. The wife had little business experience and reposed trust and confidence in her husband in financial matters and relied on him in executing the transaction. Her direct interest in the proposed development arose only from her 2.5% shareholding in the company jointly owned by the parties. To make herself personally liable for a sum in excess of £300,000 (the amount of the loan) in order to have a 2.5%

share (through the company) of any profit was held to be manifestly disadvantageous to her. From the bank's point of view, the existence of the possibility of undue influence being exercised (arising from the parties' relationship) coupled with the increased risk of its having, in fact, been exercised because the transaction was not in its face to the financial advantage of the wife, put the bank on inquiry as to her rights. (See, also, *Hill Samuel Bank v Medway* ((1994) unreported, 10 November (CA), available on Lexis), where the wife had a 50% shareholding and directorship in one of the companies and a 1% shareholding and directorship of the other.) In the light of the House of Lords' ruling in *Etridge (No 2)*, the lender will now be put on inquiry if it knew of the disproportionate allocation of the parties' shareholding in the company.

The decision in *Biddulph* may be contrasted with *Barclays Bank plc v Sumner* [1996] EGCS 65, where the husband and wife each owned half the shares in a company of which they were the only directors. They approached the bank for a joint loan in order to expand the operations of their company. Their house, with an equity of £48,000, was sold and the proceeds used to purchase another property with a mortgage from the bank for £30,000 and a further loan for the purpose of property development by the company. The bank's security was by way of an unlimited guarantee signed by both the husband and wife. The deputy judge confirmed that, where a question arose as to the advantage obtained from the guarantee by the wife, in the context of a family company, the wife's direct financial interest in the company was to be considered. Here, the wife's direct financial interest in the company was just as great as that of her husband and her involvement in the affairs of the company did not indicate anything to put the bank on inquiry. Presumably, being a joint loan case, the decision would be the same under *Etridge (No 2)* (HL).

Other cases

Prior to the House of Lords' ruling in *Etridge (No 2)*, it was a question of fact in each case whether or not the circumstances were such as to put the lender on inquiry that there might be undue influence. In *Credit Lyonnais Bank Nederland NV v Burch* [1997] 1 All ER 144 (CA), for example, a bank was held to have actual notice of the facts from which the existence of a relationship of trust and confidence between a junior employee and her employer could be inferred. It knew that the parties were in an employment relationship working in a small business and should have appreciated that the possibility of undue influence existed. Moreover, the bank was also aware that the employee was neither a shareholder nor a director of the employer's company and that she had no incentive to enter into the transaction, which was manifestly disadvantageous to her. In *Wright v Cherrytree Finance Ltd* [2001] 2 All ER (Comm) 877 (CA), the lender was held to have constructive notice of actual undue influence largely because the loan application showed the disparity between the ages of the claimant and her son-in-law and daughter. Her husband had also recently died and the claimant was seeking a loan using her only asset (her house) as security. Significantly also, the monthly payments, if the instalments fell into arrears, far outreached the income that the claimant had each month: see, also, *Steeples v Lea* [1998] 1 FLR 138 (CA), where the claimant was fixed with constructive notice of the vulnerability of the transaction because of what took place in his own solicitor's presence. As we saw in Chapter 2 (para 2.3.2), the same principles were held to apply in all other cases where there was a relationship of trust and confidence or where there was an emotional relationship between cohabitees: see *Avon Finance Co Ltd v Bridger* [1985] 2 All ER 218 (CA) (elderly parents and son); and *Massey v Midland Bank plc* [1995] 1 All ER 929 (CA) (couple in close, stable, sexual relationship but not cohabiting). In *Royal Bank of Scotland v Etridge (No 2)* [2001] UKHL 44 (HL), Lord Nicholls stressed that the *O'Brien* principle was not confined to sexual relationships. After all, 'sexual relationships are no more than one type of relationship in which an individual may acquire influence over another individual' (para 82).

According to his Lordship, as with surety wives, so with other relationships, whether a bank is put on inquiry should not depend on the degree of trust and confidence the particular person places in the other in relation to their financial affairs. A lender should not be expected to probe into the emotional relationship of the surety and debtor. As with wives, the test should be simple and straightforward. Thus, according to his Lordship, knowledge by the bank of the relationship of say, father and daughter, where the latter is standing surety for the former's debts, is enough to put the bank on inquiry. What about other relationships say, between nephew and elderly aunt (*Inche Noriah v Shaik Allie Bin Omar* [1929] AC 127) or secretary-companion and her elderly employer (*Re Craig (decd)* [1971] Ch 95)? Logically, there was no cut-off point for the application of the *O'Brien* principle and so, according to Lord Nicholls, 'the only practical way forward is to regard banks as "put on inquiry" in every case where the relationship between surety and the debtor is non-commercial': *Etridge (No 2)* (HL), para 87. However, so far as commercial relationships are concerned (for example, where a company is guaranteeing the debts of another company), his Lordship was of the view that those engaged in business 'can be regarded as capable of looking after themselves and understanding the risks involved in the giving of guarantees' (para 88). Presumably also, the lender will not be put on inquiry automatically in joint loan non-commercial cases, save where the lender knows that the loan is *de facto* for one party's benefit.

4.3 UNDUE INFLUENCE AND REGISTRATION

The foregoing principles will apply regardless of whether the land subject to the charge is registered or unregistered. Some academic commentators have argued that this is incorrect in view of the fact that the doctrine of purchaser for value without notice has no general application to registered land. Most notably, Thompson has suggested that the question of notice is only relevant when title to the property is unregistered. Where, on the other hand, the land is registered, 'a mortgagee, as a purchaser of a legal estate will only take subject to interests noted on the register and to overriding interests': Thompson, MP, 'The enforceability of mortgages' [1994] Conv 140, p 144. If the wife is in actual occupation of the property, she will have an overriding interest which will bind the lender. But, if for any reason she is no longer in occupation, her equity should not bind the lender, regardless of the question whether it had notice of her husband's fraud: see, also, Goo, SH, 'Enforceability of securities and guarantee after *O'Brien*' (1995) 15 OJLS 119, pp 123–25. Dixon and Harpum, however, have argued that this cannot be correct: Dixon, M and Harpum, C, 'Fraud, undue influence and mortgages of registered land' [1994] Conv 421. They argue that the real issue relates to the validity of the loan transaction and not whether a lender, as purchaser for value of the property, is bound by the rights of a third party (that is, the wife). They say (p 423):

> ... [the bank] is not bound by [the wife's] rights because [they] are proprietary and take effect either through notice (unregistered land) or as an overriding interest (registered land). [The bank] is bound by [the wife's] personal equity against her partner because [the bank] is tainted by [the husband's] actions through notice.

The crucial point that is being made here is that 'notice' in the *O'Brien* sense does not mean the same thing as 'notice' in the conveyancing sense used by property lawyers. Under the *O'Brien* doctrine, the courts are not concerned with the question whether the lender has failed to make inquiries of the wife so as to oblige it to take subject to any rights which such inquiries would have revealed. On the contrary, the issue is quite different, namely, 'whether the transaction ... is vitiated because the creditor is a party to a fraud or undue influence by reason of facts of which he has notice': Dixon and Harpum, p 424. In other words, the question is simply whether or not the lender is personally tainted by the undue influence or misrepresentation.

This approach, however, is not altogether free from difficulty. As has been noted by another commentator, if the 'personal culpability' of the lender is the decisive factor, it is difficult to see why constructive notice should render the creditor privy to the vitiating circumstances. Mee argues that, under general equitable principles, a person does not become 'privy' to another person's wrongdoing unless he has been guilty of a 'want of probity' (that is, dishonesty): Mee, J, 'An alternative approach to third-party undue influence and misrepresentation' (1995) 46 NILQ 147, p 154. He draws an analogy to the cases in equity on knowing assistance in a breach of trust where liability is based on actual knowledge or wilful recklessness. Constructive notice is not enough to make a stranger to a breach of trust personally liable as a constructive trustee. Mee asks, 'why should the position be different in relation to contracts induced by third-party undue influence or misrepresentation?' (p 154).

Another writer, O'Hagan, has suggested that if a legal charge is granted by a husband and wife as co-owning trustees for sale (as in *CIBC Mortgages plc v Pitt* [1993] 4 All ER 433 (HL)), the wife's equity to have the transaction set aside on the ground of undue influence is capable of being overreached, regardless of the bank's notice of the circumstances giving rise to her equity: O'Hagan, P, 'A specially protected class' (1994) 144 NLJ 765, p 767. This argument, however, has been rejected by Battersby, who rightly points out that overreaching will not occur if there is no 'conveyance to a purchaser of a legal estate' within the meaning of s 2 of the LPA 1925: Battersby, G, 'Equitable fraud committed by third parties' [1995] 15 LS 35, p 45. Although a legal mortgage is, clearly, a conveyance for this purpose, the provision must contemplate only a valid overreaching conveyance. In the words of Battersby (p 45):

> If, as in *O'Brien*, the mortgage is voidable against, and unenforceable by, the mortgagee as a result of action by the defrauded mortgagor, it is submitted that there is no conveyance which is capable of having an overreaching effect. Putting it another way, the question of the validity of the conveyance is logically prior to the overreaching effect of that conveyance.

It has also been convincingly argued by Battersby that, in a residential mortgage transaction involving a wife who stands as surety for her husband's debts, there is, in fact, only one transaction (that is, the mortgage) which can be impugned under the doctrine of undue influence, unless the lender takes for value and without notice of the wife's equity. In his view, therefore, applying the 'one transaction' analysis, there is no issue of priority between the wife's equity and that of the bank's interest since the former's right to have the transaction set aside will arise at the same moment as the mortgage itself: see, also, Mee, J, 'An alternative approach to third-party undue influence and misrepresentation' (1995) 46 NILQ 147, p 151, who also argues that there is only one transaction in this context. Prior to that time, there is no transaction in existence capable of being rescinded. In *Royal Bank of Scotland v Etridge (No 2)* [1998] 4 All ER 705 (CA), p 717, Stuart-Smith LJ endorsed this proposition in the following terms:

> There is no voidable transaction between husband and wife which is prior in time to the security which is impugned. The contract of guarantee or collateral charge is entered into by the wife directly with the bank; it is not entered into with the husband and later given by him to the bank. Normally (for there are always exceptions: see *Dunbar Bank plc v Nadeem* [1998] 3 All ER 876) there is only one transaction, not two in competition with one another; and there is no question of clearing the title, which is the function performed by the *bona fide* purchaser defence.

Support for this view can also be found in the judgment of Lord Hoffman, in *Barclays Bank plc v Boulter* [1999] 4 All ER 513, p 518, where his Lordship draws a distinction between cases concerned with the enforceability of a prior equitable interest in land and the *O'Brien* type of case. In the former category, the issue is whether a purchaser is bound by a prior equitable interest, whereas, in the *O'Brien* category, the right in question only comes into existence when the mortgage is created. There is, therefore, no prior interest which the lender needs to defeat. As another commentator has remarked, this 'broader doctrine [of notice] operates, in land law, within a wide equitable field and transcends questions of registration or overreaching': Howell, J, 'Notice: a broad view and a narrow view' [1996] Conv 34, p 35. In fact, she argues that a more apt term, in this context, would be 'knowledge' rather than 'notice' of the third party.

The doctrine of notice, as expounded in *O'Brien*, simply makes the lender 'an accomplice to the fraud' and it makes no difference, at this stage, whether title to the property is registered or unregistered. But this distinction does become significant, argues Battersby, when the lender sells (or contracts to sell) the property before the wife's successful action against the bank. In these circumstances, assuming the land is unregistered, it would become necessary to decide whether the wife's right to rescind was a mere equity. If so, any successor in title of the original lender taking without notice and for value would take free of it: see *Latec Investments Ltd v Hotel Terrigal Property Ltd* (1965) 113 CLR 265, where the High Court of Australia held that a borrower's right to rescind a lender's sale of the property was a mere equity. If, on the other hand, the mortgaged property is registered, the wife's right would rank as a minor interest which would require protection on the register. Equally, a contractual purchaser from the lender would only have a minor interest at the contract stage, which would require similar protection. On one view, not favoured by Battersby, the result in these circumstances would be that unregistered land principles would apply so that, the wife's right being a mere equity, a contractual purchaser for value without notice would defeat the wife's right to rescind. As Battersby points out, however, this would be inconsistent with s 59(6) of the Land Registration Act 1925, which provides that only on acquiring the legal estate will a purchaser defeat an unprotected minor interest. Moreover, the wife's equity, if coupled with actual occupation, may qualify as an overriding interest which may bind the purchaser in the absence of inquiry: *Blacklocks v JB Developments (Godalming) Ltd* [1982] Ch 183. In these circumstances, notice in the *O'Brien* sense, would be irrelevant. (See, further, Sparkes, P, 'The proprietary effect of undue influence' [1995] Conv 250; Milne, P, 'Lenders, co-owners and solicitors' (1999) *NLJ Practitioner*, 5 February, 168; and Lawson, A, '*O'Brien* and its legacy: principle, equity and certainty' [1995] CLJ 280, pp 284–86.)

Most recently, the House of Lords, in *Royal Bank of Scotland v Etridge (No 2)* [2001] UKHL 44, has endorsed the view that the issue between a lender and a surety wife is not one of priority of competing interests; it is a *contract* law not a property law question. As Lord Scott observed (para 146):

> It is notice of the husband's impropriety that the bank must have, not notice of any prior rights of the wife. It is the notice that the bank has of the impropriety that creates the wife's right to set aside the transaction. The wife does not have any prior right or prior equity.

4.4 WHAT STEPS MUST THE LENDER TAKE TO AVOID THE WIFE'S EQUITY?

4.4.1 Burden of proof

When the wife establishes the primary facts sufficient to put the lender on inquiry in a given case, the burden passes to the lender to show that it has taken reasonable steps to satisfy itself that the wife's consent had been properly obtained. This was the conclusion reached in the House of Lords' decision in *Barclays Bank plc v Boulter* [1999] 4 All ER 513, where the wife sought to have an 'all moneys' charge set aside on the basis that she had trusted her husband to deal with their financial affairs and that he had told her that the charge was merely to secure the money borrowed for the joint purchase of a house. Lord Hoffman (who gave the leading opinion) gave the analogy of a purchaser of a chattel, whose vendor's title is vitiated by fraud. In such a case, the defrauded owner has no proprietary interest in the chattel and so, it is not for the purchaser to establish a defence which would defeat it, but for the owner to show that the purchaser had actual or constructive notice of the fraud. In other words, the burden of proving notice is on the person (that is, the wife) who claims that the vitiating factor affects a person (that is, the bank) who is not a party to the undue influence. But once this initial burden is discharged, the onus falls on the bank to establish that it took reasonable steps to satisfy itself that her consent was free and informed: see *Davies v Norwich Union Life Insurance Society* (1999) 78 P & CR 119 (CA), where the lender took no steps at all. (See, further, Thompson, M, 'Pleading points' [2000] Conv 43.)

This obligation to take reasonable steps has been likened to an equitable duty of care on the part of the lender 'to take positive steps to safeguard the interests of person with whom the [lender] was dealing, and who came from a particular class at risk': Rickett, CEF, 'The financier's duty of care to a surety' (1998) 114 LQR 17, p 19; and see, also, *Smith v Bank of Scotland* [1997] 2 FLR 862 (HL), involving an appeal from Scotland, where Lord Clyde spoke in terms of a duty on the part of the lender, under Scots law, arising out of the 'good faith of the contract' to give independent advice. Most recently, Lord Scott, in *Royal Bank of Scotland v Etridge (No 2)* [2001] UKHL 44 (HL), concluded that a lender should be expected to take reasonable steps to satisfy itself that the surety wife understood the transaction she was entering into. His Lordship said (para 147):

If the bank did so, no longer could constructive notice of any impropriety by the husband in procuring his wife's consent be imputed to it. The original constructive notice would have been shed. If, on the other hand, a bank with notice of the risk of some such impropriety, failed to take the requisite reasonable steps, then, if it transpired that the wife's consent had been procured by the husband's undue influence or misrepresentation, constructive knowledge that that was so would be imputed to the bank and the wife would have the same remedies as she would have had if the bank had actual knowledge of the impropriety.

Although most of the cases involve a husband and wife, it is clear that the same principles will apply to heterosexual and homosexual cohabitees: *Massey v Midland Bank plc* [1995] 1 All ER 929 (CA), p 933. In *Etridge (No 2)*, the House of Lords made it clear that the *O'Brien* decision was not confined to sexual relationships, but extended to every case where the relationship between the surety and the debtor was non-commercial: para 87, *per* Lord Nicholls. In view of the decision in *Boulter*, it is now incumbent on the wife expressly to plead constructive notice on the part of the bank in her pleadings.

4.4.2 Private meeting

In *O'Brien*, Lord Browne-Wilkinson indicated that a lender is expected to take steps 'to bring home to the wife the risk she is running by standing as surety and to advise her to take independent advice' (p 429). More specifically, in respect of transactions entered into post-*O'Brien*, this meant insisting that the wife attends a private meeting (in the absence of the husband) with a representative of the lender at which she is:

(a) informed of the extent of her liability as surety;

(b) warned of the risk she is running; and

(c) urged to take independent legal advice.

His Lordship also indicated that in 'exceptional cases' (for example, where the lender has knowledge of facts which 'render the presence of undue influence not only possible but probable'), the lender must insist that the wife *actually receives* independent advice: *O'Brien*, p 430.

Significantly, the requirement of a personal interview was identified in *O'Brien* as a 'substantial step required by law' going beyond what was considered good banking practice at the time: see the Voluntary Code of Banking Practice (para 12.1) published by the British Bankers Association and adopted by lending institutions in March 1992. Indeed, Lord Browne-Wilkinson regarded this as an 'essential' element (at least, in relation to transactions post-dating *O'Brien*) because earlier case law showed that written warnings were often not read and sometimes intercepted by the husband: *O'Brien*, p 431. Moreover, in his view, a personal interview would not impose an unworkable administrative burden on banks and other lending institutions. Such a strict requirement was not, however, appropriate in relation to transactions pre-dating *O'Brien* where, in his Lordship's view, the reasonableness of the steps taken by the lender to avoid constructive notice would depend on the facts of each case. In *O'Brien* itself, although the bank manager had given instructions that Mr and Mrs O'Brien should be made fully aware of the nature and effect of the relevant documents and should take independent legal advice, those instructions were not followed by the branch staff. If Mrs O'Brien had been properly advised, she would have been told that her home was potentially at risk for the debts of her husband's company which already had an existing liability of £107,000 and which was to be given an overdraft facility of £135,000. If she had been told this, it would have dispelled her husband's misrepresentation that the liability was limited to only £60,000 and would last for only a few weeks.

In several of the cases decided since *O'Brien*, the requirement of a private meeting has been acknowledged as governing the question whether the lender is infected by the presumed exercise of undue influence. In *Northern Rock Building Society v Archer* (1998) 78 P & CR 65 (CA), Chadwick LJ concluded that the absence of a private meeting was not fatal 'at least in a case which predates the guidance given by Lord Browne-Wilkinson in *O'Brien'* (p 72). In *Midland Bank plc v Kidwai* [1995] 4 Bank LR 227 (CA), the wife had been seen by the bank official in the absence of the husband. She was advised by him to seek advice from a solicitor and she was told that her liability was potentially unlimited and that there was a possibility that she might lose her home. The Court of Appeal held that this was sufficient to bring home to the wife both the extent of the liability and the risk that she was running. The fact that she was not told of the extent of the existing debt or that the charge to which she was being asked to consent was a second charge was irrelevant. In the words of Morritt LJ:

> ... the submissions of the wife, if accepted would cast on the bank the duties of the solicitor or other independent adviser prudent banks advise those in the position of the wife to consult. Not only is the bank not required to do so by the principles expounded [in *O'Brien*] but it cannot do so for it is interested in the transaction in question and therefore not independent. Thus, it cannot enter into questions of evaluation of the risk which lead to advice whether to enter into the transaction at all. This is a matter for the independent adviser, whose duty it is to obtain all relevant information from the bank, as well as from the husband.

By contrast, in *Bank of Cyprus (London) Ltd v Markou* [1999] 2 All ER 707, although the bank's assistant manager told the wife at a meeting what she was signing, he did not explain the implications of the transaction and did not advise her to seek independent legal advice. In particular, he did not indicate the extent of her liability as a surety or warn her of the risk she was running in losing her family home if her husband's business (which was already loss making) should fail. The deputy judge concluded that the bank had failed to 'satisfy the requirement indicated by Lord Browne-Wilkinson': *Markou*, p 713.

(See, also, *Wright v Cherrytree Finance Ltd* [2001] 2 All ER (Comm) 87 (CA), where, notwithstanding that the wife had signed the various loan documents, she had not read them and the lender was held not to have explained the position to her in a private meeting. It was not enough that the lender had stated in the documentation that the wife should seek independent advice.)

However, the trend of the decisions (albeit concerning transactions pre-dating *O'Brien*) has been to place greater emphasis on the role of the solicitor in advising the wife of the effects of the transaction. In *Massey v Midland Bank plc* [1995] 1 All ER 929 (CA), for example, Steyn LJ concluded that Lord Browne-Wilkinson's 'guidance ought not to be mechanically applied' (p 934). In that case, the bank official dealing with the transaction explained (at a joint interview attended also by the debtor) that the bank would require the claimant (a cohabitee) to be independently advised by a solicitor before it would agree to proceed with the transaction. The Court of Appeal held that the bank had taken reasonable steps to ensure that the claimant's consent to grant the charge had been properly obtained and had also received confirmation from the solicitors involved that they had explained the charge to her. On this basis, therefore, the bank was held not to be fixed with constructive notice of the claimant's equity. According to Steyn LJ, the guidance given in *O'Brien* was not intended to be necessarily exhaustive so that 'if ... the objective of independent advice for the wife (or somebody in a like position) is realised, the fact that there was not an interview between a representative of the creditor and the surety, unattended by the debtor, ought not by itself to be fatal to the creditor's case': *Massey*, p 934. According to his Lordship, it was the 'substance' of the *O'Brien* guidance which mattered and not its form.

Similarly, in *Banco Exterior Internacional v Mann* [1995] 1 All ER 936 (CA), Morritt LJ observed that the requirement of a private meeting was not the only step which would avoid a bank being fixed with constructive notice of a wife's rights. In his view, it ought to be regarded as the 'best practice', but not the only means of counteracting the wife's equity. In his Lordship's view, the 'essence of the matter' was that 'the creditor should take reasonable steps to ensure in so far as he can that the undue influence of the husband is counteracted by ensuring that the wife is aware of the consequences to her of entering into the proposed transaction for the benefit of her husband': *Banco Exterior Internacional*, p 943. Here, the bank's offer of a loan to the husband's company to be secured, *inter alia*, by a second charge over the matrimonial home owned by the husband alone, yet occupied by him and his wife, was conditional on the nature of the charge being explained to the wife by her solicitor (and the solicitor certifying that he had, in fact, done so). The husband passed the loan documents on to the company's solicitor who wrote to the wife explaining that the effect of her signing the declaration was that she would thereby waive her rights in the matrimonial home in favour of the bank, to the extent that it was owed any moneys by the company. In particular, under the declaration, the wife surrendered priority of her occupation rights under the Matrimonial Homes Act 1983 and any overriding interest arising under s 70(1)(g) of the Land Registration Act 1925.

The husband and wife later attended the solicitor's office where she signed the documents in the presence of the solicitor, after he had explained the nature of the declaration. The majority of the Court of Appeal (Hobhouse LJ dissenting) held that the bank was entitled to rely on the company's solicitor to give independent advice when advising the wife. The test was how the transaction appeared to the bank, which was entitled to assume that the solicitor would regard it as his professional duty, not merely to explain the nature and effect of the documents to the wife, but also to advise her that, if the worst happened, she could lose her rights in the house and that it was for her to decide whether she was willing to take that risk or not. In this case, the bank also received confirmation from the solicitor, so there was nothing to fix it with constructive notice of any undue influence by the husband. (Consider also the facts in *Halifax Building Society v Brown* [1996] 1 FLR 103 (CA), where, although the wife's letter postponing her interest in the home in favour of the lender contained an acknowledgment that she had received independent advice, the reality was that the lender had corresponded directly with the husband's solicitors, who had simply advised him to inform his wife to seek separate advice. The Court of Appeal held that there was a triable issue of constructive notice.)

More recently, in *Royal Bank of Scotland v Etridge (No 2)* [1998] 4 All ER 705, the Court of Appeal concluded that, where the wife is not dealing with the bank through a solicitor, it is normally enough if the bank has simply urged her to obtain independent legal advice before entering into the transaction, especially if the solicitor provides confirmation that: (1) he has explained the transaction to the wife; and (2) she appeared to understand it. This is what occurred in *Bank of Baroda v Rayarel* [1995] 2 FLR 376 (CA), where the execution of the charge was witnessed by the solicitor who had acted for the couple and their son in the preparation of the document. The charge contained a certificate to the effect that the chargors had been advised of the effect of the document and acknowledging their right to independent legal advice. This certificate was signed individually by each of the parties and was witnessed by their solicitor. The Court of Appeal had no difficulty accepting that the certificate reinforced the bank's assumption that they could rely on the parties' solicitor to advise the wife properly and, in particular, to obtain independent legal advice. The wife had signed the certificate, effectively countersigned by the solicitor, to the effect that she had been given such advice. The bank had, therefore, avoided constructive notice of her rights.

Significantly, in *Etridge (No 2)* (CA), Stuart-Smith LJ observed (without apparent criticism) that lending institutions had been unwilling to adopt the personal interview procedure laid down in *O'Brien* (even in respect of transactions post-dating *O'Brien*) and ventured to suggest that such an approach would be likely 'to expose the bank to far greater risks than those from which it wishes to be protected': *Etridge (No 2)* (CA), p 720. This is presumably because, if the bank conducts a private interview with the wife and does not adequately explain the nature of the transaction to her, it may find itself unable to enforce the charge against her. Instead, lenders have adopted the practice of requiring the wife to obtain independent legal advice and then seeking confirmation that she has done so. Some academic commentators, however, have suggested that the *O'Brien* requirement of a private meeting is prescriptive and that 'it will be an ill-advised lending institution which departs from [it] on the basis of decisions concerning transactions pre-dating *O'Brien*': Draper, MJ, 'Undue influence: a review' [1999] Conv 176, p 198. (See, also, Fehlberg, B, 'The husband, the bank, the wife and her signature – the sequel' (1996) 59 MLR 675, p 684, who argues that 'allowing creditors to escape the private meeting requirement by insisting on independent advice would have the particular disadvantage for surety wives of isolating them from negotiations surrounding the loan transaction where information is exchanged, questions may be asked and misunderstandings clarified'.)

The view, however, that Lord Browne-Wilkinson's requirement of a private meeting was intended to be prescriptive has been firmly rejected by the House of Lords in *Royal Bank of Scotland v Etridge (No 2)* [2001] UKHL 44. The problem, identified in much of the academic literature, is that the independent advice, relied on by lenders to exonerate them from constructive notice of the wife's equity, has been largely perfunctory and does not adequately bring home to the wife the possible dangers of acting as surety for her husband's indebtedness. According to Lord Nicholls, therefore, a lender should be expected to take reasonable steps to satisfy itself that the wife has had brought home to her, *in a meaningful way*, the practical implications of the proposed transaction. This did not mean that a bank has to attempt to discover for itself whether a wife's consent is being procured by undue influence. A personal meeting was not the only way a bank could discharge its obligation to bring home to the wife the risks she was running. It was not unreasonable for a lender to prefer that this task should be undertaken by an independent legal adviser. Normally, therefore, it will be reasonable for a bank to rely upon confirmation from a solicitor, acting for the wife, that he has advised her appropriately. If, however, the bank knows that the solicitor has not duly advised the wife, or if the bank knows facts from which it ought to have realised that the wife has not received appropriate advice, it will proceed at its own risk.

4.4.3 Independent legal advice

Urging the wife to take legal advice

The trend of authority prior to the House of Lords' decision in *Etridge (No 2)* favoured the view that it was generally sufficient for a lender to avoid a finding of constructive notice if it urged the surety wife to take independent legal advice from a solicitor: *Massey v Midland Bank plc* [1995] 1 All ER 929 (CA), p 934; *National Bank of Abu Dhabi v Mohamed* (1998) 30 HLR 383 (CA); and *Royal Bank of Scotland v Etridge (No 2)* [1998] 4 All ER 705 (CA), p 721. However, merely stating in the loan documentation that the claimant should seek independent advice was not sufficient to dispel the effects of undue influence: *Wright v Cherrytree Finance Ltd* [2001] 2 All ER (Comm) 877 (CA). If the bank failed properly to advise the wife to seek such advice, the charge would normally be unenforceable against her: *Davies v Norwich Union Life Assurance Society* (1999) 78 P & CR 119 (CA). Even if the wife received proper advice regarding an initial transaction, there was held to be an additional requirement upon the bank to see that she received legal advice in relation to any further advance or overdraft facility which was unrelated to the original transaction: *Barclays Bank plc v Caplan* [1998] 1 FLR 532.

A good illustration of these principles is to be found in the case of *Turner v Barclays Bank plc* [1997] 2 FCR 151. The husband and wife were the joint owners of their family home, subject to a building society mortgage. The husband also owned his business premises. He needed to raise money and the bank granted a first mortgage on the business property and a second mortgage on the jointly owned home. The bank's records showed that independent legal advice had been considered by both parties, but they did not wish to take it and that both were 'fully aware of the implications of this action'. On the occasion when they both signed the charge, the bank noted that the wife was offered 'independent legal advice on this and the last occasion and this had been declined'. The wife also signed a standard form in which she acknowledged that 'if the borrower does not repay the bank it may sell the charged asset' and 'you have recommended that I obtain legal advice ... and I have declined to accept your recommendations'. Neuberger J held, on the facts, that, on at least one occasion, the bank had also spoken to the wife in the absence of the husband and recommended that she take legal advice. In all the circumstances, therefore, the bank was held to have done enough to discharge constructive notice of any undue influence on the part of the husband. Not only did it explain the effects of the charge to the wife, but also the extent of the indebtedness of the husband's business to the bank, and what would happen if the business failed. In addition, the bank had recommended to her that she get legal advice.

Exceptional circumstances

In many cases, as we have seen, lenders require (as a matter of practice) confirmation from the solicitor that independent advice has, in fact, been given. This accords with the Voluntary Code of Banking Practice, the current version of which took effect on 1 July 1997, which goes further than the *O'Brien* and *Etridge (No 2)* (CA) guidelines by actually requiring confirmation that the surety has been independently advised of the limit of her (or his) liability and that she (or he) understood the transaction. In *O'Brien*, however,

Lord Browne-Wilkinson suggested, as we have already seen, that, only in exceptional circumstances, would it be necessary for a lender to *insist* that the wife actually obtained legal advice. His Lordship said (p 430):

> I would not exclude exceptional cases where a creditor has knowledge of further facts which render the presence of undue influence not only possible but probable. In such cases, the creditor to be safe will have to insist that the wife is separately advised.

The point was also alluded to in *Etridge (No 2)* where Stuart-Smith LJ (giving the judgment of the Court of Appeal) considered it sufficient if the bank merely urged the wife to obtain independent advice without actually insisting that she did so except in 'exceptional' cases (p 720). One such exceptional case was *Credit Lyonnais Bank Nederland NV v Burch* [1997] 1 All ER 144, where the Court of Appeal held that the bank was required to ensure that the complainant actually received such advice because any competent solicitor would have advised her not to enter into the transaction. Here, a junior employee was persuaded to consent to a second charge over her flat in order to secure her employer's increased overdraft facility. She signed the charge in her employer's presence at the offices of the bank's solicitors. At no time was she told either by her employer or the bank of the former's indebtedness to the bank or the extent of the overdraft facility being granted. The bank's solicitors wrote to her pointing out that the guarantee was unlimited both in time and amount and advising her to seek independent legal advice before entering into the transaction, but she did not do so. The Court of Appeal concluded that the bank had not taken sufficient steps to avoid being fixed with constructive notice of the presumed undue influence because neither the potential extent of her liability had been explained to her, nor had she received independent advice. On the facts, the bank was required to ensure that she actually obtained such advice because any competent solicitor would have advised her against entering into the transaction. In the words of Swinton Thomas LJ (p 158):

> What the bank failed to tell her, and undoubtedly should have told her, was the extent of the company's present indebtedness and, even more important, that she was exposing herself to a potential liability of £270,000 which would, of course, involve the loss of her home. Furthermore, I have no doubt that in these circumstances they should have insisted that she took independent legal advice before entering into the charge.

Undoubtedly, this was an 'extreme' case (*per* Millett LJ, p 152) because the complainant had committed herself to a personal liability far beyond her modest means, risking personal bankruptcy, in return for no personal benefit to herself. The excessively onerous nature of the transaction would have prompted any solicitor acting on her behalf to 'warn her against it in the strongest possible terms' and to have ceased acting for her further if she persisted in the transaction against his advice: *Burch*, p 155. In these circumstances, merely urging the employee to take legal advice was held insufficient. (See, also, *Steeples v Lea* (1998) 76 P & CR 157 (CA), where the lender sought to enforce a security he had obtained upon the house of the defendant who was a junior employee of the borrower, for a loan of £50,000. The transaction here was characterised as 'extravagantly improvident'.) It is, thus, apparent, as Millett LJ emphasised in *Burch* (p 156), that independent advice 'is neither always necessary nor always sufficient'. In his view, the result of a given case did not depend mechanically on the presence or absence of such advice. The decision in *Burch*, however, was at odds with two earlier decisions (which were not cited), namely, *Bank of Baroda v Rayarel* [1995] 2 FLR 376 (CA) and *Midland Bank plc v Kidwai* [1995] 4 Bank LR 227 (CA). In both these cases, unlike *Burch*, the suggestion that the taking of 'reasonable steps' by the lender involved informing the wife of the current state of the husband's borrowing was firmly rejected. In *Kidwai*, Morritt LJ said:

> The amount of the existing loan was no measure of the extent of the liability [of the surety] and indeed reference to it might be positively misleading.

According to his Lordship, such information (including the extent of any overdraft facility) could only be extracted from the bank by the wife's independent legal adviser. The lender could not take on that role itself as it was an interested party and, in any event, it owed a duty of confidentiality to its customer (the husband) which would prevent it from disclosing such information without the latter's consent: see, also, *Massey v Midland Bank plc* [1995] 1 All ER 929 (CA).

The case of *Cooke v National Westminster Bank plc* [1998] 2 FLR 783 (CA) provides another example of 'exceptional circumstances' where the lender was held to be under a duty to insist that the wife actually obtain legal advice. The wife was asked to guarantee the liabilities of her husband's company by executing a charge over a jointly owned property to which she had contributed most of the purchase money. The bank wrote to the couple and also to their solicitors asking that the wife be given separate legal advice and requesting written confirmation that this had been done. A representative of the bank noted that, in discussions, the wife had not been 'over anxious' to give the guarantee but, nevertheless, the charge was duly executed. The bank, however, had not received any confirmation that the wife had obtained separate legal advice, despite reminding the solicitors in writing. The wife later sought to have the charge set aside on the ground that it had been obtained by her husband's undue influence and the bank counterclaimed for summary judgment on the guarantee on the basis that it was not arguable that the bank had constructive notice of her equity. The Court of Appeal disagreed; the bank ought reasonably to have satisfied itself of the wife's consent, largely because of its knowledge of the wife's reluctance to proceed with the guarantee. This concern over her position warranted confirmation that she had actually taken separate legal advice. The wife, therefore, was given unconditional leave to defend the bank's counterclaim. The case fell to be classified as 'exceptional', because the bank had knowledge of further facts (that is, the wife's reluctance to proceed with the transaction) which rendered the presence of undue influence, in the words of Lord Browne-Wilkinson in *O'Brien*, 'not only possible but probable', so that, in order to be safe, it should have insisted that the wife was separately advised.

If the lender, however, insists that the complainant actually obtains legal advice before entering into the transaction, and she (or he) actually does obtain advice but goes ahead in spite of the advice given, the lender will normally escape the consequences of notice. The reason for this (as explained by Millett LJ) is that the lender, once aware that she has been to a solicitor, is entitled to assume that the solicitor has discharged his duty and that his client has followed his advice.

Interestingly, also, in *Royal Bank of Scotland v Etridge* [1997] 3 All ER 628 (CA), p 635, Hobhouse LJ (in interlocutory proceedings) suggested that a bank was under a duty of ensuring that the wife receives independent legal advice where it employs its own solicitor to act as its agent. The rationale here was that, because the bank had effectively delegated its own task to its solicitor, it was responsible for his discharge of that duty. This, however, could no longer be considered good law following the disapproval of the decision in the subsequent Court of Appeal proceedings (*Etridge (No 2)* [1998] 4 All ER 705, pp 721–22), where it was emphasised (by a differently constituted Court of Appeal) that a bank was not normally required to question the sufficiency of a solicitor's advice even if he was instructed by the bank.

The lender's risk

In some cases, as we have seen, special circumstances were held to exist which required the lender not only to advise the wife to obtain independent legal advice but to *insist* that she did so. As one writer put it:

> ... where a bank takes reasonable steps to advise the surety to seek independent advice, it avoids constructive notice of any possible wrongdoing by the debtor because there is now, on the surface, less likelihood of such. Where additional facts indicate *probable* wrongdoing, only an insistence on independent advice can restore apparent neutrality.

(See Tijo, H, 'O'Brien and unconscionability' (1997) 113 LQR 10, p 13.)

In the absence, however, of special circumstances, it has been held to be sufficient if the bank has merely urged the wife to obtain such advice before entering into the guarantee or charge. This view was confirmed by the Court of Appeal in *Etridge (No 2)*, applying the earlier Court of Appeal decisions in *Massey* and *Rayarel* (see above). In *Etridge (No 2)*, Stuart-Smith LJ made it clear that no importance was to be attached to the fact that, in the ordinary case, the solicitor had not provided the bank with full or adequate confirmation that he had advised the wife. In his view, such confirmation was *not* an essential requirement. However, where the bank has asked a solicitor to explain the transaction to the wife and he fails to provide confirmation that he has done so, the bank would not be entitled to assume that he has, but would be put on inquiry whether the solicitor had, in fact, advised the wife. The upshot of this is that, if the bank failed to make further inquiry, it would be put on notice that the solicitor had not advised her (that is, it would not avoid constructive notice of the wife's right to have the transaction set aside). If, on the other hand, the solicitor gave advice but merely omitted to confirm this fact, then the bank would be unaffected by its failure to obtain confirmation prior to completion of the transaction: *Etridge (No 2)* (CA), p 722.

Ultimately, therefore, as acknowledged by the Court of Appeal in *Etridge (No 2)*, the issue of confirmation has revolved around the assumption of *risk* as to whether the wife has entered into the transaction as a result of her husband's undue influence. If the lender has insisted that independent legal advice should be sought and receives confirmation that, in fact, it was given, the lender could not be tainted by any impropriety. If, on the other hand, no such confirmation was forthcoming, the lender would bear the risk of being saddled with constructive notice of the wife's equity in the event that such legal advice had not, in fact, been given. Moreover, even if the lender received confirmation from the solicitor that he had advised the wife, this might not avail the lender, as we have already seen, in exceptional cases where the lender knew of other material facts not available to the solicitor, or if the transaction was so against the wife's interests that no competent solicitor could properly advise her to go ahead: *Etridge (No 2)* (CA). Interestingly, in *Barclays Bank plc v Goff* [2001] 2 All ER (Comm) 847 (CA), Mantell LJ felt some unease in applying such a stringent test since the occasions on which a competent solicitor would positively advise the giving of a charge to support the debts of another would be rare. In the words of Pill LJ:

> ... the family members do sometimes enter into unwise arrangements to assist their nearest and dearest. I do not consider that the exception was intended to cover all cases in which a solicitor would be expected to decline to give positive advice to enter into the transaction or to all cases in which the solicitor would be expected to advise that the transaction was unwise.

Instead, the Court of Appeal in *Goff* preferred a test whereby an exceptional case would be made out if there were circumstances where any reasonably competent solicitor would have positively advised a wife who was proposing to act as surety for her husband's debts not to enter into the transaction. In this case, the mere fact that the wife had been given independent advice in the presence of her husband was not a sufficiently exceptional circumstance to displace the general rule: see, further, Price, NS, 'Undue influence: *fillus nullium*' (1999) 115 LQR 9, who has argued that, in the category of exceptional cases, the wife may have an alternative claim based on the unconscionable nature of the transaction. It seems inevitable also that a lender would be fixed with the impropriety, regardless of confirmation, if it had actual notice of the borrower's undue influence or knew that the solicitor's certificate was false:

Bridge, S, 'The aftermath of *O'Brien*: carte blanche for banks, cartes jaunes for solicitors?' [1999] CLJ 28, p 29.

As we have seen, in cases where the proposed transaction was excessively onerous, it was not enough for the lender simply to encourage the wife to seek independent advice: *Burch*, pp 152 and 156, *per* Nourse and Millett LJJ, respectively. As was emphasised in *O'Brien*, where the undue influence (or misrepresentation) was 'possible', independent advice need only be urged but, where it was 'probable', such advice had to be insisted upon by the lender. (See, further, Hooley, R and O'Sullivan, J, 'Undue influence and unconscionable bargains' [1997] LMCLQ 17, p 20.) This was justified on the basis that, where undue influence was probable, there was also a strong likelihood that the wife's failure (or refusal) to obtain advice was not made freely.

Finally, it should be said that a lender has been held to be treated as acting reasonably in relying on a solicitor's confirmation that a wife had received appropriate advice, even though that confirmation was based, not on the solicitor's own knowledge, but on what another solicitor had told him. This last point was addressed recently by the Court of Appeal in *Scottish Equitable Life plc v Virdee* [1999] 1 FLR 863, where it was held that the lender was entitled to assume, on the basis of the signature of the witnessing solicitor and the covering letter from the husband's solicitors, that the wife had been properly advised by a solicitor and to believe that she had had the implications of the form of disclaimer (and the implications of signing it) explained to her. There was no requirement, in other words, that a solicitor should expressly confirm that he had *personally* advised the wife, and no need for a solicitor to be identified as acting for that person. The mere witnessing of the wife's signature by a solicitor would not, however, by itself relieve the lender from constructive notice of the husband's undue influence: *Virdee*, p 867.

The House of Lords' ruling in Etridge (No 2)

In the course of his speech, Lord Scott said (para 164):

> ... in the ordinary case the facts of which the bank is aware, or must be taken to be aware, point to no more than the existence of the inevitable risk that there may have been undue influence or some other impropriety and are not facts sufficient by themselves to give rise to a presumption of undue influence. In such a case the bank does not have to take steps to satisfy itself that there is no undue influence. It must take steps to satisfy itself that the wife understands the nature and effect of the transaction.

As mentioned earlier, the House of Lords has sought to address the various perceived deficiencies in the quality of legal advice given to surety wives under the current law. The current system of giving so called 'independent legal advice' was identified as a fiction and a charade: para 52, *per* Lord

Nicholls. Although, as we have seen, a private meeting with the wife is not essential, the bank is now expected to take reasonable steps to satisfy itself that the wife has had brought home to her, *in a meaningful way*, the practical implications of the proposed transaction. This, in turn, will involve entrusting the task of a personal meeting to an independent legal adviser. Normally, it will also be reasonable that a bank should be able to rely upon confirmation from a solicitor, acting for the wife, that he has advised her appropriately. If, however, the bank knows that the solicitor has not duly advised the wife, or if the bank knows facts from which it ought to have realised that the wife has not received the appropriate advice, the bank will proceed at its own risk: paras 54–57. Moreover, if the certificate is not forthcoming from the solicitor, the bank will not normally have reasonable grounds for being satisfied that the wife's agreement had been properly obtained. In that case, it will be subject to any equity arising from her husband's impropriety: para 122, *per* Lord Hobhouse. In addition, the bank will have no basis for rebutting the risk that the wife's signature had not been properly obtained if it is aware that she had not been separately advised by a solicitor who was acting for her: see the appeals in *Midland Bank plc v Wallace* and *Barclays Bank plc v Harris* [2001] UKHL 44.

In addition to entrusting the task of a personal meeting to a solicitor, the House of Lords identified various duties which the bank will now owe *directly to the wife* in order to ensure that she does know the purpose for which the solicitor is giving her advice. These additional duties are discussed in the next section.

4.4.4 Personal inquiries

In *Banco Exterior Internacional SA v Thomas* [1997] 1 All ER 46 (CA), it was emphasised that a bank has no business inquiring into the personal relationships between those with whom it had dealings or as to their personal motives for wanting to help one another. If, therefore, the complainant takes independent legal advice and decides still to proceed, as she is entitled to do, it is not for the bank to decline to allow her to do so. In this case, the complainant (Mrs Dempsey) agreed to a suggestion from a close personal friend (Mr Mulchay) that he would pay her a regular income if she would guarantee his borrowing and provide her house as security for an expansion of his second hand car business. The bank required her to obtain independent legal advice about the nature and effect of the proposed transaction, and she duly consulted the solicitor nominated by the bank. She later executed the guarantee and legal charge. Her former solicitor, however, advised her strongly against entering into the transaction and informed the bank of his views by telephone. He also informed the bank by letter that, despite his strong advice to the contrary, she had decided to proceed. The Court of Appeal held that it was not the bank's concern to ask itself why Mrs Dempsey was willing to stand surety for her friend's indebtedness, but merely to ensure that she knew what she was doing and wanted to do it, having received independent advice about the nature and effect of the transaction. At the time when she signed the documentation, it was apparent that she did not lack a free and informed will and, consequently, the presumption of undue influence was rebutted. Sir Richard Scott VC said (p 55):

> I would accept that the arrangement ... was one that any adviser would advise strongly against. But the purpose of advisers is to advise. The recipient of the advice does not have to accept it. He or she can decide, fully informed by the advice that has been received, whether or not to proceed with the allegedly ill-advised and improvident transaction. In the present case, Mrs Dempsey may well have been attracted by the offer of £500 per month (or £125 per week). She was of full age. She suffered from no mental infirmity. And she had the nature and effect of the transaction with the bank explained to her by an independent solicitor.

It was argued on behalf of the complainant that her signing of the documents showed that she was so fully under the influence of her friend, Mr Mulchay, that her solicitor's advice would have made no difference. His Lordship, however, dismissed this argument as being 'circuitous' since, if it was accepted, it 'would turn what is only a presumption of undue influence into an irrebuttable conclusion' (p 55). In his view, the short answer to this argument was that, once Mrs Dempsey had been separately advised, the presumption of undue influence played no further part, since it had been effectively displaced by rebutting evidence of independent advice. Moreover, the bank had no constructive notice of undue influence because it knew only that Mrs Dempsey was prepared to stand surety for her friend's indebtedness. It did not have to know why she was willing to do this. In this connection, the bank's only business was to make sure that she knew what she was doing and this they had done by requiring her to seek independent legal advice, which she did. Indeed, they had received confirmation of that advice from their nominated solicitor.

Interestingly, in *Inche Noriah v Shaik Allie Bin Omar* [1929] AC 127, the Privy Council also concluded that the receipt of independent legal advice may rebut the presumption of undue influence even though it is not acted upon. In their Lordships' view, what was necessary was proof that the transaction was the result of the free exercise of independent will. (But contrast, *Powell v Powell* [1900] 1 Ch 243, p 246, *per* Farwell J, who said: 'it is not sufficient that the donor should have an independent adviser unless he acts on his advice. If this were not so, the same influence that produced the desire to make the settlement would produce disregard of the advice to refrain from executing it, and so defeat the rule.' See, also, *Credit Lyonnais Bank Nederland NV v Burch* [1997] 1 All ER 144 (CA), p 156, where Millett LJ said: 'the cases show that it is not sufficient that she should have received independent advice unless she has acted on that advice. If this were not so, the same influence that produced her desire to enter into the transaction would cause her to disregard any advice not to do so.')

The House of Lords, in *Royal Bank of Scotland v Etridge (No 2)* [2001] UKHL 44, has now confirmed that it is no business of the lender to discover for itself whether a wife's consent is being procured by the exercise of her husband's influence. In the words of Lord Nicholls (para 53):

> To require such an intrusive, inconclusive and expensive exercise in every case would be an altogether disproportionate response to the need to protect those cases, presumably a small minority, where a wife is being wronged.

It was apparent, therefore, to the House of Lords that detailed and personal inquiries made of the complainant would be impracticable in most cases and, as suggested by the Court of Appeal in *Thomas*, an obvious intrusion and 'unwarrantable impertinence' on the bank's part: *Thomas*, p 55, *per* Sir Richard Scott VC ('a bank is not to be treated as a branch of the social services agencies'). The requirement, therefore, that the wife seeks independent legal advice is perceived as the only realistic (and practical) means of ensuring that a free and informed choice was made by the wife: see Draper, MJ, 'Undue influence: a review' [1999] Conv 176, p 183. On the other hand, it has also been argued forcefully that a 'ritual reliance' on the provision of independent legal advice does not afford adequate protection to wives (or cohabitees) standing as surety for their partner's debts: Millett, PJ, 'Equity's place in the law of commerce' (1998) LQR 214, p 220. On this view, a more detailed investigation of the facts is warranted in order to determine properly whether or not the wife understands the nature and consequences of her actions. According to Millett (p 220):

> We have substituted an inappropriate bright line rule for a proper investigation of the facts and have failed the vulnerable in the process. The Australians are turning to the jurisdiction to relieve against harsh and unconscionable bargains as an alternative, and there is much merit in this approach. It is certainly better than allowing the bank to assume that the surety has received adequate legal advice, an assumption which the bank almost always knows to be false.

This reasoning has now been substantially endorsed by the House of Lords in *Etridge (No 2)*, where the unsatisfactory feature of the current law, namely the wife's lack of real involvement in the confirmatory process, was identified by both Lords Nicholls and Hobhouse. In many cases, for example, the wife does not know the purpose for which the solicitor is giving her advice or that protective confirmation is being sent to the bank. Moreover, she may have no real choice in determining who should act for her in giving legal advice. To avoid this for the future, Lord Nicholls stressed the need for banks to take steps to check *directly with the wife* the name of the solicitor she wishes to act for her. This meant that lenders should now communicate directly with the wife, informing her that, for its own protection, it will require written confirmation from a solicitor, acting for her, to the effect that he has fully explained to her the nature of the documents and the practical implications they will have for her. She should also be told of the purpose of this requirement (that is, that thereafter she should not be able to dispute she is legally bound by the documents once she has signed them). She should also be asked to nominate a solicitor whom she is willing to instruct to advise her, separately from her husband, and act for her in giving the necessary confirmation to the bank. She should be told also that her husband's solicitor may act for her but, if she prefers, she is free to instruct a different solicitor to act regarding the bank's requirement for confirmation of legal advice. In the words of Lord Hobhouse (para 116):

> ... an essential feature of the scheme is that the wife has to be aware of what is going on, that the bank is asking for the certificate and why, that she is being asked to instruct a solicitor to advise her and that she is being asked to authorise the solicitor to provide the certificate.

In his Lordship's view, this new scheme whereby a wife will be put into a proper relationship with a solicitor, who is acting for her and accepts appropriate duties towards her, will do much to reduce the hitherto 'fiction of free and informed consent' apparent in many of the previous cases. According to his Lordship (para 121):

> If the bank follows this procedure then the fiction of independent advice and consent should be replaced by true independent advice and real consent.

Ultimately, the bank should not proceed with the transaction until it has received an appropriate response directly from the wife. As we shall see in Chapter 5, the lender is now also under an obligation to provide the solicitor, acting for the wife, with the financial information he needs for the purpose of properly advising his client. Accordingly, it should now become 'routine practice' for banks to send to the solicitor the necessary financial information: *Etridge (No 2)*, para 79, *per* Lord Nicholls. What is necessary will depend on the facts of the case. Ordinarily, this will include the following:

(a) information on the purpose for which the proposed new facility has been requested;

(b) the current amount of the husband's indebtedness;

(c) the amount of the husband's current overdraft facility;

(d) the amount and terms of any new facility;

(e) if the bank's request for security arises from a written application by the husband, a copy of that application should also be sent to the solicitor.

The bank will require the consent of its customer (the husband) to the circulation of the above confidential information. If this consent is not forthcoming, the transaction will not be able to proceed. Exceptionally, the House of Lords recognised that there may be cases where the bank believes or suspects that the wife has been misled by the husband, or is not entering into the transaction of her own free will. In such a case, the bank must inform the wife's solicitor of the facts giving rise to its belief or suspicion.

The foregoing will apply to future transactions. So far as past transactions are concerned, however, the House of Lords has intimated that a bank will ordinarily be regarded as having discharged its obligations if the solicitor gives the bank confirmation to the effect that he had brought home to the wife the risks she was running by standing as surety: *Etridge (No 2)* (HL), para 80.

4.5 LENDER'S POSITION WHERE WIFE ADVISED BY A SOLICITOR

In *Royal Bank of Scotland v Etridge (No 2)* [1998] 4 All ER 705, the Court of Appeal held that, if a wife deals with the bank through a solicitor (whether acting for her alone or for her husband, or both), the bank is ordinarily *not* put on inquiry and is not required to take any steps at all. In other words, the bank is entitled to assume that the solicitor is acting properly in advising the wife: *Bainbrigge v Browne* (1881) 18 Ch D 188, where Fry J held, in relation to a case involving a parent and child, that if a solicitor acts in the transaction on behalf of the child, a purchaser for value is entitled to assume that he has given the child proper advice, even though he is also acting as the father's solicitor. In this connection, the Court of Appeal in *Etridge (No 2)* confirms that a solicitor acts exclusively as the wife's solicitor, notwithstanding that he may also be the husband's solicitor or has agreed to act as the bank's agent (in only a ministerial capacity) at completion. In other words, the bank is entitled to expect the solicitor to regard himself as owing a duty to the wife alone when giving her advice, regardless of who introduced the solicitor to the wife. The position, of course, will be different if the solicitor at the meeting with the wife/surety acts solely for the husband/debtor: *Allied Irish Bank v Roberts* ((1995) unreported, 30 January (CA), available on Lexis).

More importantly, it has been held that the bank is under no obligation to question the sufficiency of the solicitor's advice. It is entitled to assume that a solicitor would act honestly and would give proper advice to the wife: *Bank of Baroda v Shah* [1988] 3 All ER 24 (CA). In particular, the lender is under no duty to inquire what transpired at the interview between the complainant and the solicitor by whom she was advised: *Massey v Midland Bank plc* [1995] 1 All ER 929 (CA). How far a solicitor should go in probing the matter with his client is a matter for the solicitor's professional judgment and not something which concerns the lender. This is because the lender is not involved in the nature and extent of that advice. In the words of Hoffman LJ, in *Bank of Baroda v Rayarel* [1995] 2 FLR 376 (p 386):

> The bank's legal department is not obliged to commit the professional discourtesy of communicating directly with the solicitor's client and tendering [independent] advice itself. Nor is it obliged to inform the solicitor of his professional duties.

In *Bank of Scotland v Bennett* [1999] Lloyd's Rep Bank 145 (CA), for example, the couple had been dealing with the bank through the husband's solicitor and the bank was entitled to assume that he would advise the wife on all relevant matters relating to the proposed mortgage, including whether it was necessary for her to obtain independent legal advice. Although, of course, the notice of an agent is normally imputed to his principal, this rule falls to be modified in the light of the provisions of s 199(1)(ii)(b) of the LPA 1925, which provide that:

> A purchaser shall not be prejudicially affected by notice of ... (ii) any other instrument or matter or any fact or thing unless ... (b) in the same transaction with respect to which a question of notice to the purchaser arises, it has come to the knowledge of ... his solicitor or other agent, *as such*, or would have come to the knowledge of his solicitor or other agent, *as such*, if such inquiries and inspections had been made as ought reasonably to have been made by the solicitor or other agent. (Emphasis added.)

This provision makes it clear that a lender will not be affected by notice of anything which its solicitor has discovered unless he was acting as the bank's solicitor at the time when he discovered it. The purpose of para (b) is to ensure that the actual knowledge of the lender's solicitor (acquired as such) is the actual knowledge of the lender and anything which ought to have been learned by the solicitor will be treated as having been learned by the lender. The test, however, is an objective one and will not depend on the particular instructions given to the lender's solicitors. Thus, in *Woolwich plc v Gomm* (2000) 79 P & CR 61 (CA), the wife argued that, had the lender's solicitors pursued the inquiries which ought reasonably to have been made on the basis of its particular instructions, the lender would have been fixed with constructive notice of her equity. This approach was emphatically rejected by the Court of Appeal on the ground that an objective standard had to be applied in determining whether a lender had been fixed with notice under s 199(1)(ii)(b). The particular instructions given by a lender to its solicitor were merely relevant for the purpose of deciding what a reasonably prudent lender would expect its solicitor to do.

In *Halifax Mortgage Services Ltd (formerly BNP Mortgages Ltd) v Stepsky* [1996] 2 All ER 277, the Court of Appeal held that, on the wording of s 199(1)(ii)(b), knowledge possessed by solicitors who were acting for both a borrower and a lender in the same transaction could not be imputed to the lender unless that knowledge was received by the solicitors in the capacity of solicitors for the lender 'as such' within the meaning of the sub-section. In that case, the information as to the true purpose of the mortgage transaction (that is, to pay off the husband's debts as opposed to purchase shares in a business) came to the knowledge of the solicitors while they were acting as the solicitors for the borrowers. That knowledge, once obtained, remained with the solicitors and could not be treated as coming to them again when they were instructed on behalf of the lender.

The same point arose in *Barclays Bank plc v Thomson* [1997] 4 All ER 816 (CA), where the bank obtained a charge over the wife's family home in order to secure the borrowing on the joint bank account which she held with her husband. The bank had written to the solicitors dealing with the transfer of the property, who also acted for the husband's business, instructing them to register the charge and requiring them to make the wife fully aware of its content. The solicitors duly explained to the wife (in her husband's absence) that in signing the charge she would be allowing her house to act as security for the borrowing on the joint account, and confirmed in writing to the bank that they had carried out its instructions. The wife, however, subsequently argued that the solicitors had been deficient in their advice to her and that, because they were acting as the bank's agent, knowledge of that deficiency could be imputed to the bank. Not surprisingly, the Court of Appeal rejected this argument, holding that, where a bank instructed a solicitor to act on its behalf for the purpose of discharging its duty to ensure that the wife received independent legal advice, the bank was entitled to rely on the solicitor's assurance that he had discharged his duty towards her, even where the solicitor was also acting for the husband and the bank. This is because the bank is entitled to expect that a solicitor, when advising the wife, will be acting exclusively for her when discharging his duty in giving independent legal advice, and not the lender: see, further, Thompson, MP, 'The independence of legal advice' [1997] Conv 216. This is so, even if the solicitor is acting principally for the husband, or retained by the bank, and regardless of who is paying his fee. As Simon Brown LJ observed (p 826), he 'cannot at that stage have two clients: such a notion would defeat the very purpose of [his] retainer which is to give the [wife] *independent* advice'. Interestingly, the Court of Appeal reached the same result by applying s 199(1)(ii)(b) of the LPA 1925. In the words of Simon Brown LJ (p 826):

> Knowledge acquired by solicitors whilst tendering independent advice to a signatory does not come to them as agents for the lenders. At that time their professional duty is owed to the signatory alone.

Significantly, the decision in *Bank of Credit and Commerce International SA v Aboody* [1992] 4 All ER 955 (CA) was distinguished because the knowledge sought to be imputed to the bank in that case related to the *husband's* undue influence and not the solicitor's advice tendered to the wife: see, further, Nield, S, 'Imputed notice' [2000] 64 Conv 196, p 201. A number of earlier cases were relied on in the *Thomson* decision as establishing a bank's entitlement to rely upon a solicitor's confirmation that proper advice had been given to the wife, even though the solicitor acted principally for the husband (that is, the person against whose undue influence the wife sought to be protected). Most notably, in *Midland Bank plc v Serter* [1995] 1 FLR 1034 (CA), the husband's solicitor had also explained (over the telephone) the nature of the charge to the wife. The solicitor subsequently sent a certificate to the bank stating that he had done so. The Court of Appeal held that the bank was entitled to believe that the solicitor was acting for the wife (or the husband) when advising her, in pursuance of his general professional duty. Since there was nothing from which it could be argued that the solicitor was the agent of the bank for the purpose of advising the wife, the bank was not fixed with constructive knowledge of any undue influence by the husband. In this connection, the same solicitor had been instructed by the bank merely to register the charge, and no more. Glidewell LJ said (p 1046):

> ... a solicitor, like any other agent, may be instructed specifically to act for a party for one particular purpose in relation to a transaction, but not to act for him generally for other purposes. Thus it is only knowledge which he acquires when carrying out that part of the transaction in which he is instructed to act as agent which is to be imputed to the party who for that purpose is his principal.

Equally, in both *Banco Exterior Internacional v Mann* [1995] 1 FLR 602 (CA) and *Bank of Baroda v Rayarel* [1995] 2 FLR 376 (CA), the charge was signed by the wife in the presence of a solicitor, who was also the solicitor for the husband and for his company. In both cases, the solicitor explained the nature of the charge, and in *Rayarel* he signed a certificate addressed to the bank saying that he had done so. In *Mann*, the wife herself signed a certificate to that effect, which also said that she had been told of her right to receive independent legal advice. In both cases, it was held that the bank was entitled to rely on the presence of independent legal advice, notwithstanding that the solicitor had also acted for the husband. If there was a possibility of a conflict of interest between the wife and the husband whom the solicitor was also advising, the bank was entitled to assume that the solicitor would have told her that she was free to take advice from another solicitor. The bank, as already mentioned above, is not obliged to remind the solicitor of his professional duties.

The position was confirmed by the Court of Appeal in *National Westminster Bank plc v Beaton* [1997] 30 HLR 99. Here, legal title in the family home was registered in the husband's name alone, although the wife had a beneficial interest in the property. The bank advanced £20,000 to the husband for his own business purposes, which was secured by a second charge on the home. Two years later, the couple proposed to move house and instructed a solicitor to act in respect of the purchase, which was to be in their joint names. The bank indicated to the solicitor that it was willing to release its charge over the old property conditional upon payment of a lump sum to reduce the husband's borrowings and upon the couple granting it a second charge on the new property. The bank asked the solicitor to act on its behalf in taking and registering a mortgage over the new property and to arrange for the couple to execute the requisite documentation. It also asked the solicitor to explain the meaning of the mortgage form to the wife. The solicitor duly accepted the instructions to act for the bank. The mortgage documents were duly executed at his office by the couple. The new mortgage, however, was not limited to £20,000, but was to secure all liabilities incurred by the husband. The solicitor wrote to the bank that the charge had been executed in accordance with its instructions and the wife had been advised accordingly. In subsequent proceedings by the bank to enforce the charge, the wife claimed that the solicitor had not explained that the charge gave unlimited security for her husband's liabilities. Moreover, she argued that the solicitor had been appointed as the bank's agent to advise her as to the effect of the charge and, thus, was fixed with constructive notice of any deficiencies in that advice.

The Court of Appeal, relying on the *Serter* and *Thomson* line of cases, had no difficulty in rejecting this argument. The bank had not constituted the solicitor as its agent simply by asking him to give advice to the wife, nor did it make itself vicariously liable for any deficiency in the advice given. The bank's request to the solicitor was treated as no more than a reminder of his professional duty to the wife. Significantly, the court was not prepared to infer agency when the relationship was readily explicable on some other basis. Moreover, the solicitor had given advice to the wife in his capacity as her solicitor and not in his capacity as solicitor for the bank. Thus, even though he would have had knowledge of any deficiency in his advice, this knowledge did not come to him as solicitor for the bank 'as such' so that s 199(1)(ii)(b) of the LPA 1925 could not operate to fix the bank with constructive notice of any deficiency. In the course of his judgment, Henry LJ also referred to s 199(3) of the LPA 1925, which reads:

> A purchaser shall not by reason of anything in this section be affected by notice in any case where he would not have been so affected if this section had not been enacted.

In his view, if s 199 had not been enacted, the bank would not have been affected by notice unless the solicitor was the bank's agent in advising the wife. Ultimately, therefore, all turned on whether or not the solicitor was the bank's agent for this purpose. Since, on the facts, he was not, s 199(1)(ii)(b) added nothing to the wife's argument. (Contrast *Allied Irish Bank plc v Byrne* [1995] 2 FLR 325, discussed in Chapter 5, para 5.3, where the solicitor was instructed by the bank to act on its behalf in the preparation and completion of the mortgage. Ferris J held that the solicitor was the lender's agent and his knowledge was to be imputed to the bank.)

It has been held, however, that a bank cannot assume that the solicitor has discharged his duties fully and competently if it knows (or ought to know) that this is false. Thus, if the bank is in possession of material information which is not available to the solicitor, the fact that the wife had been advised by the solicitor will not prevent the bank from being fixed with constructive notice: *Royal Bank of Scotland v Etridge (No 2)* [1998] 4 All ER 705 (CA), p 722. Thus, in *Bank of Scotland v Bennett* [1999] Lloyd's Rep Bank 145 (CA), the position would have been different if the bank knew of special facts critical to the wife's decision-making which they had no reason to believe that the solicitor was aware of: *Bennett*, p 162. In this type of situation, it seems there is nothing that the lender can do to protect itself; it is put on inquiry but cannot seemingly discharge the imputation of constructive notice by relying on the fact that the wife has taken independent legal advice.

Most recently, the House of Lords, in *Royal Bank of Scotland v Etridge (No 2)* [2001] UKHL 44, has confirmed that a solicitor, advising the wife, is acting for her alone. He is concerned only with her interests, despite the fact that he may also be acting for the husband and also the lender. As a corollary to this, knowledge of what passes between the solicitor and the wife cannot be imputed to the bank, since the solicitor is not acting as the bank's agent when he is advising the wife. Any knowledge the solicitor acquires from the wife will be confidential as between them. In the words of Lord Nicholls (paras 77–78):

> The solicitor is not accountable to the bank for the advice he gives to the wife. To impute to the bank knowledge of what passed between the solicitor and the wife would contradict this essential feature of the arrangement. The mere fact that, for its own purposes, the bank asked the solicitor to advise the wife does not make the solicitor the bank's agent in giving that advice. In the ordinary case, therefore, deficiencies in the advice given are a matter between the wife and her solicitor. The bank is entitled to proceed on the assumption that solicitor advising the wife has done his job properly.

By way of exception, as we have seen, if the bank knows that the solicitor has not duly advised the wife, or if it knows facts from which it ought to have realised that the wife has not received appropriate advice, the bank will proceed at its own risk: para 57, *per* Lord Nicholls. Moreover, if the relevant solicitor was not, in fact, acting for the wife and had not been held out by her as doing so, the conduct of the solicitor will not avail the lender: para 100, *per* Lord Hobhouse.

In most transactions, it will be apparent on the face of the documents who is the surety and who is the principal debtor. The lender, therefore, will be entitled to assume that the solicitor acting for the surety appreciates the reason why his advice was being sought and that it must be independent of the interests of the debtor. If there is nothing, however, in the documentation to alert the solicitor that his client requires advice appropriate to the position of a person standing as surety, the lender will not be entitled to avoid constructive notice of any undue influence simply by relying on the fact that a solicitor had acted for the wife: *Northern Rock Building Society v Archer* (1998) 78 P & CR 65 (CA); and Thompson, MP, 'Constructive notice of undue influence' [1999] Conv 510.

4.6 CONSUMER CREDIT ACT 1974

In some of the cases involving undue influence, an alternative plea has been put forward that the transaction is an extortionate credit bargain within the meaning of ss 137–42 of the Consumer Credit Act (CCA) 1974.

The point was first canvassed in *Avon Finance Co Ltd v Bridger* [1985] 2 All ER 281 (CA), p 286, where Lord Denning MR suggested that:

> ... if [the agreement] grossly contravenes the ordinary principles of fair dealing, and if regard is had to factors such as the age, experience and business capacity of [the parties] ... the case may well come within the provisions of the 1974 Act.

If the agreement is held to be extortionate, the court can set it aside independently of any argument based on the doctrine of undue influence. In *Coldunell Ltd v Gallon* [1986] 1 All ER 429 (CA), however, the claim that the loan agreement was an extortionate credit bargain within s 138 of the CCA 1974 was rejected since there was held to be nothing unusual about the loan. In particular, the rate of interest (20%) was not unreasonable so as to bring the agreement within s 138(1)(a) of the CCA 1974 (grossly exorbitant payments). Moreover, on the facts, the moneylenders had acted in the way that any ordinary commercial lender would be expected to act. Although s 171(7) places the burden on the creditor to show that the bargain does not grossly contravene the ordinary principles of fair dealing (see s 138(1)(b)), this had been discharged once it had been shown that the lenders had not been tainted with the son's undue influence exerted over his parents.

4.7 DUTY OF CARE TO CUSTOMER

In several cases, it has been stressed that where a lender takes on the role of adviser to a customer in respect of the nature and effect of the loan transaction, the bank is under a duty of care not to misrepresent negligently the effect of the documentation.

In *Lloyds Bank Ltd v Bundy* [1974] 3 All ER 757 (CA), the defendant, an elderly farmer, was a customer of the claimant bank. His son's plant hire company ran into financial difficulties and so he guaranteed the company's overdraft for £1,500 and charged his farmhouse to the bank to secure that sum. The company ran into further difficulties and the assistant bank manager suggested that the defendant should sign a further guarantee for £5,000 and execute a further charge for £6,000, which he did. The son's business did not improve so a further meeting was held with the bank at the defendant's home. There, he was told that the bank would only continue to support the company if he increased the guarantee and charge up to a figure of £11,000. The assistant manager at the meeting did not appreciate that there was a conflict of interest, but realised that the defendant relied on him implicitly as a bank manager to advise him about the transaction. The Court of Appeal held that the confidential relationship arising between the bank and the defendant imposed on the bank a duty of fiduciary care to ensure that the latter formed an independent and informed judgment on the proposed transaction before committing himself. This meant advising the defendant to obtain independent legal advice.

In *Cornish v Midland Bank plc* [1985] 3 All ER 513 (CA), the claimant, a customer of the bank, signed a second mortgage in favour of the bank without appreciating, and without being informed by the bank, that it was so worded as to secure not only a loan of £2,000 for renovations to a farmhouse jointly owned by herself and her husband, but also unlimited further advances made to the husband. The Court of Appeal held that the bank was required to explain to the wife that the mortgage covered further advances. Here, the bank had assumed a duty to give the claimant proper advice concerning the effect of the mortgage and had been negligent in the way it had discharged that duty. The claimant was, therefore, entitled to damages against the bank, but the charge itself was not set aside because, unlike in *Bundy*, the only relationship existing between the claimant and the bank was that of banker and customer and no unfair advantage had been taken of her and no presumption of undue influence arose.

Normally, however, a bank is under no duty to explain to a prospective guarantor the effect of what he (or she) is signing. In *O'Hara v Allied Irish Banks Ltd* [1985] BCLC 52, Harman J said (p 53):

> I cannot see that a stranger, invited to sign a guarantee (in respect of some matter in which the stranger has a commercial interest) by a third party – perhaps a bank – who has advanced money to the person whose account is to be guaranteed, is owed any duty whatever at that point of time.

Thus, the duty not to misstate negligently the effect of a mortgage (as in *Cornish*, above) only arises when a bank takes it upon itself to advise a customer as to the nature and effect of a mortgage prior to the customer executing the mortgage. Here, the bank will assume the risk to its customer of not giving a proper explanation of the nature and effect of the transaction. In *Cornish*, therefore, the bank official had chosen to give an explanation and, hence, he was under a duty not to act negligently. In *Barclays Bank plc v Khaira* [1992] 1 WLR 623, Mr T Morrison QC (sitting as a deputy High Court judge) put the matter this way (p 637):

> There may be circumstances where it is clear that the bank is being looked to for advice or is in some close relationship with the prospective guarantor of a kind where questions of undue influence might arise. In such special circumstances, the court might be prepared to hold that the bank had assumed responsibility in law to the individual either to proffer advice as to the effect of what was being signed or to advise that he take separate legal advice.

The deputy judge stressed, however, that in the normal course of events, a bank owes no duty of care in tort or contract to proffer explanations to those who come to their premises to sign securities. Nevertheless, as a matter of good business practice, banks should be encouraged to explain the nature and effect of such documents to prospective guarantors: *Khaira*, p 637. In reality, however, because of the potential liability involved, banks have opted not to advise guarantors personally but to delegate this task to a solicitor.

ROLE OF THE SOLICITOR

5.1 INTRODUCTION

Although in *Barclays Bank plc v O'Brien* [1993] 4 All ER 417 (HL), Lord Browne-Wilkinson suggested that the bank itself was obliged to warn the wife at a private meeting (not attended by the husband) of the extent of her liability, the risks involved and the need to take independent legal advice, more recent case law, as we have seen, has placed greater emphasis on the role of the solicitor in advising the wife of the effects of the transaction. In *Massey v Midland Bank plc* [1995] 1 All ER 929 (CA), p 934, for example, Steyn LJ concluded that the *O'Brien* 'guidance ought not to be mechanically applied'. In *Royal Bank of Scotland v Etridge (No 2)* [1998] 4 All ER 705, the Court of Appeal concluded that it was enough if the bank has urged the wife to obtain independent legal advice before entering into the transaction, especially if the solicitor provides confirmation that: (1) he has explained the transaction to her; and (2) that she appeared to understand it. This accords with current lending practice and shifts the burden of advising the wife away from the lender in favour of the solicitor acting on her behalf. Most recently, the House of Lords, in *Royal Bank of Scotland v Etridge (No 2)* [2001] UKHL 44, has acknowledged that Lord Browne-Wilkinson's requirement of a private meeting was not intended to be prescriptive, accepting that lenders have been reluctant to assume the responsibility of advising the wife at such a meeting.

It was said in *Wright v Carter* [1903] 1 Ch 27 (CA), p 57, that a solicitor who is asked to advise a client who may be subject to undue influence 'takes upon himself no light nor easy task'. The nature of the duty has been described in another early case as 'a very delicate business': *Bainbrigge v Browne* (1881) 18 Ch D 188, p 198. Although, in most cases, independent legal advice will be crucial to absolving the lender from the taint of undue influence, this will not always be so. As Millett LJ observed in *Credit Lyonnais Bank Nederland NV v Burch* [1997] 1 All ER 144 (CA), p 156:

> Such advice is neither always necessary nor always sufficient. It is not a panacea. The result does not depend mechanically on the presence or absence of legal advice.

A similar view was expressed by Lord Nicholls in *Etridge (No 2)* (HL) (para 20):

> Proof of outside advice does not, of itself, necessarily show that the subsequent completion of the transaction was free from the exercise of undue influence. Whether it will be proper to infer that outside advice had an emancipating effect, so that the transaction was not brought about by the exercise of undue

influence, is a question of fact to be decided having regard to all the evidence in the case.

Much, as we shall see, will depend on the nature of the transaction and the relationship between the parties. What is evident is that the task of advising the wife 'carries a heavy responsibility': *Royal Bank of Scotland v Etridge (No 2)* [1998] 4 All ER 705 (CA), p 717, *per* Stuart-Smith LJ. This is because, in the majority of cases, the wife's only substantial asset (the matrimonial home) is being put at risk.

5.2 NATURE OF ADVICE TO BE GIVEN TO WIFE

In the Court of Appeal, in *Etridge (No 2)*, Stuart-Smith LJ alluded to the fact that, in many cases decided since *O'Brien*, the protection apparently afforded to wives by the requirement of independent legal advice had proved 'illusory'. In his view (p 711):

> The advice which the wife has received has often been perfunctory, limited to an explanation of the documents and yet inadequate to dispel her misunderstanding of the real extent of the liability which she was undertaking, and not directed to ensure that she was entering into the transaction of her own free will rather than as the result of illegitimate pressure from her husband or blind trust in him.

The 'perfunctory' nature of the advice often given under the current law was also highlighted by the House of Lords in *Etridge (No 2)*. In particular, it was stressed that such advice did not always adequately bring home to the wife the possible dangers of acting as surety for her husband's debts. The purpose, therefore, of seeking independent legal advice is to ensure that the wife enters the transaction after 'full, free and informed thought': *Zamet v Hyman* [1961] 1 WLR 1442 (CA), p 1446, *per* Lord Evershed MR. As Hobhouse LJ observed, in *Banco Exterior Internacional v Mann* [1995] 1 All ER 936 (CA), 'the problem is ... not lack of intelligence or education, but the lack of independence' (p 946). A full explanation will, thus, normally release the weaker party (usually the wife) from the undue influence of the dominant party.

In *Etridge (No 2)* (pp 715–17), the Court of Appeal, in order to dispel any misconceptions as to the purpose of providing independent legal advice, took the opportunity to set out comprehensive guidelines as to the nature of the duties of a solicitor when instructed to advise a person who may be the subject of undue influence. Although the guidance was specifically aimed at a wife who may be under the influence of her husband, it was apparent that the propositions therein stated were of general application. It will be convenient first to give a summary of the Court of Appeal guidelines and then see how these have been modified by the House of Lords' ruling in *Etridge (No 2)*:

1 According to the Court of Appeal, it was not enough that the wife understands the legal effect of the transaction and intends to enter into it: *Credit Lyonnais Bank Nederland NV v Burch* [1997] 1 All ER 144 (CA), p 156;

and *Naidoo v Naidu* (2000) *The Times*, 1 November. The point was addressed in *Powell v Powell* [1900] 1 Ch 243 (p 247), involving a parent and child, where Farwell J said that 'the solicitor does not discharge his duty by satisfying himself simply that the donor understands and wishes to carry out the particular transaction'. What he must also do is satisfy himself that 'the gift is one that it is right and proper for the donor to make under all the circumstances'. (See, also, *Wright v Carter* [1903] 1 Ch 27 (CA), pp 57–58, where Stirling LJ said: 'a solicitor would fail in his duty if he neglected to inform himself of the circumstances in which the transaction was taking place', and gave the example of a poor man divesting himself of all his property in favour of a solicitor.) This, in turn, required the solicitor to be fully informed of all the material facts: *Permanent Trustee Co of New South Wales Ltd v Bridgewater* [1936] 3 All ER 501 (PC), p 507; and *Inche Noriah v Shaik Allie Bin Omar* [1929] AC 127 (PC), pp 135–36. In *Bank of Scotland v Bennett* [1999] Lloyd's Rep Bank 145 (CA), p 162, for example, it was held that the bank was entitled to assume that the solicitor acting for the wife would not purport to advise her without first informing himself as to the financial position of her husband's company.

2 The solicitor's duty was to satisfy himself that his client was free from improper influence: *Burch*, p 156. The first step, therefore, was to discover whether the transaction was one which the wife could sensibly be advised to enter if free from such influence. If the answer was yes, he could safely advise his client to proceed. However, if the answer was no, his duty was to advise her not to enter into the transaction. In *Burch* itself, it was held that no competent solicitor would have advised the complainant to enter into a guarantee on the terms she did. Any such solicitor would be bound to have inquired of the reason why the bank required additional security. He would then have discovered that it was to enable the limit of her employer's overdraft to be increased from £250,000 to £270,000. Armed with that information, he would be bound to have advised his client that an unlimited guarantee was unnecessary. Moreover, if his client still felt obliged to accede to her employer's wishes, he could then have advised her that she should offer only a limited form of guarantee. If given such advice, the court concluded that the complainant would have chosen an alternative option which was less onerous to her while still meeting the bank's requirements.

3 If the solicitor was not satisfied that the transaction was one which his client should enter into, he should refuse to act further for his client in the implementation of the transaction if she persisted: *Powell v Powell* [1900] 1 Ch 243, p 247, *per* Farwell J. In this eventuality, he would be obliged to inform the other parties (including the bank) that he has seen his client and given her certain advice (thereby preserving the confidentiality of his advice) and that, as a result, he has declined to act for her any further. This

would then alert the lender that all is not well and prompt it to refuse to go ahead with the loan or, alternatively, renegotiate new terms which were more acceptable.

4 The solicitor must advise his client that she is under no obligation to enter into the transaction at all and, if she still wishes to do so, that she is not bound to accept the terms of any document which has been put before her. In *Bullock v Lloyds Bank Ltd* [1955] 1 Ch 317, p 326, Vaisey J said that the solicitor should explain 'first, that she could do exactly as she pleased and, secondly, that the scheme put before her was not one to be accepted or rejected out of hand but to be discussed, point by point, with a full understanding of the various alternative possibilities': see, also, *Willis v Barron* [1902] AC 271 (HL), p 281. The solicitor should also discover on her behalf, where appropriate, whether less onerous terms might be obtained from the lender: *Burch*, p 156. In this connection, he should not assume that the lender's offer is on a 'take it or leave it' basis, or that it has an impregnable negotiating position. In *Etridge (No 2)* (CA), Stuart-Smith LJ opined, in this context, that the wife's position may be relatively strong given that '(i) she is not obliged to give security (ii) any security is better than none and (iii) the bank cannot afford the risk of taking a security which it knows the wife's solicitor has advised her she should not give' (pp 715–16).

5 Where the bank is asking for a continuing 'all moneys' unlimited guarantee/charge, the solicitor will not discharge his duty to the wife by simply telling her that the liability is unlimited. What he must do is to 'bring home to her that she is being asked to undertake liability for the existing indebtedness (even though this was previously unsecured by her) as well as for future indebtedness to an unlimited extent, and not merely liability for the amount of the contemplated advance or increase in the overdraft': *Etridge (No 2)* (CA), p 715. He should also warn her that she will have no control over the extent of her liability because the bank will be entitled to advance further credit at any time without reference to her. As already mentioned above, he should discuss with her the possibility of alternatives (for example, giving only a limited guarantee/charge) and, if necessary, he should offer to negotiate with the bank on her behalf. It seems, therefore, that it is part of the solicitor's duty to point out that there may be more prudent courses of action: see *Permanent Trustees v Bridgewater* [1936] 3 All ER 501 (PC), p 507, where a mortgage was set aside because there 'was no bargaining or inquiry for a better market by anyone on the [complainant's] behalf'.

6 How far the solicitor should probe into the matter in order to satisfy himself that his client is able to make a free and informed decision is a matter of professional judgment and will depend on all the circumstances of the case: *Massey v Midland Bank plc* [1995] 1 All ER 929 (CA), p 934. In that case, the solicitor explained to his client the nature and extent of the

second charge, but gave no advice about the financial standing of her partner's proposed business. This fact was considered irrelevant by the Court of Appeal as the depth of the solicitor's investigation was 'a matter for the solicitor's professional judgment and a matter between himself and his client' (p 934). (See, further, Chandler, A, 'Undue influence and the function of independent advice' (1995) 111 LQR 551, who questions this approach on the ground that the advice given in *Massey* was, by its very nature, incomplete. In his view, citing Vaisey J in *Bullock v Lloyds Bank Ltd* [1955] Ch 317, p 326, the transaction could only stand 'if executed under the advice of a competent adviser capable of surveying the whole field with an absolutely independent outlook'.)

7 Good practice dictates that the solicitor should see his client (the surety) alone (that is, unattended by the debtor): *Massey v Midland Bank plc* [1995] 1 All ER 929 (CA), p 934. However, so long as the client receives independent legal advice, failure to hold a private interview, in the absence of the debtor, will not be fatal to the lender's case: *Massey*, p 935. Moreover, it will not matter that the debtor himself arranged for his own solicitors to advise the surety because the lender is entitled to assume that the solicitors will act honestly and give proper advice to their client: *Massey*, p 935.

8 It will also be a matter for the solicitor's professional judgment to decide whether he should himself advise the wife on the wisdom of the transaction or, alternatively, invite her to obtain other advice (for example, from an accountant). In exercising that judgment, it will usually be necessary for him to inform himself of: (1) the circumstances of the proposed transaction; (2) the amount of the existing indebtedness and new advance; (3) the reasons for the new advance or the bank's request for additional security; and (4) the stability of the marriage. In *Clark Boyce v Mouat* [1994] 1 AC 428 (PC), it was held that a solicitor is under no duty himself to advise on the wisdom of the transaction, but he may be liable for breach of contract to his client if he fails to advise her as surety to investigate the financial situation of the borrower. Lord Jauncey said (p 437): 'When a client in full command of his faculties and apparently aware of what he is doing seeks the assistance of a solicitor in the carrying out of a particular transaction, that solicitor is under no duty whether before or after accepting instructions to go beyond those instructions by proferring unsought advice on the wisdom of the transaction. To hold otherwise could impose intolerable burdens on solicitors.'

9 At the very least, the solicitor must warn his client that that by entering into the transaction she could be putting at risk the one substantial asset on which she could rely should the marriage fail: *Etridge (No 2)* (CA), p 717. In *Banco Exterior Internacional v Mann* [1995] 1 All ER 936 (CA), p 950, Sir Thomas Bingham said: 'It is an ordinary incident of a solicitor's duty to explain the obvious potential pitfalls of legal transactions to those about to take part in them, and there is no clear dividing line between

explanation and advice. If the certifying solicitor did his job with reasonable competence ... [the wife] would appreciate quite clearly that if the worst happened she could lose her rights in the house and that it was for her to decide whether she was willing to take that risk or not.' A solicitor will not, therefore, discharge his duty to the wife unless he identifies 'the risks and advise[s] how those risks can be reduced or avoided': *Northern Rock Building Society v Archer* (1998) 78 P & CR 65 (CA), p 79, *per* Chadwick LJ.

10   If the solicitor feels himself torn between conflicting duties to the wife and other interested parties for whom he is acting, then he should refuse to act for the wife and make way for another solicitor not subject to that conflict: *Banco Exterior Internacional v Mann* [1995] 1 All ER 936 (CA), p 950. (See, also, *Steeples v Lea* [1998] 1 FLR 138 (CA), p 150, where it was indicated that the transaction might have been saved had the solicitor suggested to the complainant that she should seek independent advice.)

It is apparent from the foregoing that, according to the Court of Appeal, the solicitor's duty when acting for the wife went beyond merely explaining the documentation to her and ensuring that she understood the nature of the transaction and wished to carry it out. The guidelines went further in requiring the solicitor to be satisfied that the transaction was one which the wife could sensibly be advised to enter into, if free from undue influence: see propositions 1 and 2, above. If the solicitor was not satisfied that this was the case, according to the Court of Appeal, he was obliged to advise her not to enter into it and to refuse to act further for her in the implementation of the transaction if she persisted: see proposition 3, above. According to Lord Nicholls, however, in the House of Lords in *Etridge (No 2)*, this went much too far: see, also, Lord Scott (paras 180–82). In his view, the observations of Farwell J in *Powell v Powell* [1900] 1 Ch 243 (p 247), referred to in proposition 1 above, 'should not be pressed unduly wide' and 'cannot be regarded as of general application in all cases where a solicitor is giving advice to a person who may have been subject to undue influence': *Etridge (No 2)* (HL), para 59. It was not for the solicitor to veto the transaction. If he considers the transaction is not in the wife's best interests, he should give her reasoned advice to that effect. At the end of the day, however, the decision whether to proceed or not is that of the client, not the solicitor. According to his Lordship, 'a wife is not precluded from entering into a financially unwise transaction if, for her own reasons, she wishes to do so': *Etridge (No 2)* (HL), para 61. This mirrors the approach taken in several of the earlier cases. In *Banco Exterior Internacional v Mann* [1995] 1 All ER 936 (CA), for example, Sir Thomas Bingham intimated that that there was no duty on a solicitor to advise his client not to sign. He said (p 950):

It was enough if she would receive such advice as to leave her in no doubt of her right to decide whether she was willing in all the circumstances to take a risk which had been explained to her.

Similarly, in *Re Coomber* [1911] 1 Ch 723, Moulton LJ said (pp 729–30):

> [The solicitor] is not bound to say 'I will advise you to do it', or 'if I were you I would do it', or 'if I were you I would not do it'. Nothing of that kind is necessary for competent and independent advice ... All that is necessary is that some independent person, free from any taint of the relationship ... should put clearly before the person what are the nature and consequences of the act. It is for adult persons of competent mind to decide whether they will do an act, and I do not think that independent and competent advice means independent and competent approval. It simply means that the advice shall be removed entirely from the suspected atmosphere; and that from the clear language of an independent mind, they should know precisely what they are doing.

The above passage was cited with approval by Lord Nicholls as accurately representing the extent of the solicitor's duty in the context of advising a surety wife. His Lordship did, however, recognise that there may be exceptional circumstances where 'it is glaringly obvious' that the wife is being 'grievously wronged' (para 62). In those circumstances, the solicitor should clearly decline to act further: *Wright v Carter* [1903] 1 Ch 27 (CA), pp 57–58; and *Powell v Powell* [1900] 1 Ch 243, p 247. Ultimately, the responsibilities of the solicitor who is advising the wife stem from his retainer. In this connection, the lender's concern is to receive confirmation from the solicitor that he has brought home to the wife the risks involved in the transaction. The content of the advice required from a solicitor before giving such confirmation sought by the bank will depend on the circumstances of the case. The following matters were regarded by his Lordship as 'the core minimum':

(a) the solicitor will need to explain to the wife the purpose for which he has become involved. He should explain that the bank may rely upon his involvement to counter any suggestion that the wife did not properly understand the implications of the transaction. He must also explain that he will need to obtain confirmation from the wife that she wishes him to act for her in the matter and to advise her on the legal and practical implications of the transaction;

(b) he will need to explain the nature of the documents and the practical consequences these will have for the wife if she signs them (for example, she could lose her home or be made bankrupt if her husband's business does not prosper);

(c) he will need to point out the seriousness of the risks involved. The wife should be told the purpose of the proposed facility, the amount and principal terms of the new facility and that the bank might increase the amount of the facility, or change its terms, or grant a new facility, without reference to her. She should be told the amount of her liability under the guarantee. He should discuss her financial means, including her understanding of the value of the property being charged. He should also discuss whether she, or her husband, has any other assets out of which repayment could be made if the husband's business fails;

(d) he must state clearly that the wife has a choice as to whether or not to proceed with the transaction. The decision is hers and hers alone. An explanation of the choice facing the wife will require some discussion of the present financial position, including the amount of the husband's present indebtedness and the amount of his current overdraft facility;

(e) he should check whether the wife wishes to proceed. She should be asked whether she is content that the solicitor should write to the bank confirming he has explained to her the nature of the documents and the practical implications they may have for her, or whether, for example, she would prefer him to negotiate with the bank on the terms of the transaction. The solicitor should not give any confirmation to the bank without the wife's authority.

Lord Scott also gave useful guidance as to what the solicitor's duty should be towards the wife (para 169):

(a) he should try to discover from the wife her understanding of the proposed transaction so as to remedy any possible misconceptions;

(b) he should explain to the wife the steps the bank might take to enforce its security;

(c) he should make sure the wife understands the extent of her liabilities under the security;

(d) he must explain the likely duration of the security;

(e) he must ascertain whether the wife is aware of any existing indebtedness that will, if she grants the security, be secured under it;

(f) he should explain to the wife that he may need to give the bank a written confirmation that he has advised her about the nature and effect of the proposed transaction and obtain her consent to his doing so.

His Lordship also alluded to the need for the solicitor to confirm with the bank that his instructions extend to advising her about the nature and effect of the transaction. This is because, in his Lordship's view, a lender was not entitled to assume, without more, that a solicitor's instructions necessarily extended to advising the wife on these matters: *Etridge (No 2)* (HL), para 168. However, once such confirmation had been obtained, the bank was entitled reasonably to believe that the solicitor will have advised her properly and that, accordingly, she has had an adequate explanation and understanding of the transaction: *Etridge (No 2)* (HL), para 171.

It was also intimated by Lord Hobhouse, in particular, that lenders should not require an unlimited guarantee and that a solicitor, acting for the wife, should advise her that any security should be subject to a stated monetary limit on her liability as surety: *Etridge (No 2)* (HL), para 112. In addition, it was stressed by the House of Lords that the meeting with the wife should take place in the absence of the husband and the solicitor's explanations should be couched in non-technical language. Above all, the solicitor's task should not be viewed as purely a formality or a charade.

A solicitor who fails to advise his client properly on the merits of a proposed mortgage transaction may be liable in tort and in breach of his contractual duty to his client. Although the duties owed by a solicitor are high, the courts do not require him to go beyond the scope of what he is requested and undertakes to do. The test is always what the reasonably competent practitioner would do having regard to the standards normally adopted in his profession. His duty is directly related to the confines of his retainer: *Midland Bank Trust Co Ltd v Hett, Stubbs & Kemp* [1979] 1 Ch 384, p 403, *per* Oliver J. The standard of care owed was set out by Lord Hailsham in *Inche Noriah v Shaik Allie Bin Omar* [1929] AC 127 (PC), in the following terms (pp 135–36):

> [The advice] must be given with a knowledge of all relevant circumstances and must be such as a competent and honest adviser would give if acting solely in the interests of the donor.

One commentator has suggested that this formulation places a greater burden on the solicitor in not only explaining the nature and effect of the transaction but also 'an assessment of the viability of the transaction and whether it is in the surety's interest to sign': Wong, S, 'No man can serve two masters: independent legal advice and solicitor's duty of confidentiality' [1998] Conv 457, p 460. This, as we have seen, was considered to be a matter for the solicitor's professional judgment in the Court of Appeal in *Etridge (No 2)*: see proposition 8, above.

Wong, however, has argued that this does not go far enough and that the purpose of independent advice is to protect the surety against, what he calls, 'advantage-taking'. This, in his view, can only be achieved if the surety is given advice which covers, not only a full understanding of the terms of the transaction and the risks in giving the security, but also the viability of the transaction: Wong, p 462; and see, also, O'Hagan, P, 'Legal advice and undue influence: advice for lawyers' (1996) 47 NILQ 74, p 77. As Wong recognises, if a solicitor is to advise on the wisdom of the transaction, he must have sufficient information to advise the surety and 'the contention that [he] may act for two parties becomes harder to sustain' (p 462). At the very least, the solicitor must be informed of the extent of the husband's borrowings and his current facility in order properly to assess the extent of his client's potential liability. But, this may lead to problems of confidentiality if the information is obtained whilst the solicitor is also acting for the lender or husband (borrower). As Wong says (p 463):

> The conflicting duties of confidentiality and disclosure ultimately results in the solicitor resolving the issue by offering mere technical legal advice to the surety, rather than partisan advice on the viability of the transaction. His conflicting duty of confidentiality will form an effective barrier to his giving such partisan advice.

He has argued that, even if the necessary consent to the disclosure of such information is obtained from the lender/borrower, this does not resolve the problem since the consent 'does not eradicate the existing conflict between the parties' respective interests and the solicitor's need to balance those interests in terms of his advice to each client': Wong, p 464. Despite consent, therefore, the solicitor will still be tempted to limit his advice to 'mere technical advice' or avoid any conflict of interest by simply refusing to act further for the wife. Another reason for this, of course, is that the solicitor may not have sufficient expertise to give detailed financial advice of the kind required from say, an accountant or business adviser. The point has been made by Fehlberg, another academic writer, who states:

> Even if truly independent advice is sought, solicitors are unlikely to view themselves as being in a position to provide financial or accounting advice to sureties, due to their lack of appropriate qualifications and their lack of information about the business for which the security is provided. As a general rule, solicitors are likely to confine themselves to providing a basic explanation of the legal terms of the document and a warning to the wife that she could lose everything, including her home.

(See Fehlberg, B, 'The husband, the bank, the wife and her signature – the sequel' (1996) 59 MLR 675, p 688.)

It is interesting to observe that some of these concerns have now been addressed by the House of Lords in *Etridge (No 2)*. As we have seen, the solicitor's duty to the wife is now largely confined to explaining the documentation and ensuring that she understands the nature of the transaction and wishes to carry it out. To this end, however, the House of Lords has recognised that the solicitor should obtain any information he needs from the lender and, if the latter fails to provide it, he should decline to provide the requisite confirmation sought by the bank. In this connection, Lord Nicholls considered that it should become 'routine practice' for lenders to send to the solicitor the necessary financial information (that is, regarding the purpose of the loan, the current amount of the husband's indebtedness, the amount of his current overdraft facility and the amount and terms of any new loan): *Etridge (No 2)* (HL), para 79. If the bank's request for security arises from a written application by the husband, the bank should send a copy of that application to the solicitor. The consent of the bank's customer (the husband) will be required for this purpose and, if this is not forthcoming, the transaction will not be able to proceed: see, also, *Etridge (No 2)* (HL), para 114, *per* Lord Hobhouse and paras 189–90, *per* Lord Scott, who also suggested that the husband's proposal that the wife stand as surety for his debts would constitute an implied authority to the bank to disclose details to the wife. Indeed, if the husband refuses to give his consent to give out information, this will, no doubt, be a clear indication to the bank and the solicitor 'that something may be amiss' and that it ought not to rely on the wife being bound by the transaction: para 114, *per* Lord Hobhouse. Alternatively, in these circumstances, the bank may need to insist that the wife receive legal advice from a solicitor independent of her husband: para 190, *per* Lord Scott.

If, exceptionally, the bank believes or suspects that the wife has been misled by her husband (or is not entering into the transaction of her own free will), it must inform the wife's solicitor of the relevant facts. This guidance is applicable to future transactions (that is, post-*Etridge (No 2)*) and is intended to ensure that a solicitor does not give a certificate to the lender unless it conforms to the reality. So far as *past* transactions are concerned, the bank will ordinarily be regarded as having discharged its obligations if a solicitor, acting for the wife, gave the bank confirmation to the effect that he had brought home to the wife the risks she was running acting as surety for her husband's debts.

It will be apparent that, at the forefront of their Lordships' minds in *Etridge (No 2)* has been the need to provide clear and practical guidance to both lenders (see Chapter 4) and solicitors involved in residential mortgage transactions where a wife is being asked to stand surety for her husband's indebtedness. In particular, Lord Nicholls' scheme (see Chapter 4, para 4.4.4) whereby a wife will be put into a proper relationship with a solicitor, who is acting for her and accepts appropriate duties towards her, is likely to do much to reduce the hitherto 'fiction of free and informed consent' apparent in many of the earlier cases. In the words of Lord Hobhouse (para 116):

> ... an essential feature of the scheme is that the wife has to be aware of what is going on, that the bank is asking for the certificate and why, that she is being asked to instruct a solicitor to advise her and that she is being asked to authorise the solicitor to provide the certificate. This is a far cry from the situation which has been tolerated in the past where the wife has not appreciated that she had any solicitor or was being advised and did not know of the existence of the certificate or its significance.

The approach taken by the House of Lords also has the benefit of not imposing any greater burden on lenders than hitherto required under *O'Brien*, yet, at the same time, being entirely consistent with the duties of the solicitor towards both the lender and the surety wife.

A good illustration of the differing views expressed by the Court of Appeal and House of Lords on the question of the extent of a solicitor's duty towards a surety wife for which he is acting is to be found in the case of *Kenyon-Brown v Desmond Banks & Co* [2000] Lloyd's Rep Bank 80, one of the conjoined appeals heard by the House of Lords together with *Etridge (No 2)*. In that case, the solicitor had acted for the husband on many occasions. He also acted for both husband and wife on the purchase of a holiday home and also the matrimonial home, both of which had been purchased with the aid of a mortgage. The husband decided to repurchase the controlling interest in his company. In order to raise the money, he and his wife granted a second mortgage over their family home. She had been opposed to the repurchase, but had been persuaded by her husband to go ahead. Before the mortgage was executed, the lending bank required an assurance that the wife had received legal advice. Such advice was given by the parties' solicitor, who stated in his attendance note that the wife had decided to proceed because she trusted her husband. However, he failed to discover that she had been overborne by her husband when agreeing to the proposed repurchase. The bank later required further security and a second mortgage was taken out over the holiday home. Again, the solicitor was asked for confirmation that legal advice had been given to the wife. This time, he saw both the husband and wife, and advised on the second mortgage. He recorded that the wife was happy to consent to the mortgage, that she appeared to understand it fully and that she seemed totally unconcerned that the transaction would solely benefit her husband.

The Court of Appeal held that the solicitor had been negligent in failing to recognise the risk of undue influence (in view of his knowledge of the trust placed by the wife in her husband at the time of the second mortgage) and also in failing to decline to act further and advise the wife to seek alternative advice. The court also concluded that he had failed to take into account a number of considerations which were vital to the evaluation of whether it made sense for the wife to enter into the mortgage and to make a balanced decision whether to do so, free of any undue influence by the husband. Mance LJ said (p 281):

> There was no suggestion, or likelihood ... that he had ascertained the amount outstanding, its origin and the circumstances in which it came to be outstanding, let alone the prospects of its repayment or of the additional security over the holiday home being called upon. Nor did he ask why [the wife] was willing to grant such additional security. Still less, therefore, did he know that her husband had told her that she would be bankrupted if she did not enter into the mortgage, nor did he elicit the fact that she did not consider the marriage to have any long term future, but wished, on the other hand, to avoid bringing it to an end until her son ... was older and to maintain a tolerable atmosphere at home in the meantime while she was living with her husband.

Significantly, the fact that the wife did not want comprehensive advice and appeared totally unconcerned about the warnings which the solicitor gave was not, in his Lordship's view, conclusive of the matter. Even though the wife was clear as to what she was doing by entering into the second mortgage and wanted to do so, this related to her understanding of and wish to enter into the mortgage, not to the issue of whether that wish was freely induced or was the result of undue influence. A solicitor's duty was to perform his retainer with reasonable care and, in the context of a residential mortgage transaction, that meant carrying out the duties indicated by the Court of Appeal in *Etridge (No 2)*. According to Mance LJ, therefore, in considering whether the solicitor should himself advise on the wisdom of the transaction or invite his client to obtain other financial advice, the solicitor was obliged to inform himself of a number of matters, including the circumstances of the proposed transaction, the amount of the existing indebtedness and new advance, the reasons for the new advance and the stability of the marriage.

Otherwise, according to his Lordship, there would be a 'gap' in the protection against undue influence available to a wife; the bank would be entitled to assume that a solicitor had considered and, where appropriate, negatived any risk of undue influence but the solicitor, on the other hand, would be entitled to accept his client's instructions not to go into the matter in any detail and yet confirm to the bank that he had given appropriate legal advice. A solicitor giving such confirmation to a bank did so in his capacity as solicitor for his client, namely, the wife. The solicitor's fault, therefore, in this case, lay not in confirming to the bank the giving of inappropriate advice, but the non-performance of his duties to his client.

By contrast, the House of Lords, as we have seen, concluded that the normal duty of a solicitor instructed to advise a surety wife is to explain the nature and effect of the loan documentation in order to try and make sure that the surety knows what she is doing rather than that she is free from undue influence. The particular circumstances of a case may add to (or reduce) the extent of the duty owed by the solicitor but, in the ordinary case, he will not have reason to suspect undue influence simply because he knows a wife has trust and confidence in her husband and is proposing to give a charge over her property to support his financial position: para 374, *per* Lord Scott. On the facts in *Kenyon-Brown*, therefore, the solicitor was entitled to treat the wife 'as a mature lady able to make up her own mind as to whether to allow her share in [the property] to become security for her husband's debts' (para 375). There was no obligation on him to make the sort of detailed inquiries referred to in the above-cited passage of Mance LJ. His only concern was to make sure that she understood the nature and effect of the document she was being asked to sign. Since this is what he had done, the appeal was allowed.

5.3 SOLICITOR ACTING FOR OTHER PARTIES

Acting also for lender

In some 'three party' cases (that is, involving a surety, borrower and lender), the solicitor will be acting for the wife alone. It may be, however, that in other three party cases, he will also be acting for the husband (debtor) and/or even the lender. In the Court of Appeal in *Etridge (No 2)*, it was stressed that, when giving advice to the wife, the solicitor is acting exclusively as her solicitor and that it made no difference that he was also the husband's solicitor or that he was acting as the bank's ministerial agent at completion of the transaction: *Etridge (No 2)* (CA), p 721. Even if he accepts the bank's instructions to advise the wife, he will still be acting as her solicitor when he interviews her. (Contrast the position where the solicitor is asked to advise in a 'two party' transaction: see Chapter 2, para 2.4.) In the words of Stuart-Smith LJ (p 721):

> Whoever introduces the solicitor to the wife and asks him to advise her, and whoever is responsible for his fees, the bank is entitled to expect the solicitor to regard himself as owing a duty to the wife alone when giving her advice.

However, where he is also instructed by the bank (other than in a purely ministerial capacity), there may be a real danger of a conflict of interest arising. In these circumstances, it has been acknowledged that the solicitor cannot provide the wife with independent advice and, even if he does, any knowledge acquired by him may well be imputed to the lender: see, further, Nield, S, 'Imputed notice' [2000] Conv 196, pp 203–04, who highlights the fact that 'the precise nature of the solicitors' instructions from each of the parties they represent ... becomes all-important'. Thus, where the solicitor's instructions to act on behalf of the bank go beyond a mere ministerial capacity, the solicitor should decline to act for the wife: *Etridge (No 2)* [1998] 4 All ER 705 (CA), p 716. In *Allied Irish Bank plc v Byrne* [1995] 2 FLR 325, for example, although the charge had been executed in the presence of a solicitor, the solicitor had been retained by the bank and had not been supplied with all relevant information. Ferris J held that the solicitor could not be regarded as independent and, since the bank had not advised the wife to take independent legal advice, the transaction could not stand. His Lordship said (p 353):

> The essential information which any adviser needed in order to protect Mrs Byrne was information concerning the amount and purpose and terms of the relevant facility or facilities. The bank had this information but did not pass it onto Mr Kidd ... Moreover, Mr Kidd was not in any relevant sense an independent solicitor ... He was the agent of the bank in addition to being the solicitor for Mrs Byrne.

The case highlights the potential difficulty of the same solicitor acting for both the wife and the lender, particularly where he does not have all the information necessary properly to advise the wife on the merits of entering into the transaction: see, also, *Bank Melli Iran v Samadi-Rad* [1995] 1 FCR 465, *per* Mr Robert Walker QC (sitting as a deputy judge of the High Court), reversed on appeal on different grounds: [1995] 3 FCR 735 (CA) who said that the advice should be independent of both the source of the potential influence and of any conflicting interest or duty to another client.

The point arose also in *National Westminster Bank plc v Breeds* [2001] Lloyd's Rep Bank 98. Here, the husband owned a business with his partner, which they operated through a limited company. Their solicitor was also the company secretary. The husband made a number of misleading representations to an officer of the company's bank in order to obtain continued funding for the company. He also made misrepresentations and applied pressure on his wife in order to induce her to grant the bank a mortgage over their house to secure the funding. The issue was whether the bank was entitled to rely on a statement by the solicitor that he had explained the transaction to her, when he was not only acting for both lender and borrower, but was also the company secretary and an active participant in its quest for finance and banking facilities. Lawrence Collins J held that the bank had constructive notice of the husband's misrepresentations and undue influence, even though the solicitor had certified that the wife had understood the nature of the charge. There was a strong probability of a conflict of interest and the solicitor could not possibly have given independent advice to the wife. His Lordship said (p 111):

> A solicitor should not act for two clients where there is a real risk of a conflict of interest between them. Independence includes the ability to advise, without fear, that the wife should not enter into the transaction, or that she should not accept the bank's terms without a fight.

The principle that emerges from this case is that, where there is an obvious potential for a conflict of interest, the bank is not entitled to assume that the solicitor had discharged his duty because it knows or ought to know that its assumption is false. (See, also, *Bank of Montreal v Stuart* [1911] AC 120 (PC), pp 137–39, where the solicitor acted not only for the bank, but also for the husband and was a director and shareholder of the company, which made it virtually impossible for him to act fairly towards the wife.) The view taken in *Breeds* is reflected in r 6 of the Solicitors' Practice Rules 1990, which expressly prohibits a solicitor from acting for both lender and borrower in a private mortgage transaction, unless there is no conflict of interest.

The House of Lords, in *Royal Bank of Scotland v Etridge (No 2)* [2001] UKHL 44, has essentially approved much of the foregoing reasoning. Lord Nicholls, for example, accepted that, in advising the wife, a solicitor is acting for her alone. He is concerned only with her interests despite the fact that he may also be acting for the husband and even the lender. As a corollary to this, knowledge of what passes between the solicitor and the wife cannot be imputed to the bank, since the solicitor is not acting as the bank's agent when he is advising the wife. Any knowledge the solicitor acquires from the wife will be confidential as between them. In the words of Lord Nicholls (para 77):

> [It] is central to this arrangement that in advising the wife the solicitor is acting for the wife and no one else. The bank does not have, and is intended not to have, any knowledge of or control over the advice the solicitor gives the wife. The solicitor is not accountable to the bank for the advice he gives to the wife. To impute to the bank knowledge of what passed between the solicitor and the wife would contradict this essential feature of the arrangement. The mere fact that, for its own purposes, the bank asked the solicitor to advise the wife does not make the solicitor the bank's agent in giving that advice.

Significantly, however, Lord Scott drew an important distinction between the case where the solicitor, as well as having instructions from the bank, is solicitor for the wife and the case where the solicitor's only instructions come from the bank and the bank is his only client. In the latter case, the solicitor does not become the wife's solicitor simply through his holding himself out unilaterally as her solicitor. In *Midland Bank plc v Wallace* (one of the conjoined appeals heard by the House of Lords in *Etridge (No 2)*), for example, the solicitor represented to the bank that he had advised the wife but, in fact, the solicitor had given no advice to her and she had no reason to regard him as acting for her. In those circumstances, the solicitor, according to Lord Scott, was acting for the bank alone and his knowledge that no one had given the wife any explanation or advice about the security could properly be attributed to the bank (para 179). Thus, where the solicitor is acting only for the bank and never becomes the solicitor for the wife, his knowledge of what had (or had not) taken place regarding advice to the wife can be imputed to the bank (para 180).

If the solicitor acts in breach of his professional obligation to the wife, her remedy will be against him and not against the bank. In this connection, it has already been suggested by various commentators that the combined effect of the *O'Brien* and *Etridge (No 2)* decisions has been to shift the onus of responsibility away from lenders towards that of solicitors advising the parties. Bridge, for example (see [1999] 58 CLJ 28, p 30) makes the pertinent remark:

> Instead, wives will sue their solicitors, less satisfactory in many ways for the wives as well as the solicitors. Raising the *O'Brien* defence saves the family home, at least in the short term, and frequently brings the bank to the negotiating table with offers of time and even compensatory payments. Suing the solicitor is a lengthy and expensive process, and it will not stop the bank.

Acting also for the debtor

It was recognised in the Court of Appeal in *Etridge (No 2)* that a transaction under which the wife is asked to guarantee her husband's indebtedness need not necessarily be to her disadvantage and, therefore, one into which she could not properly be advised to enter. In the words of Stuart-Smith LJ (p 716):

> If the marriage is secure and the indebtedness has been incurred by the business which provides the husband's livelihood and on which the prosperity of his wife and family depends, there may be no real conflict between the interests of the husband and the wife. In such a case it may not matter whether the business is carried on by the husband personally or through the medium of a small company; or whether the wife holds 50% or indeed any of the shares in the company. It may be a very difficult question in any particular case whether it is worth putting the roof over their heads at risk in order to continue to carry on the business. But if it is, then the transaction may be as much in the interest of the wife as of the husband; and if it is not, it may be as much against his interest as against hers.

The above passage clearly indicates that there may be no conflict of interest between the husband and wife, so that a solicitor may not be disqualified from acting for the wife merely because he is also acting for the husband in the same transaction. Here again, it will be a matter for the solicitor's professional judgment to decide whether he should proceed and act for both parties, or advise the wife to consult a separate solicitor. In *Clark Boyce v Mouat* [1994] 1 AC 428 (PC), the claimant mother agreed to mortgage her house to secure a loan to her son. She was unaware that the son's own solicitor had declined to act in the matter and was informed by a partner in the defendant firm of solicitors (who had agreed to act for both mother and son) that her position as mortgagor providing the security was substantially different from that of her son as recipient of the loan. He suggested that she ought to obtain independent legal advice, but she declined to do so. He also pointed out that she would lose her house if her son failed to meet the mortgage repayments. The Privy Council held that a solicitor could properly act in a transaction for two parties with conflicting interests provided that he had obtained the informed consent of both parties, which meant that each party knew that there was a conflict between himself and the other party which might result in the solicitor being disabled from disclosing his full knowledge of the transaction or from giving one party advice which conflicted with the interests of the other. Lord Jauncey said (p 436):

> In determining whether a solicitor has obtained informed consent to acting for parties with conflicting interests it is essential to determine precisely what services are required of him by the parties. In this case [the trial judge] was satisfied that Mrs Mouat was not concerned about the wisdom of the transaction and was merely [seeking] the service of the solicitor to ensure that the transaction [was] given proper and full effect by way of ascertaining questions of title and ensuring that by appropriate documentation the parties [achieved] what they [had] contracted for.

In this case, therefore, the claimant had required the defendants to do no more than carry out the mortgage transaction and explain its consequences. She had also been made aware of the consequences of mortgage default and had rejected independent legal advice. In those circumstances, the defendants were under no duty to provide unsought advice on the wisdom of entering into the transaction to a client in full command of her faculties. (Contrast *Northern Rock Building Society v Archer* (1998) 78 P & CR 65 (CA), where the solicitors were required to explain the risk of entering into the transaction.) Similarly, in *Bank of Baroda v Rayarel* [1995] 2 FLR 376 (CA), the execution of the charge was witnessed by the solicitor who had acted for the wife, the husband and their son in the preparation of the charge. The charge document contained a certificate to the effect that the chargors had been advised on the effect of the deed and acknowledging their right to independent legal advice. The Court of Appeal held that the bank was entitled to assume that each of the three defendants would be properly advised. In particular, that the solicitor would advise the wife of the importance of separate legal advice. The wife had signed a certificate, countersigned by the solicitor, to the effect that she had been given such advice. Here, again, it was stressed that the nature and extent of the solicitor's advice was not a matter for the lender, but a matter between solicitor and his client alone. In the words of Hoffman LJ (p 386):

> If there is a possibility of a conflict of interest between the surety and the other parties whom the solicitor is also advising, the bank is entitled to assume that the solicitor will have told her that she was entitled to take independent advice. The bank's legal department is not obliged to commit the professional discourtesy of communicating directly with the solicitor's client and tendering such advice itself. Nor is it obliged to inform the solicitor of his professional duties.

Significantly, the solicitors' guidelines dealing with conflicts of interest and confidentiality do not prohibit multiple representation in potential conflict situations provided that the consent of the parties is obtained: see the Law Society's *Guide to the Professional Conduct of Solicitors* (1993). See, further, Tobin, R, 'Intolerable burden or good conveyancing practice?' [1994] Conv 404. Similarly, the House of Lords in *Etridge (No 2)* recognised that, in practice, the solicitor advising the wife will be the solicitor acting also for her husband, either in the particular transaction or generally: para 69, *per* Lord Nicholls. Although his Lordship recognised that there were various factors favouring the need for a solicitor to act for the wife alone (for example, she may be inhibited in discussion with a solicitor who is also acting for the husband, particularly if she feels that her interests rank lower in the solicitor's scale of priorities than the interests of the husband), there were stronger reasons, on balance, for retaining the current practice. In particular, his Lordship stated (para 73):

> A requirement that a wife should receive advice from a solicitor acting solely for her will frequently add significantly to the legal costs. Sometimes a wife will be happier to be advised by a family solicitor known to her than by a complete stranger. Sometimes a solicitor who knows both husband and wife and their histories will be better placed to advise than a solicitor who is a complete stranger.

The upshot, therefore, of the House of Lords' ruling on this point is that, when a solicitor accepts instructions to advise the wife, he will assume responsibilities directly to her. He will be concerned solely with her interests but, if he feels that there is a real risk of a conflict of duty or that it would not be in her best interests for him to accept instructions from her, he must decline to act for her. Lord Scott, in particular, did allude to the difficulties inherent in a solicitor acting for both wife and debtor husband: '... it is, after all, the existence of the risk of undue influence or misrepresentation by the husband that requires the bank to be reasonably satisfied that the wife understands the nature and effect of the transaction': *Etridge (No 2)*, para 174. Accordingly, if there is some reason known to the bank for suspecting undue influence (or other impropriety) by the husband, the bank should insist on advice being given to the wife by a solicitor independent of the husband (para 174). In the ordinary case, however, his Lordship confirmed the view that:

> ... the bank is entitled to rely on the professional competence and propriety of the solicitor in providing proper and adequate advice to the wife notwithstanding that he, the solicitor, is acting also for the husband.

5.4 WHO CAN GIVE THE ADVICE TO THE WIFE?

The question as to who can properly give independent legal advice to the wife was canvassed recently in *Barclays Bank plc v Coleman* [2000] 1 All ER 385 (CA). The husband wanted to acquire a property as an investment and obtained a loan from the bank to fund the purchase. The loan was secured by a legal charge over the family home, owned jointly by the husband and his wife. The charge was an 'all moneys' charge, securing not only the funding of the property transaction, but also any future borrowings by the husband from the bank. The charge was executed by the parties in the presence of a legal executive, who returned the charge to the bank, together with a signed endorsement in which he confirmed that the contents of the charge had been explained to the wife, that she had understood them and that she had signed the document of her own free will. It was clear on the face of the endorsement that it had been signed by a legal executive rather than a solicitor. The Court of Appeal held that the bank did not have constructive notice of the wife's equity to have the charge set aside because it was entitled to rely on the legal executive's certificate. This was in accordance with the realities of a solicitor's practice, where the responsibility for dealing with such matters was frequently delegated to legal executives. Advice given by such persons was legal advice and there was no reason for holding it to be inadequate, provided that it was independent of the bank and given with the authority of the legal executive's principal. In particular, where a solicitor allowed his legal executive to give advice from his practice address, he necessarily held the legal executive out as having authority to do so.

The decision of the Court of Appeal on this point has been confirmed by the House of Lords: *Etridge (No 2)* [2001] UKHL 44. Lord Scott said (para 293):

> It would reasonably have appeared to the bank, from the typed endorsement on the legal charge, that Mrs Coleman had received advice from a legally qualified person acting for her, so as to enable her to understand the contents and effect of the document she was signing. The fact that the advice had been given by a legal executive and not by a qualified solicitor is not, in my opinion, material. An experienced legal executive in a firm with a conveyancing practice is well able to give full and adequate advice as to the contents and effect of a straightforward legal charge.

5.5 DUTY OF CARE TO LENDER

The duty of care owed by a solicitor acting for a lender in a mortgage transaction has been clarified in several recent cases. Here again, the solicitor may be acting for both lender and borrower and a potential conflict of interest may arise because he will owe a duty of confidentiality to each client, but the existence of this duty will not affect his duty to act in the best interests of the other client. In most cases where the solicitor acts for the lender, his instructions will normally require him to investigate title, prepare the necessary loan documentation, check and inform the lender of any discrepancies and report any matter affecting value. Normally, if the lender has asked the solicitor to advise the wife on the proposed loan transaction, it will also require the solicitor to provide confirmation that he has done so.

In the event that the confirmation is given negligently (and the wife succeeds in her *O'Brien* defence), the lender may have a good claim against the solicitor, either for breach of contract or in tort: see *Allied Finance & Investment Ltd v Haddow* [1983] NZLR 22 (duty of care owed where a certificate was given by a solicitor on which the lender was expected to act).

A solicitor is under an implied duty to inform the lender of any matters that a reasonably competent conveyancing solicitor would conclude might be relevant to the valuation of the property or some other aspect of the lender's decision whether to lend and, if so, how much. In *Mortgage Express Ltd v Bowerman & Partners* [1996] 1 EGLR 126 (CA), the solicitor was instructed to act for both the borrower and the lender in relation to the acquisition of a flat for £220,000 and the creation of a mortgage to secure a loan of £180,150. When instructed by the lender, the solicitor was sent a copy of the valuation of the flat in the sum of £199,000. The borrower's vendor was simultaneously acquiring the flat for £150,000 which was known to the solicitor, but he did not inform the lender. The borrower defaulted in his mortgage repayments and the lender repossessed the flat and sold it for £96,000. The parties agreed that, at the date of sale to the borrower, the value of the flat was £120,000, that had the lender been informed of the sale to the borrower's vendor at £150,000, it would have arranged a second valuation and that that valuation would have been sufficiently different from the first that the lender would have withdrawn the original mortgage offer. The Court of Appeal held that, where a solicitor acts for both purchaser and lender, and learns of information common to both, the question whether he should pass it on to one client or the other (or both or neither) depended entirely on the relevant interest of each client. In this case, the fact of the simultaneous sale at a figure £50,000 below the valuation relied on by the lender might have caused the lender to doubt the valuation and, accordingly, the solicitor should have informed it of this fact. In the course of his judgment, Sir Thomas Bingham said (pp 128–29):

> A client cannot expect a solicitor to undertake work he has not asked him to do, and will not wish to pay him for such work. But if, in the course of doing the work he is instructed to do, the solicitor comes into possession of information which is not confidential and which is clearly of potential significance to the client, I think that the client would reasonably expect the solicitor to pass it on and feel understandably aggrieved if he did not.

It is apparent, however, that the solicitor's duty to the lender does not extend to providing information regarding the strength of the borrower's covenant. In *National Home Loans Corp plc v Giffen Couch & Archer* [1997] 3 All ER 808 (CA), the lender offered a married couple a loan secured by a remortgage on the borrowers' property. The defendant solicitors agreed to act for both the lender and the borrowers and they were sent detailed (printed) instructions by the lender, which required them to investigate title to the property and advise if any condition of the offer of a loan had not been (or could not be) complied with. They were also required to report on title on the lender's form, which required them to certify that they were not aware of any material change in the borrowers' circumstances subsequent to the date of the offer and to conduct a bankruptcy search. However, there was no requirement to report on the state of the account on any existing mortgage. The solicitors became aware that there were substantial arrears on the existing mortgage in respect of which legal proceedings had been threatened, but they did not pass this information on to the lender.

The Court of Appeal held that, where a solicitor, in the course of acting for both the borrower and lender, discovered information casting doubt on the borrower's ability to repay the loan, he was not under a duty to report that information to the lender, unless his instructions specifically required him to do so. In the instant case, the information on the arrears and threat of legal proceedings did not relate to title, adequacy of security or any other matter on which the defendant was instructed to report or advise, and so the defendant was not in breach of duty in failing to pass that information on to the lender. The decision highlights the general rule that the extent of a solicitor's duty towards his client depends on the terms and limits of his retainer and any implied duty of care must be related to what he has been instructed to do: *Midland Bank Trust Co Ltd v Hett Stubbs & Kemp* [1979] Ch 384, p 402, *per* Oliver J; and *Carradine Properties Ltd v DJ Freeman & Co* (1962) SJ 157 (CA).

It has been held recently that the *Bowerman* reporting obligation will ordinarily be implied as between a solicitor (acting for a lender) and the lender unless it is inconsistent with the express terms of the solicitor's retainer, or with the surrounding circumstances of the relationship between the parties. This means, therefore, that, in addition to any express duties provided for by his instructions, a solicitor is obliged to report information obtained by him in the course of investigating title (or preparing for completion) which is not confidential and which a solicitor of ordinary competence would regard as information which might cause the lender to doubt the correctness of the valuation or the *bona fides* of the borrower.

In *Nationwide Building Society v Balmer Radmore* [1999] Lloyd's Rep PN 241, the claimant lender brought proceedings against various solicitors alleging breach of contract, negligence and breach of fiduciary duty regarding the conduct of numerous conveyancing transactions where the solicitors acted for both the lender and the borrower in connection with the advance of loans for the purpose of purchasing or remortgaging residential property. In each case, the borrower had defaulted and the claimant's security had proved deficient. All the cases exhibited one or more of the following features: (1) an excessive valuation of the security; (2) back to back or sub-sale arrangements involving the borrower and an intermediary vendor or vendors; (3) direct payments to the vendor; (4) late variations in the ostensible purchase price; and (5) use of the property otherwise than as the borrower's residence once the transaction had been completed. In several of the cases, the claimant was the victim of a 'sub-sale fraud' committed by the borrower involving a dishonest representation by the borrower as to the true purchase price of the property. The solicitors were alleged to have been in breach of duty in failing to disclose these matters to the claimant.

Blackburne J held that the solicitors' instructions had included 'reporting duties' which went beyond mere matters of title and ensuring that a proper security was obtained. In particular, these duties included reporting on matters bearing upon the value of the property, its prospective marketability (if and when the sale of the security had to be enforced) and whether or not the value of the security would be preserved pending its realisation. But, in addition to his express duties, the solicitor had an implied reporting duty to each of his clients, the extent of which was confined to matters within the scope of the respective client's interest and which was to be determined primarily by reference to the express terms and limits of the retainer. If the solicitor was in any doubt as to whether he was free to disclose any such matter because it might be confidential to the borrower, he ought to obtain the borrower's consent and, if that was not forthcoming in circumstances where the solicitor had a duty to the lender to report the information, then the solicitor's duty was to cease to act for one, if not both, of his clients.

On the facts, there was a duty to disclose information indicating that the borrower was intending to defraud the lender. There was also an express duty to report reductions in the price to be paid but, in any event, a solicitor who signed the claimant's report on title impliedly warranted that he had made those inquiries which a competent solicitor, acting reasonably would make in order to satisfy himself that the purchase price stated in the report was the true purchase price. The solicitor was also under a duty to report a sub-sale to the lender, in particular, where the property market was in decline and he was aware that the price of the earlier sale was the same or less than the proposed advance to the purchaser as such information might have caused the lender to doubt the correctness of its valuation. As to the existence of a direct payment to the vendor, a solicitor would normally require confirmation of this and, provided it was forthcoming, he would be entitled to rely on it and to continue to act without reporting adversely to the lender. If, however, circumstances indicated that he ought to take the view that the risk of fraud was such that he could not safely rely on that confirmation when informing the lender that the stated purchase price was indeed the purchase price, then he must disclose what he knows or cease to act. Significantly, Blackburne J distinguished the *Giffen Couch* case, referred to above, on the ground that there the scope of the lender's instructions to the solicitor regarding creditworthiness was far more limited.

As to the measure of loss for breach of contract or negligence, his Lordship identified three separate scenarios. First, where the lender would not have been willing to make the loan to the borrower, irrespective of the value and marketability of the security, the lender would be entitled (subject to mitigation and contributory negligence) to the entirety of its loss. (This was the finding in seven of the cases.) Secondly, where the lender would have made a lesser advance, the measure of loss would normally be the difference between what the lender had actually lost and what it would have lost had it lent the lesser amount, subject again to any issue of mitigation or contributory negligence. (This was the outcome in two of the cases.) Thirdly, if the lender would have proceeded in any event (regardless of the non-reporting of the information) on the same terms, then no loss would be incurred from the failure to provide that information. (This was the finding in one case.) Where, however, the allegation against the solicitor was couched in terms of a breach of fiduciary duty, different principles applied. In the first place, in order to make good a case of breach of fiduciary duty, the lender had to show that the solicitor was 'consciously disloyal' (that is, that his conduct was intentional): *Bristol & West Building Society v Mothew* [1998] Ch 1 (CA) (mere incompetence was not enough). Moreover, if a solicitor was found to be in breach of duty, he was then disabled from claiming that the loss recoverable by way of equitable compensation should be diminished on the basis that the lender had contributed to the loss flowing from the breach. As to causation where the breach was deliberate but not dishonest, the correct approach to equitable compensation was to assess what actual loss, applying common sense and fairness, had resulted from the breach having regard to the scope of the duty broken. In this connection, the lender is entitled to be placed in the position it was before the breach, as long as it can show that the breach caused the loss.

It has also been stressed recently that, in the absence of any agreement to the contrary, the normal standard of responsibility of a solicitor towards his lender client is to exercise reasonable skill and care. In *Midland Bank plc v Cox McQueen* [1999] 1 FLR 1002 (CA), the solicitor had been instructed by the lender to advise the wife and obtain her signature to the loan documentation. This was duly returned to the lender, apparently properly completed, with the wife's signature shown as being witnessed by a legal executive. It was later discovered that the documents had not been signed by the wife but by an impostor, who had been introduced by the husband to the legal executive as his wife. The lender then issued proceedings claiming damages against the solicitor arguing that his failure to obtain the wife's signature was in breach of his retainer. In this case, the obligation had not been to 'properly execute' the documents, but merely to obtain the signature of the husband and his wife and to certify (as opposed to undertake) that the wife understood the document and signed it of her own free will. The solicitor's obligation was, therefore, not an absolute one. If the lender had wanted to impose such an absolute obligation on a solicitor, this had to be done in the clearest terms so that the latter could appreciate the extent of the obligation he was accepting. (Contrast *Zwebner v Mortgage Corp* ((1998) unreported, 18 June (CA)) where the solicitor's retainer required him to 'properly execute' the loan documents.) Lord Woolf MR summarised the legal position in the following terms:

> The question is, did the bank intend to ask for and did the solicitors intend to give a promise to answer for the fraud of the customer even if that fraud could not be detected by exercising all proper care? In my view the answer to the question should be no, unless the language used compellingly indicates otherwise.

Where a lender sues its solicitor for having negligently given incorrect advice or for having negligently given incorrect information, it is sufficient for the lender to prove that it relied on the advice or information (that is, that it would not have acted as it did if it had not been given negligent advice or information). In *Bristol & West Building Society v Mothew* [1998] Ch 1 (CA), the defendant solicitor acted for a husband and wife in the purchase of a house and also for the claimant society to whom the purchasers had applied for a loan to finance the purchase. The society offered to advance the money but only on the express condition that the balance of the purchase price was provided by the purchasers without resort to further borrowing. It instructed its solicitor to report, prior to completion, any proposal that the purchasers might create a second mortgage, or otherwise borrow, in order to finance the rest of the purchase price. In fact, the solicitor knew that the purchasers were arranging for an existing bank debt to be secured by a second charge on the property, but, due to an oversight, he stated in his report to the claimant that the balance of the purchase price was being provided by the purchasers without resort to further borrowing. When the purchasers defaulted on the mortgage repayments, the claimant enforced its security and the house was sold at a loss.

The Court of Appeal held, *inter alia*, that the claimant had relied on the solicitor's report in advancing the loan and, therefore, that was enough to show the necessary link between the solicitor's negligence and the loan advance. The position would have been different had the lender sued the solicitor for having negligently failed to give proper advice. In that situation, the lender would need to show what advice should have been given and, if such advice had been given, that it would not have entered into the transaction or would not have entered into it on the terms it did. The same principle applies where the lender's complaint is that the solicitor failed in his duty to give material information. In *Mothew*, on the other hand, the solicitor did not merely fail to report the borrowing arrangements to the society; he expressly represented in his report that no such arrangements existed.

CHAPTER 6

REMEDIES

6.1 SETTING ASIDE THE TRANSACTION

The effect of a finding of undue influence (whether actual or presumed) is to render the transaction voidable, as opposed to void. Thus, a victim of undue influence is entitled to set the transaction aside as against the wrongdoer. As we have seen, the transaction may also be unenforceable as against a third party (for example, a lender) who has notice (actual or constructive) of the wrongdoing, or (less likely) where the wrongdoer acted as agent for the third party. In addition, it is evident that the right of rescission does not cease on the death of the claimant but may pass to his personal representatives: see *Mitchell v Homfray* (1881) 8 QBD 587 (CA), where, if the donor had been entitled when he died to have the gift set aside, his executors would have succeeded to his rights and obtained the relief sought.

The transaction will normally be rescinded in its entirety. In *Allied Irish Bank v Byrne* [1995] 2 FLR 325 (CA), the wife was induced to mortgage a house of which she was the sole owner as security for her husband's indebtedness by a false representation made by him that her liability was limited to £35,000. In reality, the charge was for an unlimited sum. Ferris J held that setting aside a charge was an 'all or nothing process' and, accordingly, the wife had the right to have the whole charge set aside as against her husband and that the bank had constructive notice of that right. His Lordship said (pp 354–55):

> It seems to me that setting aside must refer to setting aside in its entirety ... This is consistent with the fact that a party who complains of having entered into a transaction on the basis of a misrepresentation is saying that if he had been aware of the truth, he would not have entered into the transaction. If this claim is upheld, the court seeks to put that party into the position in which he would have been if the representation had not been made. This involves ascertaining what the position would have been if the transaction had not taken place. It does not involve reforming the transaction to accord with the representation.

The same conclusion was reached by the Court of Appeal, in *TSB Bank plc v Camfield* [1995] 1 All ER 951. Here, the husband was a partner in a motor vehicle leasing business. The bank provided the husband with an overdraft facility of £30,000 secured by a charge over the family home. His wife executed the charge, thereby charging her beneficial interest with an unlimited liability to meet the debts of the partnership. Her impression, however, fostered by an innocent misrepresentation by her husband, was that the maximum liability under the charge would be only £15,000. The bank lent

£30,000 to the partnership and subsequently made further advances. At first instance, the judge held that the wife was prepared to risk her interest in the house to the extent of £15,000 and, accordingly, entered judgment against the wife for that amount and ordered possession subject to payment of that figure within six months. The Court of Appeal, however, disagreed with this approach and concluded that the charge should be set aside in its entirety as against the wife. On the facts, the wife would not have entered into the charge if she had known its true nature and, since her ignorance of the true nature of the transaction resulted from the bank's failure to take reasonable steps to see that she was properly advised, there was no room for the charge to be partially set aside or set aside on terms that it was a valid security for the specified amount (that is, £15,000) for which the wife thought she was at risk. (See, also, *Bank Melli Iran v Samadi-Rad* [1995] 3 FCR 735 (CA), p 738, to the same effect.)

The rationale underlying the Court's reluctance in *Camfield* to permit a partial setting aside of the transaction was held to stem from the nature of the right to rescind itself. Thus, according to Roch LJ, such right is that of the representee, not that of the court. Although the court does have a discretion in some cases to refuse rescission and award damages in lieu thereof under s 2(2) of the Misrepresentation Act 1967, this does not convert rescission into an equitable remedy subject to the court's discretion. Consequently, the court's function is to decide whether the representee (usually the wife) has lawfully rescinded the transaction or is entitled to rescind it and not to grant equitable relief to which terms may be attached. According to his Lordship, such an analysis was consistent with the workings of s 1 of the Misrepresentation Act 1967, which implicitly recognises that the right to rescind for misrepresentation is that of the person to whom the misrepresentation has been made. But for s 2(2), the court does not have the power to declare the contract to be subsisting when the representee has already exercised the right to set aside the transaction: *Camfield*, p 960.

It is submitted, however, that much of this reasoning is open to question given that, in equity, the charge entered into with the bank would have to be cancelled, requiring the inevitable intervention of the court: see O'Sullivan, J, 'Undue influence and misrepresentation after *O'Brien*: making security secure', in Rose, Francis D (ed), *Restitution and Banking Law*, 1998, Oxford: Mansfield, pp 66–69. Moreover, it appears to be at odds with an analogous line of cases, in particular, *Bristol & West Building Society v Henning* [1985] 1 WLR 778 (CA) referred to by Ferguson: see Ferguson, P, 'Partial rescission for misrepresentation rejected' (1995) 111 LQR 555. She argues strongly that:

> In these cases, the claimant of a beneficial interest in a property purchased with the aid of a mortgage was held impliedly to have consented to the subordination of any beneficial interest to the rights of the mortgagee. The mortgagee's claim was in all cases upheld to the extent of the claimant's

understanding of the amount of the proposed mortgage; and in one case in which the mortgage advance was far beyond what the claimant believed would be raised, the mortgagee was nonetheless permitted to recover in full [see *Abbey National Building Society v Cann* [1991] 1 AC 56 (HL)]. The contrast with *Camfield*, in which the chargee received nothing at all, is striking.

In her view, although the wife in *Camfield* would not have executed the charge had she known that it was not limited to £15,000, nevertheless, 'it is also true that she *would* have done so if it *had* been limited to that amount': Ferguson, p 558. Applying the *Henning* doctrine, therefore, there was actual consent by the wife to the bank's priority up to that limit and 'a strong argument that she is estopped from claiming rescission except insofar as the liability exceeded the £15,000 she was – to the bank's knowledge – willing to risk': Ferguson, p 558. The better view, therefore, it is submitted, is that rescission is not 'an all or nothing process' (effectively providing the claimant wife with an unwarranted windfall), but that the court has power to set aside the transaction upon appropriate terms: see, further, Virgo, G, 'Undue influence and misrepresentation after *O'Brien*: making security secure – a commentary', in Rose, Francis D (ed), *Restitution and Banking Law*, 1998, pp 76–77. Indeed, this is the approach which has been accepted in Australia where the decision in *Camfield* has not been followed: *Vadasz v Pioneer Concrete (SA) Property Ltd* (1995) 184 CLR 102 (High Court of Australia).

The decision in *Camfield* was, however, applied in *Castle Phillips Finance v Piddington* (1995) 70 P & CR 592 (CA). Here, the wife executed a charge over the family home, of which she was the sole freehold owner, in favour of Lloyds Bank as security for a £1,000 loan to her husband and his overdraft facility of £1,700. A year later, she executed a further charge over the house in favour of Barclays Bank to secure, as she thought, a loan of £2,000 for roof repairs. In fact, the charge secured payment of all sums due to Barclays on all accounts of the husband. Barclays had already paid off the husband's debt to Lloyds (£3,114) and the Lloyds charge had been cancelled. The husband used the roof repair account for his own purposes and exceeded the limits on his other accounts. When Barclays called in the debts, the husband borrowed £15,000 from the claimant finance company, at an interest rate of 48% per year with the house as security, which was transferred into the joint names of the husband and wife. A friend of the husband impersonated the wife and forged her signature. Neither the wife nor the claimant had notice of the husband's fraud. The indebtedness to Barclays was cleared and the Barclays charge was cancelled. Eventually, the husband defaulted on the loan agreement and the claimant sought possession of the house. The Court of Appeal held that it was not possible to set aside the loan agreement in part, only on terms that a new equitable mortgage in a limited sum be created. Following *Camfield*, it had to be set aside *in toto*, but the effect of this was mitigated by subrogating the claimant to the Lloyds charge. This was because, when the claimant discharged the debt to Barclays, it became entitled only to the same security as

Barclays, namely, the Lloyds charge. Peter Gibson LJ, giving the leading judgment of the court, felt unable to draw any distinction between misrepresentation (alleged in *Camfield*) and undue influence in the case before him.

It is important to stress, however, that, in *Camfield*, the wife obtained no benefit from the loan transaction. There was nothing for the wife to give back and no cause for her to make restitution as a condition of granting relief: see, also, *MacKenzie v Royal Bank of Canada* [1934] AC 468 (PC), p 476. In cases, however, where the wife has received a benefit, the right to rescission has been held to be conditional upon her making *restitutio in integrum* or counter-restitution. In *Dunbar Bank plc v Nadeem* [1998] 3 All ER 876 (CA), the husband applied to the bank for further funds to purchase, jointly with his wife, a new leasehold of the matrimonial property of which he was at that time the sole lessee. The bank indicated that it would be prepared to lend up to £260,000 against the property, which was valued at £400,000. Eventually, the bank made the advance to the husband and wife which was secured by an 'all moneys' charge against the property under which the wife became liable, not only for her joint debts with the husband but also for his personal debts to the bank. One of the arguments raised by the bank in response to the wife's claim to have the charge set aside unconditionally as a result of her husband's undue influence (of which the bank had constructive notice) was that the transaction could not be set aside unless the wife accounted to the bank for the benefit she had received from the use of its money. In this connection, the joint leasehold in the property was purchased using £210,000 of the loan (the balance being used to clear the husband's outstanding personal arrears with the bank). The Court of Appeal agreed with the bank's contention holding that the wife was obliged to make restitution in respect of all that she had obtained from the transaction. This meant restoring, as a condition of rescission, the beneficial interest in the lease (and not a proportion of the debt secured by the legal charge).

A close analysis of the facts revealed that there were, in effect, two transactions in this case. First, there was an agreement made between the husband and wife whereby the former agreed that he would purchase for his wife a half interest in the property on terms that she join with him in charging the property. Under this agreement, she obtained a half interest in the equity of redemption subject to the bank's charge over the property. Secondly, there was the agreement between the couple and the bank whereby the wife obtained (jointly with her husband) an advance of £260,00, on the terms that £210,000 would be used for the specific purpose of acquiring a leasehold interest in the property. The extent, therefore, of her enrichment (in the event of the legal charge being set aside) was not the money which was advanced jointly to her and her husband, but the interest in the equity of redemption which she obtained by the use of the bank's money. In other words, it was not part of the bargain between the parties that there should be a several loan to the wife of any proportion of the joint loan of £260,000. Had that been the case, the appropriate form of restitution would have been repayment of that part of the loan available for her own use. In the instant case, however, the matter was further complicated by the fact that there was a subsequent valid charge over the property granted by the husband and wife in favour of another bank, which rendered it impossible for the wife to restore to her husband the unencumbered interest which she had obtained from him under the first agreement. Had she been able to do so, however, then her beneficial interest would have come within his charge to the bank with the result that the bank would have had a charge over the whole of the beneficial interest in the lease as security for the whole liability. In the words of Morritt LJ (pp 887–88), this would have produced a 'just result' because:

> The wife's personal liability would be extinguished in exchange for the removal of her beneficial interest, being the two consequences to her of the two transactions ... But the further consequence would be that the wife could have no defence to the claim of the bank made against her for possession of the property comprised in the lease and charged to the bank.

The *Nadeem* case suggests that 'benefit' in this context falls to be fairly narrowly construed as meaning 'something received directly under the contract to be set aside or one inextricably linked with it', as opposed to an indirect benefit such as that 'received by a wife through the successful operation of her husband's business for a period before the creditor sought to enforce the charge': *Chitty on Contracts*, Vol 1, 28th edn, 1999, London: Sweet & Maxwell, p 446, n 6.

A further illustration of the court's power to set aside a transaction on terms that the complainant make counter-restitution as a condition of relief is to be found in *Cheese v Thomas* [1994] 1 All ER 35 (CA). In this case, the claimant and the defendant (his great nephew) agreed to buy a house for £83,000 for the purpose of providing accommodation for the claimant for the remainder of his life. The claimant contributed £43,000 towards the purchase price and the defendant contributed £40,000, by means of a building society mortgage. The house was purchased in the defendant's sole name and it was agreed that the claimant would live there until his death and it would thereafter belong to the defendant. When the defendant failed to keep up the mortgage payments, the claimant brought proceedings seeking rescission of the transaction on the ground of undue influence and repayment of the £43,000. The trial judge ordered that the house should be sold and the proceeds of sale divided between the parties in the same proportions as they had contributed to the purchase price before the building society mortgage was repaid. The difficulty, however, was that the house was sold for only £55,000, resulting in a loss of over £27,000 on the purchase price. The claimant, therefore, argued that he should be entitled to recover the whole of the £43,000 paid to the defendant regardless of the fall in the value of the property. The Court of Appeal, however, disagreed, holding that the defendant should not be required to bear the whole of the loss brought about by the fall in market value and, accordingly, upheld the judge's order that each party should get back a proportionate share of the net proceeds of sale of the house and thereby shoulder the loss in value equally. Sir Donald Nicholls VC set out the governing principles in this way (pp 40, 41 and 42):

> If the transaction is set aside, the plaintiff also must return what he received. Each party must hand back what he obtained under the contract. There has to be a giving back and a taking back on both sides ... It is well established that a court of equity grants this type of relief even when it cannot restore the parties precisely to the state they were in before the contract. The court will grant relief whenever, by directing accounts and making allowances, it can do what is practically just ... As with the jurisdiction to grant relief, so with the precise form of the relief to be granted, equity as a court of conscience will look at all the circumstances and do what fairness requires.

In this case, the transaction could not be viewed simply as a payment of £43,000 by the claimant to the defendant in return for the right to live in the latter's house. If that had been the correct way to characterise the transaction, there would have been a 'strong case for ordering repayment of £43,000 ... regardless of the subsequent fall in the value of the house': *Cheese v Thomas*, p 40. In those circumstances, a straightforward return of the benefits received under the impugned transaction would have been appropriate: *Newbiggin v Adam* (1886) 34 Ch D 582 (CA), p 595, *per* Bowen LJ ('there ought ... to be a giving back and a taking back on both sides'). But, according to the Vice Chancellor, the transaction was not one of simple exchange, but, essentially, a joint venture involving the purchase of a property in which both parties would contribute and have rights. In this case, therefore, restoring the parties to their original positions meant selling the house and returning to each a proportionate share of the net proceeds at the date the transaction is set aside. Clearly, also, the Court of Appeal was prompted to reach this conclusion because of the absence of any wrongdoing by the defendant: see Chen-Wishart, M, 'Loss sharing, undue influence and manifest disadvantage' (1994) 110 LQR 173, p 176, who highlights that the defendant was characterised as an 'innocent fiduciary' in this case. In particular, the court concluded that it would be 'harsh' to require the defendant, who had been anxious to provide his great uncle with a home, to bear 'the whole of the loss flowing from the problems which have beset the residential property market for the last year or two': *Cheese*, p 43. (See, also, Dixon, M, 'Looking up a remedy for inequitable conduct' [1994] CLJ 232, for a critique of the decision.)

It has been emphasised academically, however, that the decision in *Cheese* is not an authority for loss apportionment. It should be viewed correctly as an example of a restitutionary claim for the value of the benefit conferred: Goff, R and Jones, G, *Law of Restitution*, 8th edn, 1988, London: Sweet & Maxwell, pp 366–67. This was, indeed, the approach taken in *Langton v Langton* [1995] 2 FLR 890, where the deputy judge, in setting aside a gift, considered whether it would be appropriate to 'compensate' the wrongdoer for any expenditure he had incurred in pursuance of the transaction as part of the process of restoring the *status quo* between the parties. In this connection, the defendants had sought to recover half of their expenditure in respect of the property since the execution of the deed of gift. This, however, fell to be balanced against the attendance allowance which the claimant gave to the defendants for looking after him since the date of the gift. The total of such payments was well in excess of the expenditure claimed by the defendants and, hence, the deputy judge held it would not be 'practically just' to make any payment to the defendants in respect of their expenditure on the property.

Where, as we have seen, *restitutio in integrum* is impossible, the court seeks to do what is practically just in all the circumstances and may order the complainant to make counter-restitution by means of a monetary equivalent. This gives the court considerable flexibility to rewrite the terms of the transaction and to permit a range of remedial devices to be used in balancing the interests of the parties. In *Midland Bank plc v Greene* [1994] 2 FLR 827, for example, the parties were the joint owners of their matrimonial home. They mortgaged the property to the bank with an 'all moneys' security provision. The major part of the borrowing was for the purpose of purchasing a leasehold interest, but the charge also secured any future debts of the husband. The parties later decided to improve the house and obtained from the bank a mortgage advance supported by the earlier security. In this case, it would have been inequitable for the wife to be able to avoid the mortgage without discharging the debts which she had incurred in order to procure her interest in the property. Moreover, the later loan supported by the same mortgage was held to be to the wife's advantage and was, therefore, not voidable, on the same basis as the earlier charge. The court, therefore, ordered the wife to pay a sum corresponding to the sums due on the home loan account established under the later mortgage as a condition of setting aside that transaction. (See, also, generally, *O'Sullivan v Management Agency and Music Ltd* [1985] 1 QB 428 (CA), referred to below.)

It should be borne in mind that the mere fact that the lender has treated the loan transaction as binding and has acted on it does not preclude the granting of relief: *MacKenzie v Royal Bank of Canada* [1934] AC 468 (PC), p 476. In other words, even though the transaction has been fully executed, this will not by itself bar rescission. It has also been held that the right to set aside a transaction for undue influence is assignable to a third party: *Dickinson v Burrell* (1866) LR 1 Eq 337.

It is also worth noting that the difficulties arising out of 'all moneys' security provisions are likely to be much diminished because, after 1 July 1997, a bank or building society is expected to comply with the Code of Banking Practice which prohibits unlimited guarantees or securities and requires lenders to advise proposed sureties of the limit of their liabilities.

6.2 SEVERANCE

Although the court will not partially set aside a charge affected by undue influence, it does have power to order severance of distinctly separate guarantees.

In *Barclays Bank plc v Caplan* [1998] 1 FLR 532, the bank agreed to grant an overdraft facility of £300,000 to the company of which the husband was a director. The facility was secured by the husband's personal guarantee supported by a charge over the jointly owned home of the husband and wife. This involved refinancing the existing charge over the house. A year later, the husband's borrowing was increased significantly and the debts of other companies were guaranteed at the same time. A side-letter to this effect was agreed and executed by the husband and wife, substantially extending their liabilities in respect of the husband's business interests. Significantly, the side-letter referred to two other distinctly identified guarantees and the sums guaranteed were not interdependent. Accordingly, it was held that they could be severed from the rest of the transaction with the result that the liabilities initially agreed with the bank could be enforced against the wife whilst the further liabilities (added a year later) could not. Mr Jonathan Sumption QC (sitting as a deputy judge of the High Court) explained the position thus (p 546):

> At common law, where an instrument contains legally objectionable features which are unenforceable against one party, they may be severed from the rest of the instrument if (i) the unenforceable feature is capable of being removed by the excision of words, without the necessity of adding to or modifying the wording of what remains, and (ii) its removal does not alter the character of the instrument or the balance of the rights and obligations contained in it.

Corresponding principles fall to be applied in the equitable context, especially as 'what the courts are concerned with is the enforceability, not of pieces of paper, but of covenants and dispositions in pieces of paper which may contain more than one': *Caplan*, p 546.

Significantly also, the deputy judge pointed out that, in many cases, the effect of severing part of a transaction will not differ significantly from exercising the court's power to set aside the transaction on terms as to making counter-restitution (see above). Moreover, it was stressed that the severance in the context of undue influence cases was likely to be rare since the finding of undue influence (or misrepresentation) inevitably vitiates the victim's consent. If there is no free consent, 'the courts will not normally construct for [the wife] a different transaction to which she would have consented': *Caplan*, p 546. This is apparent from cases such as *Byrne* and *Camfield*, referred to above. In *Byrne*, for example, if the charge had been enforced against the wife up to £35,000, the court would effectively be holding the wife to a rewritten contract. Similarly, in *Camfield*, to permit the bank to enforce the charge up to £15,000 (as understood by the wife) would have been to rewrite the transaction for the parties. Although in most cases, therefore, the setting aside of the charge is an 'all or nothing process', this may not always be the case where 'the objectionable features of the document can readily be severed from the rest without rewriting it': *Caplan*, p 546.

6.3 BARS TO RELIEF

As we have already seen, the gift or transaction which is liable to be set aside on the ground of undue influence is treated as voidable and not void. Hence, the right to rescind may be barred by affirmation, delay amounting to acquiescence, or estoppel.

In *Mitchell v Homfray* (1881) 8 QBD 587 (CA), for example, involving a gift made by a patient to her doctor, it was held that, after the confidential relationship had ceased, the donor had intentionally elected to abide by the gift and, accordingly, it could no longer be set aside after her death. The case illustrates the importance of the affirmation taking place after the influence has ceased: *Moxon v Payne* (1873) LR 8 Ch App 881, p 885, *per* James LJ. Moreover, it suggests that independent legal advice is not a necessary prerequisite of affirmation. In that case, the complainant had not received independent advice, but was nevertheless held to have confirmed the gift during her lifetime. It seems also that a positive act is not essential to show that the donor had elected to affirm the gift; all that is necessary is 'proof of a fixed, deliberate, and unbiased determination that the transaction should not be impeached': *Wright v Vanderplank* (1856) 8 De GM & G 133, p 147; 44 ER 340, p 345, *per* Turner LJ, involving a case of father and daughter.

It has been held recently that it is an abuse of process for a wife to seek a property adjustment order on the basis that a valid charge had been executed over the matrimonial home whilst, at the same time, defending possession proceedings brought by the lender on the ground of undue influence in respect of that charge. In *First National Bank plc v Walker* [2001] 1 FLR 505 (CA), the wife pursued her claim in ancillary relief proceedings on the basis of the validity of the charge secured on the family home, but, eight days later, defended the bank's possession proceedings on the basis that the mortgage was voidable on the ground of her husband's undue influence. It was inferred that the wife (or her solicitors) must have known prior to the ancillary proceedings that she would raise a defence of undue influence against the bank. In those circumstances, the Court of Appeal held that the wife had precluded herself from asserting against her husband that the charge was voidable because of his undue influence. In particular, it was pointed out that a spouse had to pursue her remedies in both the matrimonial and the possession proceedings consistently. In the words of Andrew Morritt VC (p 520):

> It is not acceptable to pursue a claim for ancillary relief on the footing that the charge is valid and to defend a claim for possession on the footing that it is

voidable, the more so as the bank will seldom know of the course of events in the matrimonial proceedings.

Delay (or laches) on the part of the complainant amounting to proof of acquiescence has been raised in a number of the early cases on undue influence: see, for example, *Turner v Collins* (1871) LR 7 Ch App 329 (seven years' delay). In some cases, laches is taken to mean undue delay on the claimant's part in prosecuting his claim and no more. More accurately, however, in the present context, it is used 'to mean acquiescence in its proper sense, which involves a standing by so as to induce the other party to believe that the wrong is assented to': *Goldsworthy v Brickell* [1987] 1 Ch 378 (CA), p 410, *per* Nourse LJ.

It is apparent, therefore, that lapse of time on its own will not constitute a bar to relief unless it provides evidence of acquiescence in circumstances where the complainant fails to take steps to rescind the transaction within a reasonable time after he (or she) is no longer subject to the undue influence: *Hatch v Hatch* (1804) 9 Ves 292, p 617; 32 ER 615, p 617; *Kempson v Ashbee* (1874) LR 10 Ch App 15, p 21; *Powell v Powell* [1900] 1 Ch 243, p 245; and *Re Pauling's Settlement Trusts* [1964] 1 Ch 303 (CA). In *Mutual Finance Ltd v Wetton & Sons Ltd* [1937] 2 KB 389, p 397, Porter J stated that the crucial date was the moment at which the undue influence had ceased to operate; in other words, the complainant was obliged to repudiate the transaction at that time or be held to the bargain. It is submitted that this *dictum* does not represent the trend of the authorities, which merely require that the victim of undue influence raise objection within a reasonable time. Of course, while the influence persists, the complainant will not be debarred from taking proceedings, no matter how long this is done after the transaction: *Hatch v Hatch* (1804) 9 Ves 292; 32 ER 615 (20 years, where a ward remained under the influence of her guardian for part of this time and then of her husband for the rest).

In *Allcard v Skinner* (1887) 36 Ch D 145, for example, involving a gift made by a novice to the mother superior of a convent, there was evidence that the former, when she left the convent, made no attempt to demand the return of her property until some six years later. Because of the delay in bringing an action, the Court of Appeal held that her claim based on undue influence was barred by laches and acquiescence since she left the sisterhood. Apart from lapse of time and inactivity, however, there was also conduct on her part amounting to confirmation of the gifts. Lindley LJ laid down the following proposition (p 187):

> A gift made in terms absolute and unconditional naturally leads the donee to regard it as his own; and the longer he is left under this impression the more difficult it is justly to deprive him of what he has naturally so regarded. So long as the relation between the donor and the donee which invalidates the gift lasts, so long is it necessary to hold that lapse of time affords no sufficient ground for refusing relief to the donor. But this necessity ceases when the relation itself comes to an end; and if the donor desires to have his gift declared

invalid and set aside, he ought, in my opinion, to seek relief within a reasonable time after the removal of the influence under which the gift was made. If he does not the inference is strong, and if the lapse of time is long the inference becomes inevitable and conclusive, that the donor is content not to call the gift in question, or, in other words, that he elects not to avoid it, or, what is the same thing in effect, that he ratifies and confirms it.

There can be no affirmation unless the victim of the undue influence knew (or ought to have known) of his (or her) right to rescind: *Bullock v Lloyds Bank Ltd* [1955] 1 Ch 317, pp 321–22 (where a delay of four years after the influence ceased and discovery of the remedy was held to be no bar); and *Re Pauling's Settlement Trusts* [1964] 1 Ch 303 (CA), p 353 (where the claimants could not be criticised for failing to realise what their rights were until they were advised that the advances made in that case might have been improper). In *Allcard*, on the other hand, the evidence suggested that the claimant was aware of her right to avoid the gifts at the time when she left the convent, but the majority of the Court of Appeal concluded that, even if that were not the case, it was enough that she was aware that she might have rights and deliberately determined not to inquire what they were or to act upon them. In this connection, it was apparent that she had been in touch with her brother, who was a barrister, and also a solicitor who remarked to her that the gift 'was too large a sum to leave behind without asking for it back', thereby clearly inviting her to consider her rights. As Lindley LJ observed (at p 188): 'Ignorance which is the result of deliberate choice is no ground for equitable relief nor is it an answer to an equitable defence based on laches or acquiescence.' More recently, however, it has been suggested that 'there is no hard and fast rule that ignorance of the right [to set aside] is a bar to the defence of acquiescence, but that the whole of the circumstances must be looked at to see whether it is just that the [complainant] should succeed': *Goldsworthy v Brickell* [1987] 1 All ER 853 (CA), p 873, *per* Nourse LJ, relying on the analogous case of a right to set aside a purchase by a trustee of trust property – see *Holder v Holder* [1968] 1 All ER 665 (CA) and *Re Pauling's Settlement Trusts* [1961] 1 All ER 713. Indeed, this approach was adopted by Nicholls J in *John v James* ((1985) unreported, 29 November), involving an undue influence claim. (See, also, *Lloyds Bank plc v Lucken*, heard with *Royal Bank of Scotland v Etridge (No 2)* [1998] 4 All ER 705 (CA), pp 748–51.)

The defence of estoppel has also been pleaded in undue influence cases. In *Allcard*, Bowen LJ referred to the principle of estoppel as a defence to a claim based on undue influence in the following terms (pp 191–92):

... if her delay has been so long as reasonably to induce the recipient to think, and to act upon the belief that the gift is to lie where it has been laid, then, by estoppel, it appears to me that the donor of the gift would be prevented from revoking it.

In *Goldsworthy v Brickell* [1987] 1 All ER 853 (CA), the defence of promissory estoppel was raised against a claim of undue influence relating to a tenancy agreement which an elderly farmer had been persuaded to sign by his neighbour who had been involved in the former's business and testamentary affairs. The tenancy agreement contained an option to purchase the farm on the farmer's death at a very advantageous price to the neighbour. All the elements of an undue influence claim were made out and the farmer's claim to have the tenancy agreement set aside was upheld, even though he had accepted rent from the neighbour under the agreement and had stood by whilst the latter expended a substantial sum in improving the farm. Promissory estoppel was held to require: (1) a clear and unequivocal representation (by words of conduct) that the claimant would not enforce his right to set the tenancy agreement aside; (2) that the representation was made with the knowledge or intention that it would be acted on by the defendant in the manner in which it was acted on; and (3) that the defendant, in reliance on the representation, acted to his detriment, or in some other way which would make it inequitable to allow the claimant to go back on his representation: *Goldsworthy*, pp 872–73, *per* Nourse LJ. In *Goldsworthy*, the requisite elements of representation and detriment were both lacking and, consequently, the plea of estoppel failed. On the issue of detriment, the payment of rent was no detriment because this was something that the neighbour would have to pay in any event as the price for occupation of the farm. As to the expenditure, this had been incurred prior to the date when any material representation by the farmer could have been made. The result, therefore, was that there was no bar to the tenancy agreement being set aside. (See, also, *Peyman v Lanjani* [1984] 3 All ER 703 (CA), pp 725–28.)

It is evident that if the victim of the undue influence is barred from having the transaction or gift set aside during his lifetime, his personal representatives cannot do so after his death: *Wright v Vanderplank* (1856) 8 De GM & G 133; 44 ER 340; and *Mitchell v Homfray* (1881) 8 QBD 587 (CA).

It seems that a party who has acted honestly but is, nevertheless, presumed to have exerted undue influence over another may be entitled to a defence of change of position in appropriate circumstances. The possibility of such a defence was alluded to in *Allcard v Skinner* (1887) 36 Ch D 145, where Lindley LJ said (p 186) that the claimant 'was entitled to invoke the aid of the court in order to obtain the restitution from the defendant of so much of the [claimant's] property as had not been spent in accordance with the wishes of the claimant, but remained in the hands of the defendant': see, also, Kekewich J, at first instance (p 164) and Cotton LJ (p 171). No doubt, a court applying the defence in the context of an undue influence claim would be guided by the principles laid down by the House of Lords in *Lipkin Gorman v Karpnale Ltd* [1991] 2 AC 548, where, in particular, Lord Goff stated (p 580) that a defence of change of position:

> ... is available to a person whose position has so changed that it would be inequitable in all the circumstances to require him to make restitution, or alternatively to make restitution in full.

His Lordship stressed, however, that the mere fact that the recipient had spent the money (wholly or in part) would not of itself trigger the defence; this was because the expenditure might have been incurred in any event in the ordinary course of things. The defence is also not available to a person who has changed his position in bad faith, for example, where the recipient has paid away the money with knowledge of the facts entitling the claimant to restitution. Clearly, it is also not open to a wrongdoer to raise the defence. It is apparent, therefore, that no such defence would be available to a person who has exercised *actual* undue influence on the complainant. Interestingly, however, it has been suggested that the defence could have been invoked in *Cheese v Thomas* [1994] 1 All ER 35 (CA), referred to above, in so far as 'while Mr Thomas was unjustly enriched to the extent of a £43,000 contribution to the purchase of the house, this enrichment has been reduced by the subsequent loss to the value of the house in the recession': Chen-Wishart, M, 'Loss sharing, undue influence and manifest disadvantage' (1994) 110 LQR 173, pp 177–78. In that case, it will be recalled, the defendant had acted entirely innocently and his personal conduct towards the claimant was not open to criticism by the court.

By way of completeness, it should, of course, also be mentioned that the remedy of rescission will not be available against a purchaser for value without notice of the facts giving rise to the claim of undue influence: *Cobbett v Brock* (1855) 20 Beav 524; 52 ER 706; *Bainbrigge v Browne* (1881) 18 Ch D 188, p 197, *per* Fry J; and *O'Sullivan v Management Agency Ltd* [1985] QB 428 (CA), pp 459–60, *per* Dunn LJ (where it was held that a recording company could keep music tapes acquired for consideration without knowledge of any undue influence). So far as gifts are concerned, however, the position is different. A third party donee will be obliged to restore the gift, however innocent he may have been in receiving it: *Bridgeman v Green* (1755) Wilm 58, pp 64–65; 97 ER 22, p 25, *per* Lord Wilmot who stated: 'let the hand receiving it be ever so chaste, yet, if it comes through a polluted channel, the obligation of restitution will follow it.' This, of course, is subject to any defence based on change of position, see above. (See, also, *Morley v Loughnan* [1893] 1 Ch 736, pp 757–58, *per* Wright J.)

As we saw in Chapter 4, notice for the purpose of rendering a third party liable may be actual, imputed or constructive. A lender is treated as having constructive notice of everything which a reasonably prudent person in his position would have discovered: s 199(1)(ii)(a) of the Law of Property Act 1925. Moreover, where the lender is put on inquiry as to the existence of another's rights, if he makes no inquiry he will be fixed with constructive notice of what he would have discovered had he made reasonable inquiry. But, if he has made reasonable inquiries, he will take free of the other's rights, if as a result of those inquiries any suspicions have been reasonably dispelled: *Woolwich plc v Gomm* (2000) 79 P & CR 61 (CA). The upshot is that a bank (or other lending institution) may rely on a defence closely resembling that of the *bona fide* purchaser defence applicable in the wider context of a third party who is a successor in title of the wrongdoer. But, in the present context, there is invariably no voidable transaction between husband and wife which is prior in time to the lender's security which is impugned by the undue influence. The charge is entered into by the wife directly with the bank; it is not executed with the husband and later given by him to the bank. Thus, in such cases, there is normally only one transaction, not two in competition with one another, so the question of 'clearing the title' (the function of the *bona fide* purchase defence) does not strictly arise for consideration. Instead, the lender is entitled to call in aid the doctrine of notice which, to all intents and purposes, has much the same effect: *Royal Bank of Scotland v Etridge (No 2)* [1998] 4 All ER 705 (CA), pp 717–18. (See, further, Chapter 4, para 4.3.)

6.4 ACCOUNT OF PROFITS

One of the remedies available to a victim of undue influence is an account of profits made from the transaction, subject to a reasonable allowance for work and expenditure incurred by the person exercising the influence.

Such an order was made in *O'Sullivan v Management Agency Ltd* [1985] QB 428 (CA). Here, a young singer, wholly inexperienced in business matters, entered into a series of management agreements with an internationally recognised manager and producer of popular music. The agreements were signed by the singer without obtaining or being advised by the manager to seek independent legal advice. It was apparent that there was a fiduciary relationship between the manager and the singer and, accordingly, the agreements were held to be obtained by undue influence. The issue was what remedy was available to the singer, since neither party could now be restored to their original position because all the agreements had been performed. The Court of Appeal concluded that, where *restitutio in integrum* was no longer possible, the court had jurisdiction to make such orders as were practically just between the parties. In the instant case, it was just to order the agreements to be set aside and to order the manager to account for his profits, subject to credit being given for his skill and labour in promoting the singer and making a significant contribution to his success. This meant that the manager was entitled to a reasonable remuneration including a small profit element, but one that was considerably less than he would have received had the singer obtained legal advice before entering into the agreements. (Whether a profit element would be awarded today is unlikely in view of the subsequent House of Lords' decision in *Guiness plc v Saunders* [1990] 2 AC 663.) Dunn LJ stated the relevant principle in the following terms (p 458):

> ... the principle of *restitutio in integrum* is not applied with its full vigour in equity in relation to transactions entered into by persons in breach of a fiduciary relationship, and that such transactions may be set aside even though it is impossible to place the parties precisely in the position in which they were

before, provided that the court can achieve practical justice between the parties by obliging the wrongdoer to give up his profits and advantages, while at the same time compensating him for any work that he has actually performed pursuant to the transaction.

The principle that the doctrine of *restitutio in integrum* is not to be applied too literally in the context of equity applies equally to cases of *abuse* of fiduciary relationship as it does to cases involving misrepresentation and breach of fiduciary relationship: *O'Sullivan*, p 466, *per* Fox LJ. Thus, if, for example, a person is persuaded by undue influence to make a gift of a house to another and that other spends money on improving it, there is no reason why credit could not be given for the improvements. The court simply does what is 'practically just' as between the parties, even though they cannot be restored to their original position.

6.5 DAMAGES IN LIEU OF RESCISSION

It is apparent from the judgments in *TSB Bank plc v Camfield* [1995] 1 All ER 951 (CA), that the wife may be entitled to damages in lieu of rescission under s 2(2) of the Misrepresentation Act 1967 in circumstances where it would be appropriate to declare the transaction subsisting between herself and the bank. In *Camfield* itself, an award of damages under s 2(2) was dismissed by Roch LJ as being an 'empty remedy' on the ground that 'the loss to [the wife] by upholding the legal charge in exchange for an award of damages against her husband would have far outweighed the loss that rescission would cause to [the husband]': *Camfield*, p 960.

It seems, however, that the lender (as opposed to the misrepresentor husband) cannot invoke s 2(2) directly as against the wife. This is because the 1967 Act does not expressly concern itself with the effect of a misrepresentation on a third party. As between misrepresentee (wife) and third party (bank), the law remains that prior to 1967. The result, of course, is anomalous in that the innocent lender may find itself in a potentially worse position than the wrongdoer: *Camfield*, p 956, *per* Nourse LJ.

6.6 EQUITABLE COMPENSATION

Although, as we have seen, the normal remedy in undue influence cases is for the transaction to be set aside in its entirety (if necessary on terms), the court does also have jurisdiction to award equitable compensation to the claimant where the parties cannot be restored to their former respective positions and the party who exerted the influence did not retain any profits from the transaction. Accordingly, this is a separate and distinct remedy from ordering an account of profits (see para 6.4, above).

The leading authority, albeit at first instance, is *Mahoney v Purnell* [1996] 3 All ER 61. In this case, the claimant operated a hotel business in partnership with his son-in-law. The business was incorporated as a company and each party held approximately 50% of the shares. The son-in-law indicated that he wanted to run the hotel on his own and began negotiations with the claimant with a view to buying out his shares in the company. Eventually, the parties agreed a price of £200,000, but the company accountant proposed a scheme of annual payments to the claimant of £20,000 over 10 years, which effectively valued the claimant's shares at only £64,000, together with an advanced repayment of his loan account with the company. The claimant agreed to the scheme without seeking independent legal advice. Later, the son-in-law sold the hotel for £3.27 m and the claimant, arguing that he had been induced to enter into the scheme by the son-in-law's undue influence, sought rescission of the transaction and equitable relief consisting of a money judgment, either directly, or in the taking of an account. Since the hotel had been sold and the company was now in liquidation (with some £80,000 still outstanding under the scheme in favour of the claimant), it was apparent that the claimant could no longer recover his shares in the company. It was held, therefore, that the claimant was entitled to compensation in equity equal to the value of what he had surrendered under the scheme with appropriate credit being given for what he had already received. The more usual remedy in such circumstances of the taking of an account of profits, advocated in the earlier case of *O'Sullivan v Management Agency and Music Ltd* [1985] 1 QB 428 (CA), see para 6.4, above, was considered by May J to be inappropriate given that, in the instant case, the company was in liquidation and there was no quantifiable profit remaining in the hands of the son-in-law personally. According to his Lordship, therefore (p 89):

> ... where [the taking of an account] will not achieve practical justice, an analogous permissible route to that end may be to balance the value which the plaintiff surrendered against any value which he has received and to award him the difference. That is not, I think, to award him damages, but fair compensation in equity as an adjunct to setting aside the agreement.

Significantly, he rejected the traditional view that equity did not permit an award of compensation in the nature of damages other than by the application of s 2 of the Chancery Amendment Act 1858 (damages in lieu of an injunction) or s 2(2) of the Misrepresentation Act 1967 (damages instead of rescission for misrepresentation). Instead, he relied heavily on the House of Lords' decision in *Nocton v Lord Ashburton* [1914] AC 392, where relief in the form of equitable compensation (other than by means of an account) was held to be founded on the breach of a fiduciary duty. In that case, the claimant sought to be indemnified against loss which he had sustained by having been improperly advised by his solicitor to release part of a mortgage security, whereby the security became insufficient. Compensation, therefore, was awarded on the basis of a breach of duty arising from the fiduciary relationship between solicitor and client. In *Mahoney*, May J considered the requirement of a breach of fiduciary duty as essential to found a claim for equitable compensation and concluded that, in the case before him, the relationship between the claimant and his son-in-law (from which undue influence was to be presumed) was 'based upon trust and may be described as fiduciary': *Mahoney*, pp 90–91. In his view, although the claim was not conventionally framed in the language of breach of duty, nevertheless, the ground for relief was founded on abuse of trust. Moreover, any difference between an abuse (as opposed to a breach) of trust was, according to May J, 'semantic only' and, accordingly, in his view, compensation in equity was available where the transaction is set aside for undue influence as well as for breach of a fiduciary duty. In the words of McLachlin J, in the Supreme Court of Canada in *Canson Enterprises Ltd v Boughton & Co* (1991) 85 DLR (4d) 129, p 163, relied on by May J in the *Mahoney* case (p 163):

> ... compensation is an equitable monetary remedy which is available when the equitable remedies of restitution and account are not appropriate. By analogy with restitution, it attempts to restore to the plaintiff what has been lost as a result of the breach, ie, the plaintiff's lost opportunity.

Another case in which equitable compensation was awarded in the context of a breach of fiduciary duty consisting in the exercise of undue influence is the New Zealand case of *Coleman v Myers* [1977] 2 NZLR 255. Significantly here, Cooke J viewed the facts of the case as being closely analogous to undue influence (p 332). The problem, however, as we have seen, is that not all cases of undue influence necessarily involve a breach of fiduciary obligation. To what extent, therefore, does the remedy of equitable compensation extend (if at all) to transactions entered into by a wrongdoer who is not a fiduciary, but to whom the presumption of undue influence is applied in a class 2B case? Interestingly, Heydon cites the Australian case of *United States Surgical Corp v Hospital Products International Property Ltd* [1982] 2 NSWLR 766 as authority that 'equitable compensation is available outside the fiduciary field': Heydon, JD, 'Equitable compensation for undue influence' (1997) 113 LQR 8, p 10. He refers, in particular, to the judgment of McLelland J (p 816), who described the court's power to grant relief as being 'by way of monetary compensation for breach of fiduciary or other equitable obligation'.

Significantly, also, in *Mahoney*, May J was not prepared to make any distinction as between class 2B undue influence cases and those where there was a recognised fiduciary relationship existing between the parties. On this latter point, some judicial doubt exists as to whether equitable compensation is available in every case of undue influence or only those in which there is an equivalent fiduciary relationship of say, solicitor and client or trustee and beneficiary. In particular, in *Bank of Credit and Commerce International SA v Aboody* [1992] 4 All ER 955 (CA), Slade LJ considered such cases to be different from normal cases of undue influence and stated that much of the confusion in the law might have been avoided if certain of the earlier decisions (for example, *Tate v Williamson* (1866) LR 2 Ch App 55 and *Rhodes v Bate* (1866) LR 1 Ch App 252) 'had drawn a clear distinction between the rather different principles applicable in the two classes of case': *Aboody*, p 973. The point is also made in Goff, R and Jones, G, *Law of Restitution*, 8th edn, 1988, London: Sweet & Maxwell, p 369, where the learned authors state that not every breach of confidence or trust necessarily falls to be characterised as a breach of fiduciary duty. One solution to this difficulty is to treat equitable compensation as a broader mechanism allowing for pecuniary restitution of unjust enrichment in all cases of undue influence. This permits rescission to take place, even though the property under the transaction can no longer be returned, on the basis that restitution can be effected in the form of a money equivalent. This is the view taken in an influential article by Birks, who argues that the phrase 'equitable compensation' is a misnomer, because undue influence is not a wrong and, therefore, an award of damages (or its equitable equivalent) is not appropriate in this context: Birks, P, 'Unjust factors and wrongs: pecuniary rescission for undue influence' [1977] RLR 72. In his view, undue influence is merely an 'unjust factor' which triggers a right to restitution which may be effected in money where rescission of the transaction has been prevented because the property can no longer be returned *in specie*: Birk, p 78.

Birks' premise, however, that undue influence is not a wrong may be questioned, given that a person who exercises actual undue influence must be acting wrongfully. As we saw in Chapter 2, para 2.2, the underlying rationale is that 'no one shall be allowed to retain any benefit arising from his own fraud or wrongful act': *Allcard v Skinner* (1887) 36 Ch D 145, p 171, *per* Cotton LJ. More recently, in *CIBC Mortgages plc v Pitt* [1993] 4 All ER 433 (HL), p 439, Lord Browne-Wilkinson defined actual undue influence as 'a species of fraud'. It seems difficult, therefore, to reconcile Birks's view that actual undue influence is merely an unjust factor as opposed to a civil wrong. There are difficulties also, it is submitted, in accepting Birks's assertion that presumed undue influence can be assimilated with innocent misrepresentation and non-disclosure: see Goff, R and Jones, G, *Law of Restitution*, 8th edn, 1988, p 369, n 12, citing *Great Pacific Investments Property Ltd v Australian National Industries Ltd* (1996) 39 NSWLR 143.

6.7 PROPRIETARY REMEDIES

It may be possible for the victim of undue influence to pursue an equitable tracing claim against the recipient of the money or property, provided he is able to show the existence of an initial fiduciary relationship between himself and the wrongdoer. As mentioned above, not all relationships falling within the presumed undue influence category will necessarily be fiduciary in the strict sense. Moreover, a prerequisite to a tracing claim is the need to show that the party unduly influenced has retained an equitable title to the property or, at least, that title is revested in him on the rescission of the transaction induced by the undue influence.

The requirement of a breach of a fiduciary obligation as a prerequisite to an equitable tracing claim has, however, been judicially relaxed. In *Chase Manhattan Bank NA v Israel-British Bank (London)* [1979] 3 All ER 1025, Goulding J held that, where money was paid under a mistake of fact, the receipt of such money, without more, constituted the recipient a trustee. Thus, the payer retained an equitable interest in the funds and the conscience of the recipient was subject to a fiduciary duty to respect that proprietary interest.

If such a claim is made out, the claimant will be entitled to follow the property (or its product) in the hands of the defendant: see, further, Goff, R and Jones, G, *Law of Restitution*, 8th edn, 1988, p 375.

CHAPTER 7

LENDER'S BACKDOOR TACTICS

7.1 INTRODUCTION

In the landmark cases of *Barclays Bank plc v O'Brien* [1994] 1 AC 180 and *Royal Bank of Scotland v Etridge (No 2)* [2001] UKHL 44, the House of Lords clarified the circumstances in which a lender will be put on inquiry as to the circumstances giving rise to a presumption of undue influence and, if it is, the steps it should reasonably take to satisfy itself that the wife's consent to act as surety was properly obtained. The so called '*O'Brien* defence', as we have seen, has enabled many wives to resile from the mortgage transaction in circumstances where the lender has failed to rebut the presumption of undue influence by proof that the charge was executed as a result of her free will, usually as a result of her having received independent legal advice.

The recent Court of Appeal decision in *Alliance & Leicester plc v Slayford* [2000] EGCS 113 has, however, highlighted a means by which the lender may successfully circumvent the *O'Brien* defence so as to force a sale of the matrimonial home, notwithstanding the wife's equity arising from her husband's undue influence. This chapter focuses on the practical implications of the Court of Appeal ruling.

7.2 SUING ON THE BORROWER'S PERSONAL COVENANT

A lender has a number of remedies available to it designed to enforce payment of the mortgage debt, which may be pursued either concurrently, as soon as the mortgagor is in default, or successively, until payment is recovered: *UCB Bank plc v Chandler* (1999) 79 P & CR 270 (CA); and see, generally, Cooper, S, 'Creditor's remedies against the family home' (1995) JBL 384, pp 388–90. Possession of the mortgaged property is, of course, normally sought initially, the lender acting as a secured creditor under the legal charge. But there is nothing to prevent the mortgagee from electing to sue the mortgagor on his personal covenant and obtaining a money judgment, thereby abandoning his security and acting as an unsecured creditor in any future bankruptcy proceedings. Indeed, the Court of Appeal, in *Alliance & Leicester plc v Slayford* [2000] EGCS 113, recognised this as an 'entirely sensible' practice in many cases.

It is necessary to set out the facts of this case in some detail. In November 1987, the claimant bank lent £20,000 to Mr Slayford on the security of his house in Halstead, Essex, to enable him to purchase his first wife's interest in the property. It was a condition of the loan that the property was in Mr Slayford's sole name. His partner, Mrs Slayford, who was not yet married to him, but was also in occupation of the property, agreed in writing that the rights she had, or might acquire, in the property would be subject to the rights, interests and remedies of the bank as mortgagee. She also undertook not to assert against the bank any right or interest over the property. A month later, Mr Slayford charged to the bank the entire legal and beneficial interest in the property as security for all moneys owing by him to the bank. The legal charge contained the usual personal covenant to repay the loan (and interest thereon) by monthly instalments. Subsequently, five further advances were made to Mr Slayford by the bank (between 1988 and 1989) increasing the mortgage loan to a total of £36,700.

In 1991, Mr Slayford became unemployed and fell into arrears with the mortgage instalments and the bank commenced proceedings, but claiming only possession of the property. The county court judge held that Mrs Slayford had an equitable interest in the house (by virtue of her capital contributions) and that Mr Slayford had misled her over the consent which she had signed and that she had not received independent legal advice before signing the consent, which was to her disadvantage. Accordingly, he held that her interest was not postponed to the bank's legal charge and refused the application for possession against her.

In 1998, the bank obtained leave to amend its particulars of claim to seek a money judgment against Mr Slayford in respect of the substantial arrears owing under the charge. Mr and Mrs Slayford then applied for the amended pleadings to be struck out as an abuse of process. The county court judge allowed the application, concluding that the pursuit by the bank of a money claim against Mr Slayford, with a view to bankrupting him and thereby obliging Mrs Slayford to relinquish the property, was an impermissible attempt to achieve by the back door what could not be achieved by the front door, and that it flouted the refusal to grant the order for possession. He, accordingly, struck out the bank's amended particulars of claim.

The Court of Appeal (Peter Gibson, Mummery and Latham LJJ) held that the judge had fallen into error. It was not an abuse of process for a bank, which had been met with a successful *O'Brien*-type defence taken by the wife of the mortgagor, to choose to pursue its remedies against the mortgagor by suing on the personal covenant, with a view, as an unsecured creditor, to bankrupting him. The crux of the Court of Appeal's reasoning lies in the recognition that the enforcement of a money judgment against Mr Slayford (as debtor) would not directly affect his wife, since her equitable interest in the property would either be left untouched or, if Mr Slayford were to be made bankrupt and the trustee in bankruptcy were to seek a sale of the property, she would not be deprived of any defences available to her by virtue of her interest.

The point arose in the earlier case of *Zandfarid v BCCI* [1996] 1 WLR 1420, where the bank sought to obtain possession of the matrimonial home owned by the wife and husband. The wife raised the defence of undue influence and an order for possession was refused. The bank then served statutory demands on the husband and wife and petitioned for bankruptcy, giving up its security under the legal charge. The wife claimed that the bankruptcy proceedings were an abuse of process because the bank was seeking to circumvent the wife's equity in the home by obtaining an order for sale by the back door as an unsecured creditor. Jonathan Parker J rejected this argument on the ground that the wife would be in no worse position in facing an application for a sale of the property by a trustee in bankruptcy under s 30 of the Law of Property Act (LPA) 1925 (now s 14 of the Trusts of Land and Appointment of Trustees Act (TLATA) 1996), than in facing a similar application by a mortgagee as a secured creditor. His Lordship concluded that, in both cases, the interest of the creditors would prevail save in exceptional circumstances.

7.3 APPLYING FOR AN ORDER FOR SALE

The criteria to be applied to all applications by a trustee in bankruptcy under s 14 of the 1996 Act are currently set out in s 335A(2) of the Insolvency Act 1986 (inserted by Sched 3 to the TLATA 1996). These reflect the repealed provisions in s 336(3) of the Insolvency Act (IA) 1986 as they formerly applied to trustee in bankruptcy applications under s 30 of the LPA 1925. As in s 336(5), there is provision in s 335A(3) that, in the absence of exceptional circumstances, on an application a year after the property vests in a trustee in bankruptcy, the interests of the bankrupt's creditors outweigh all other considerations: see, also, *In Re Citro* [1991] Ch 142 (CA) (decided before s 336 of the IA 1986 was applicable to the facts of the case).

Although the Court of Appeal appears to have assumed in *Slayford* that a wife will not be prejudiced in raising her *O'Brien* defence, regardless of the nature of the proceedings brought by the lender (see, also, Jonathan Parker J in *Zandfarid* (p 1429): 'the balancing act which the court is required to undertake will be precisely the same'), it is evident that, in the majority of cases, this will not prevent the ultimate repossession of the mortgaged property. Success by the wife on her defence to the bank's possession proceedings will still leave the bank a secured creditor of the husband with a valid and enforceable charge over *his* interest in the property (though it would no longer have any claim against *her* interest in it). In these circumstances, it would still be open to the bank to enforce the charge against the husband's share and itself apply to the court for an order for sale under s 14 of the TLATA 1996 as a secured creditor with a legal (or equitable) charge. Alternatively, the bank could give up its security and bring bankruptcy proceedings against the husband (relying on the personal covenant as an unsecured creditor) with a view to the trustee applying for an order for sale. Whichever route is adopted by the bank, the exercise of the court's discretion when hearing the application under s 14 will be the same and governed, in the majority of cases, by the overriding (statutory) presumption that the interests of the bank should outweigh all other considerations: s 335A of the IA 1986, above.

The *O'Brien* defence, if established, will not give rise to any positive right in the wife beyond that of a mere defence which will prevent the charge being executed against her (as opposed to her husband). In other words, it will operate merely to put her in the position as if *she* had not executed the charge in the first place, but it will not, it is submitted, place her in any better position in regard to a claim for possession based on her husband's insolvency. In the words of Millett LJ, hearing the wife's application in *Zandfarid* for permission to appeal to the Court of Appeal: 'If she is evicted as a result of the bank's application under s 30 … she will be evicted … because, unhappily, she is married to a judgment debtor who cannot satisfy the judgment debt except out of the proceeds of sale of his interest in the property.'

Although, under s 335A(2) (formerly s 336(4) of the IA 1986), the court must have specific regard to the needs and financial resources of the bankrupt's spouse and the needs of any children in determining what order to make under a s 14 application, it must also consider the interests of the bankrupt's creditors, the conduct of the bankrupt's spouse, so far as contributing to the bankruptcy, and all the circumstances of the case, other than the needs of the bankrupt. As we have already seen, where the application is made after one year (from the vesting of the bankrupt's estate in the trustee), the court is to assume that the creditor's interests prevail over all such considerations, in the absence of exceptional circumstances: s 335A(3). In the majority of cases, therefore, the court will be bound to order a sale, thereby giving preference to the husband's creditors.

In all but one of the pre-1986 bankruptcy decisions relating to matrimonial homes (the exception being *Re Holliday* [1981] Ch 405 (CA)), it has been held that the interests of the husband's creditors should prevail over the interests of the wife and any children: see, further, Brown, D, 'Insolvency and the matrimonial home – the sins of the fathers: *In Re Citro (A Bankrupt)*' (1992) 55 MLR 284, pp 286–88. In *Re Citro* [1991] Ch 142 (CA), after a review of this earlier case law, Nourse LJ said (p 157):

> Where a spouse who has a beneficial interest in the matrimonial home has become bankrupt under debts that cannot be paid without the realisation of that interest the voice of the creditors will usually prevail over the voice of the other spouse and a sale of the property ordered within a short period. The voice of the other spouse will only prevail in exceptional circumstances.

The earlier cases referred to in *Re Citro* (see *Re A Debtor ex p the Trustee v Solomon* [1966] 3 All ER 255; *Boydell v Gillespie* (1970) 216 EG 1505; *Re Turner (A Bankrupt) ex p the Trustee of the Bankrupt v Turner* [1975] 1 All ER 5; *Re Densham*

(A Bankrupt) ex p the Trustee of the Bankrupt v Densham [1975] 3 All ER 726; *Re Bailey (A Bankrupt) ex p the Trustee of the Bankrupt v Bailey* [1977] 2 All ER 26; and *Re Lowrie (A Bankrupt)* [1981] 3 All ER 353) are, clearly, still material in interpreting the criteria under s 335A of the TLATA 1996. Indeed, the Law Commission in its Report (*Transfer of Land: Trusts of Land*, Law Comm, No 181 (1989)) recognised that there was considerable value in the existing body of law: Law Commission, para 12.9. In *Re Citro* itself, Nourse LJ explained that it was not uncommon for a wife (and children) to face eviction and be unable to buy a comparable home nearby (or elsewhere) and that this would be upsetting for the children's education. This would not, however, be enough to attract the court's sympathy. According to his Lordship (p 157):

> Such circumstances, while engendering a natural sympathy in all who hear of them, cannot be described as exceptional. They are the melancholy consequences of debt and improvidence with which every civilised society has been familiar.

Accordingly, sale of the various houses in *Re Citro* were postponed for no longer than six months. The decision was applied and followed in *Lloyds Bank plc v Byrne* [1993] 1 FLR 369, where the Court of Appeal, in a case where the application for sale (under s 30 of the LPA 1925) was made by the bank as chargee and not by a trustee in bankruptcy, reiterated that the voice of the bank must prevail over that of the wife in the absence of any exceptional circumstances. In that case, the bank was faced with an ever mounting debt which could only be satisfied by a sale of the matrimonial home, whilst still leaving the wife (and her debtor husband) with enough to rehouse themselves. Parker LJ said (p 375):

> In my judgment this is wholly a matter of discretion and there is no difference in principle between the case of a trustee in bankruptcy and that of a chargee.

Similarly, in *Barclays Bank plc v Hendricks* [1996] 1 FLR 258, the wife failed to show any exceptional circumstances because she was the owner of another house in the same area. In that case, the husband, who owed various sums to the claimant bank, was separated from his wife and left the matrimonial home (of which the wife was a co-owner) to move into another house owned by the wife alone. The bank obtained a charging order against the husband's interest in the first house and sought an order for sale, pursuant to s 30 of the LPA 1925. The wife asked the court to exercise its discretion to defer a sale until her children reached the age of 18 or finished full time education. She argued that, if she were forced to vacate her present home, she would have to compel her husband to leave the second house to make way for her, which might bring their present amicable arrangements to an end so that he would cease to make the mortgage repayments on the first house. Moreover, the children did not wish to leave their current home which was nearer to their school and friends. Laddie J rejected the wife's contention, holding that where there was a conflict between the chargee's interest in a family home and the interests of the innocent spouse, the interest of the chargee prevailed except in exceptional circumstances. In this case, the wife was in a comparatively favourable position. She had another house which she owned and moving her children would not even involve them changing schools. Although the accommodation would be less attractive than the current home (and more travelling would be involved), these were considered 'comparatively small' matters and not by any means exceptional: *Hendricks*, p 263. The fact that the bank would recover almost 20% of its debt was also considered relevant on this issue.

Moreover, any reliance that the wife might have placed on the contention that the house was held on trust for sale subject to a collateral purpose (that is, that it should be the spouses' matrimonial home) was invalidated because the collateral purpose had ended both by the husband's departure and because his interest as co-owner had been charged to the bank. (Contrast *Abbey National plc v Moss* [1994] 1 FLR 307 (CA), where the collateral purpose of the arrangement between Mrs Moss and her daughter was that the former could remain in occupation until she died. The Court of Appeal held that the collateral purpose had not been destroyed by the daughter's loss of her own beneficial interest in the house.) In deciding the length of the moratorium period, his Lordship said that sufficient time should be allowed to facilitate the wife's departure from the house without adding unnecessarily to the dislocation suffered by her and her children. In the instant case, this meant that the period should be 'as short as possible' in the circumstances and 'any period more than a few weeks should be avoided if it is likely to cause significant hardship to the chargee': *Hendricks*, p 264.

Although it has now been recognised that s 15 of the TLATA 1996 has changed the law on the way in which the court will exercise its power to order a sale at the suit of a *chargee* of the interest of one of the owners of the beneficial interest of the property, the position regarding cases where one of the co-owners is bankrupt remains unchanged under the new s 335A of the IA 1986: *Mortgage Corp v Shaire* [2001] 4 All ER 364. Thus, although now the court has greater flexibility (because the court is obliged to have regard to a number of factors), under s 15 of the TLATA 1996, as to how it exercises its jurisdiction on an application for an order for sale of land subject to a trust of land in cases where a co-owner has charged his interest, this is not so in cases involving an application for sale by a trustee in bankruptcy. Indeed, Neuberger J, in *Shaire*, emphasised that it was 'quite clear that Parliament now considers that a different approach is appropriate in the two cases' (p 378).

So in what circumstances will the wife's voice be heard in the present context? The case of *Re Holliday* [1981] Ch 405 appears to be the only reported bankruptcy decision prior to the TLATA 1996 in which a sale was not ordered. In that case, however, the bankruptcy petition had been presented by the husband himself as a tactical move to avoid a transfer of property order in favour of his wife, at a time when no creditors were pressing for payment and he was in a position (in the next year or so) to discharge his debts. (In fact, none of the creditors thought fit themselves to present a bankruptcy petition against the husband.) Not surprisingly, the circumstances were viewed as being exceptional, not least because no real hardship would be caused to creditors by postponing sale for a period of five years. Interestingly, Nourse LJ, in *Re Citro*, considered this to be the one 'special feature' of the case which distinguished it from the other bankruptcy cases. In his view, without that feature, the circumstances in *Re Holliday* would not have been treated as exceptional.

It is apparent also, from more recent authority, that the wife's illness may qualify as an exceptional circumstance. In *Judd v Brown* [1998] 2 FLR 360, the wife was undergoing a course of chemotherapy which was likely to continue for five to six months, and she claimed that her chances of recovery would be damaged by stress if the matrimonial home was sold. Harman J, refusing an order for sale, held that the wife's sudden and serious attack of ovarian cancer was an exceptional event and clearly distinguishable from problems such as organising substitute housing and rearranging children's schooling, which were foreseeable and long term conditions. Merely postponing the operation of an order for sale for eight months (suggested by the trustee in bankruptcy) was not appropriate because, at the end of that time, the wife's health problems might not have been resolved and she would still have the stress associated with an impending move.

Similarly, in *Re Ravel* [1998] 2 FLR 718, the wife had suffered for many years from paranoid schizophrenia, and although she was stable and living at home her doctor advised her that 'adverse life events' (for example, a move to a smaller property away from supportive friends and family) could cause a relapse in her condition. At first instance, the registrar accepted that the wife's illness was an exceptional circumstance, but ordered sale and possession of the family home postponed for only six months on the basis that such a period was sufficient time for the local authority to earmark suitable alternative accommodation for her. On appeal, Blackburne J held that the wife's circumstances justified a postponement of the order for sale for one year to enable suitable alternative accommodation to be found for her by the local authority. In his view, six months was insufficient time and postponement of the order for five years (as contended by the wife) would be too long for the creditors to wait for their money. The case is authority for the proposition that the wife's illness need not be sudden and short term to merit the exercise of the court's discretion in her favour. Indeed, Blackburne J opined that circumstances where a person who suffers from terminal cancer but whose life expectancy cannot be judged, and whose illness, therefore, could properly be described as long term and of indeterminate duration, could still be characterised as exceptional, justifying no order or, alternatively, a postponement of sale indefinitely. (Contrast *Bank of Ireland Home Mortgages Ltd v Bell* [2000] EGCS 151, where the Court of Appeal held that the wife's health could only be taken into account as a relevant consideration to the postponement of an order for sale, not as a reason for refusing sale.)

In *Claughton v Charalamabous* [1999] 1 FLR 740, the husband's trustee in bankruptcy sought an order for sale of the family home, which the wife resisted. The trial judge concluded that the wife's renal failure and chronic osteoarthritis, the latter imposing severe restrictions on her mobility, amounted to exceptional circumstances under s 335A of the TLATA 1996. He, therefore, suspended the order for possession indefinitely (in effect, so long as the wife should continue to live in the property), having regard also to the fact that the husband's creditors would receive nothing from the sale of the house of which the proceeds would be consumed in costs. Jonathan Parker J, on appeal, upheld the judge's order, stating that he was entitled to take the view that the wife's health and immobility, with her associated special housing needs and her reduced life expectancy, amounted to exceptional circumstances. His Lordship also held that the terms of the suspension order were essentially a matter for the discretion of the judge and that an appellate court would not normally interfere, unless it was clear that a judge had misdirected himself in law or erred in principle, which had not happened in this case. He also opined that it would be 'entirely inappropriate' to attempt to lay down guidelines as to what circumstances might be exceptional under s 335A when Parliament itself had not chosen to do so. He said (p 745):

> What is required of the court in applying s 335A(3) is, in effect, a value judgment. The court must look at all the circumstances and conclude whether or not they are exceptional. That process leaves, it seems to me, very little scope for the interference by an appellate court.

Reference may also be made to *Re Mott* [1987] CLY 212, where Hoffman J postponed sale until after the death of the bankrupt's mother, who was 70 years old, in poor health, and who had lived in the house for over 40 years. The evidence of her doctor was that she would deteriorate if she was forced to move from her home. His Lordship characterised the case as one of extreme hardship, especially as the son's creditors were largely the State in the form of the Inland Revenue and the Department of Health and Social Security.

It remains to be seen to what extent lending institutions adopt the practice of suing the husband debtor upon his personal covenant with a view to forcing a sale of the matrimonial home by his trustee in bankruptcy, notwithstanding the wife's equity arising from a successful *O'Brien* defence. What is evident is that the court's discretion to refuse (or postpone) sale is very limited in such cases and the lender will normally be able to achieve by the back door what it would not have been able to do by the front door, namely, force the wife to leave her home so as realise its security. Only in extreme cases, it is submitted, will the wife's voice prevail over that of the bank. As one commentator has noted:

> At the end of the day, it would seem that, despite the additional protection given to wives as a result of *O'Brien*, the end result may well be that the ultimate sale of the family home is postponed rather than averted.

(See Thompson, MP, 'The enforceability of mortgages' [1994] Conv 140, p 145.)

Quite different considerations, however, will apply if the wife has commenced divorce proceedings against her husband and is seeking a transfer of her husband's interest in the family home as part of her divorce settlement. Here, the court must strike a fair balance between the competing claims of the divorced wife and the husband's creditors and a postponed enforcement order may be the only way of achieving justice between the parties. In *Austin-Fell v Austin-Fell* [1990] 2 All ER 455, the bank obtained judgment against the husband for £7,900 in respect of his unpaid overdraft and secured a charging order attached to his half-share of the matrimonial home. The wife was granted leave to intervene in the action for the charging order in order to apply to discharge the order. At the same time, she had commenced divorce proceedings against her husband and applied for financial relief. The registrar, hearing both applications and exercising the unfettered discretion, conferred by both s 25(1) of the Matrimonial Causes Act 1973 and s 1(5) of the Charging Orders Act 1979, to have regard to 'all the circumstances of the case', set aside the charging order and directed the husband's half-share of the family home be transferred to the wife on the ground that the wife's claim to the home was overwhelming as against the husband and should prevail over a creditor's claim for security. Significantly, the value of the house was £75,000 and the equity in it was about £60,000. The bank's debt amounted to £11,000.

On appeal, Waite J held that where the equity was insufficient to enable a charging order in favour of the husband's creditor to be enforced immediately, while leaving sufficient funds available to provide adequate protection for the wife's accommodation, the court had to weigh the expectations of the creditor against the possible hardship to the wife which would be caused if a charging order were made. This approach was in preference to deciding which claim should have predominance to the exclusion of the other. In this case, a postponed enforcement order represented the fairest balance between the competing claims of the wife and the creditor: see, also, *Harman v Glencross* [1986] 1 All ER 545 (CA).

CHAPTER 8

UNDUE INFLUENCE AND UNCONSCIONABILITY

8.1 INTRODUCTION

In *Credit Lyonnais Bank Nederland NV v Burch* [1997] 1 All ER 144 (CA), Nourse LJ said (p 151):

> Equity's jurisdiction to relieve against [unconscionable] transactions, although more rarely exercised in modern times, is at least as venerable as its jurisdiction to relieve against those procured by undue influence.

To what extent would it be desirable to subsume the doctrine of undue influence under a wider notion of unconscionability? As we saw in Chapter 1, para 1.10, Lord Denning MR, in the well known case of *Lloyds Bank Ltd v Bundy* [1974] 3 All ER 757 (CA), attempted to bring together the law on duress, unconscionable bargains and undue influence under the one umbrella of 'inequality of bargaining power'. In his formulation, the concepts of unconscionability and exertion of excessive power or coercion by a stronger party over a weaker one were regarded as key elements. Unconscionability, however, as a unifying doctrine has found little support in this country on the ground that the need for a more general formulation of principle (such as that enunciated by Lord Denning in *Bundy*) is a matter for legislative reform rather than judicial development: see *National Westminster Bank plc v Morgan* [1985] 1 All ER 821 (HL), p 830, *per* Lord Scarman. More recently, however, in *Burch*, p 151, Nourse LJ appears to have accepted that unconscionable bargains and cases involving undue influence may come under the general heading of 'inequality of bargaining power', citing Balcombe LJ, in *Backhouse v Backhouse* [1978] 1 All ER 1158, p 1166. Also, in *Langton v Langton* [1995] 2 FLR 890, Mr AWH Charles QC (sitting as a deputy High Court judge) opined that the rationale underlying the doctrine of unconscionable bargains was closely linked to that behind a class 2B presumed undue influence relationship. He stated (p 908):

> ... it seems to me that the 'unconscionable bargain' cases which arise as to particular transactions with poor and ignorant people could, and should, now be treated on the basis of, or by analogy to, the undue influence cases as one of the relationships where in all the circumstances a presumption that the transaction was procured by undue or improper influence arises and therefore has to be justified by the purchaser.

In the deputy judge's view, what underlies equity in both the presumed undue influence and unconscionable bargain cases, 'is the identification of a relationship which gives rise to a presumption that the donor, or recipient, should have the onus of establishing the righteousness of the transaction': *Langton*, p 909.

It will be convenient to examine briefly the doctrine of unconscionable bargains under English law before considering developments in other Commonwealth jurisdictions.

8.2 UNCONSCIONABLE BARGAINS

The classic English formulation of this doctrine is to be found in the judgment of Kay J, in *Fry v Lane* (1888) 40 Ch D 312, p 322:

> The result of the decisions is that where a purchase is made from a poor and ignorant man at a considerable undervalue, the vendor having no independent advice, a Court of Equity will set aside the transaction ... The circumstances of poverty and ignorance of the vendor, and the absence of independent advice, throw upon the purchaser, when the transaction is impeached, the onus of proving ... that the purchase was 'fair, just and reasonable'.

It has been held that the modern equivalent of 'poor and ignorant' is 'a member of the lower income group ... less highly educated': *Cresswell v Potter* [1978] 1 WLR 255, p 257, *per* Megarry J. This broadening of the class of claimant eligible for relief has increased considerably the potential availability of the doctrine to a wider range of transactions where the terms are unconscionable and the victim did not receive independent legal advice. In *Boustany v Pigott* (1995) 69 P & CR 298, for example, the Privy Council was asked to consider whether, on the facts, a lease should be set aside on the grounds that it was an unconscionable bargain. In that case, Miss Pigott, who was 71, had been diagnosed as suffering from Parkinson's disease, but her intellect was considered normal. She leased to the appellant (Mrs Boustany) a property for a term of five years at a monthly rent of $833.33 with an option to renew the lease for a further period of five years at a rent to be agreed or fixed by an independent party. Subsequently, the responsibility for managing Miss Pigott's properties was taken over by her cousin, the respondent, who was an accountant. Whilst he was temporarily away, Mrs Boustany requested a lawyer to renew the lease at a rent of $1,000 per month, effective for 10 years and renewable at the same rent for a further 10 years. At a meeting with Miss Pigott, Mrs Boustany and her husband, the lawyer raised the disadvantageous nature of the proposed renewal. However, he executed a new lease incorporating the renewal terms at Miss Pigott's insistence. Later, Miss Pigott signed a power of attorney in favour of the respondent, who brought proceedings seeking a declaration that the new lease was unconscionable and an order that it be declared void. The Privy Council held that the trial judge had been fully entitled to infer that Mrs Boustany and her husband had prevailed upon Miss Pigott to agree to grant a lease on terms which they knew they could not extract from her cousin, the respondent, or anyone else.

Accordingly, the new lease was set aside. In the course of his speech, Lord Templeman expressed 'general agreement' with the following five propositions of law:

1   It is not sufficient to attract equity's jurisdiction to prove merely that a bargain is hard, unreasonable or foolish. It must be shown to be unconscionable, in the sense that 'one of the parties to it has imposed the objectionable terms in a morally reprehensible manner, that is to say, in a way which affects his conscience': *Multiservice Bookbinding Ltd v Marden* [1979] Ch 84, p 110, *per* Browne-Wilkinson J (contractual terms in a mortgage transaction, providing for repayments of capital or interest linked to the value of the Swiss franc, held not to be unconscionable).

2   The word 'unconscionable' relates not only to the terms of the bargain, but also to the behaviour of the stronger party, which must be characterised by some moral culpability or impropriety: *Alec Lobb (Garages) Ltd v Total Oil (Great Britain) Ltd* [1983] 1 WLR 87, pp 94–95, *per* Peter Millett QC (sitting as a deputy High Court judge). In this case, a transaction involving a lease and lease-back was held not to be harsh or unconscionable since, on the evidence, no unfair advantage had been taken by the defendants of the company's desperate financial position. Moreover, there was no element of undervalue in the price paid for the lease of the site as a tied site, nor could the mutual break clauses and the absolute prohibition on assignment in the underlease (which was in a standard form) be regarded as unconscionable, or even unreasonable.

3   Unequal bargaining power (or objectively unreasonable terms) provides no basis for equitable interference in the absence of unconscientious or extortionate abuse of power where exceptionally, 'it was not right that the strong should be allowed to push the weak to the wall': *Alec Lobb (Garages) Ltd v Total Oil (Great Britain) Ltd* [1985] 1 WLR 173, p 183 (CA), *per* Dillon LJ.

4   A contract cannot be set aside in equity as an unconscionable bargain against a party who is innocent of actual or constructive fraud. Even if the terms of the contract are 'unfair' in the sense that they are more favourable to one party than the other (that is, contractual imbalance), equity will not provide relief unless the purchaser is guilty of unconscionable conduct: *Hart v O'Connor* [1985] AC 1000, p 1017 (PC), *per* Lord Brightman (contract for sale of land).

5   It is necessary for the claimant who seeks relief to establish unconscionable conduct, namely, that 'unconscientious advantage has been taken of his disabling condition or circumstances': *Commercial Bank of Australia Ltd v Amadio* (1983) 151 CLR 447 (High Court of Australia), *per* Mason J.

(See, further, Bamforth, N, 'Unconscionability as a vitiating factor' [1995] LMCLQ 538, who considers the decision in *Boustany* at some length.)

The above principles reiterate that equity may set aside a transaction whenever unfair advantage is taken of a person who is poor, ignorant or weakminded, and that weakness is exploited in some morally culpable manner resulting in the transaction being not merely hard or improvident but oppressive, so as to shock the conscience of the court. In *Backhouse v Backhouse* [1978] 1 All ER 1158, the wife, in the course of divorce proceedings, executed a deed transferring her interest in the matrimonial home to her husband without seeking independent legal advice. She received no consideration for the transfer except release from her liability under the mortgage. Balcombe J, in considering (*obiter*) whether the transfer was an unconscionable bargain, adopted Megarry J's formulation of 'ignorant and poor' in *Cresswell* and stated (p 1166):

> Where a marriage has broken down, both parties are liable to be in an emotional state. The party remaining in the matrimonial home, as the husband did in this case, has an advantage. The wife is no doubt in circumstances of great emotional strain. It seems to me that she should at least be encouraged to take independent advice so that she may know whether or not it is right for her ... to transfer away what is her only substantial capital asset ... [T]his transaction is an example of something which is done where the parties did not have equal bargaining power ...

Here, again, a generous interpretation of the phrase 'poor and ignorant' was applied to a wife who was not 'ignorant' but 'an intelligent woman' and 'certainly not wealthy': *Backhouse*, p 1165. All three elements necessary to set aside the transaction on the ground that it was an unconscionable bargain were present. In this case, the parties' marriage had broken down. The wife executed a conveyance by which she conveyed all her interest in the family home to her husband in return for an indemnity against the liabilities under a mortgage of the property, but for no other consideration. Balcombe J held that the wife had been 'ignorant' in the context of property transactions generally and, in particular, the execution of the conveyancing document. Secondly, there was, clearly, a 'sale at an undervalue' in that the wife had given no real consideration for her interest in the house. Thirdly, she had not received independent advice. (The fact that she knew how to get independent advice if she wanted it made no difference.) Significantly, his Lordship also intimated that, apart from these three elements (taken from the judgment of Kay J in *Fry v Lane*), there may be other 'circumstances of oppression or abuse of confidence which will invoke the aid of equity': *Cresswell*, p 257, *per* Megarry J.

More recently, in *Credit Lyonnais Bank Nederland NV v Burch* [1997] 1 All ER 144 (CA), a case involving a claim of undue influence brought by a junior employee against her employer, both Nourse and Millett LJJ suggested that the claimant might have brought an alternative claim directly against the bank to set aside the charge on the grounds of unconscionability. The transaction was manifestly disadvantageous to her and the bank had not explained the potential extent of her liability, nor had she received independent advice. Nourse LJ, whilst accepting that the case was not pleaded on the basis of an unconscionable bargain, nevertheless stated that 'the unconscionability of the transaction remains of direct materiality to the case based on undue influence': *Burch*, p 151. Indeed, in his view, the transaction was 'so harsh and unconscionable as to make it hardly necessary for a court of equity to rely on [*O'Brien*] as a basis for avoiding the transaction' (p 146). Millett LJ also alluded to the similarities between the two doctrines and concluded that, if the claimant had sought to have the transaction set aside as a harsh and unconscionable bargain, she would have had to show 'not only that the terms of the transaction were harsh and oppressive, but that one of the parties to it has imposed the objectionable terms in a morally reprehensible manner, that is to say, in a way which affects his conscience': *Burch*, p 153. The recognition in *Burch* that the *O'Brien* principle is an application of unconscionability has prompted some academic writers to suggest that the true basis of the decision was not the absence of the claimant's real consent (that is, undue influence) but the unconscionable conduct on the part of the bank in accepting a transaction which was so heavily unbalanced: see, for example, Chen-Wishart, M, 'The *O'Brien* principle and substantive unfairness' [1997] CLJ 60, p 63.

As we have already seen (Chapter 1, para 1.5.3), the Court of Appeal was given a further opportunity to consider the interaction between undue influence and unconscionable bargains in *Portman Building Society v Dusangh* [2000] 2 All ER (Comm) 221. Here, the building society granted a mortgage to the defendant, who was elderly (72 years of age), illiterate and on a very low income. The mortgage was guaranteed by the defendant's son, who received the bulk of the sum advanced and used it to purchase a supermarket. The same solicitor acted for all parties. The supermarket business was not a success and the son fell behind with the mortgage repayments. When the building society sought possession of the property, the defendant argued that he was entitled to set aside the charge directly against the society as an unconscionable bargain. On the facts, the defendant's argument failed since all the requisite ingredients of an unconscionable bargain were found to be lacking. The defendant was not at a serious disadvantage to the building society (having no existing indebtedness towards it), his situation was not exploited by the society, and the society had not acted in a morally reprehensible manner. Accordingly, the transaction, although improvident, was not oppressive and the conscience of the court was not shocked. In the words of Simon Brown LJ (p 229):

> I simply cannot accept that building societies are required to police transactions of this nature to ensure that parents (even poor and ignorant ones) are wise in seeking to assist their children.

The judgment of Ward LJ is particularly illuminating on the interrelationship between the two doctrines. His Lordship considered that the defendant's case could be put in two different ways. First, unconscionable conduct by the son affecting the building society and, secondly, the unconscionable conduct by the building society itself. So far as the conduct of the son was concerned, there was nothing to suggest that he had taken unconscientious advantage of his father's illiteracy, lack of business acumen or parental generosity.

Although the son gained all the benefit from the mortgage and the father took all the risk, this did not by itself characterise the son's actions as 'morally wrong and reprehensible'. Moreover, the building society had no notice of any impropriety so as to be put on inquiry of the defendant's equity and, in any event, the latter had received independent advice. What is interesting about this aspect of Ward LJ's judgment is his open recognition that unconscionable conduct was a vitiating factor, similar to undue influence, and that the doctrine of notice (as explained in *Barclays Bank plc v O'Brien* [1994] 4 All ER 417 (HL)) could apply in this context, so as to bind the lender in the same way as in a case involving undue influence. Significantly, his Lordship relied on a passage in Lord Browne-Wilkinson's speech in *O'Brien* where he stated (p 428) that a wife who has been induced to stand as a surety for her husband's debts 'by his undue influence, misrepresentation *or some other legal wrong*' had an equity as against him to set aside the transaction. In his view, unconscionable conduct was 'some other legal wrong' and, therefore, the principles in *O'Brien* on the issue of notice and third parties was equally applicable in cases involving unconscionable bargains: *Dusangh*, pp 233–34. His Lordship also cited the following extract from Millett LJ's judgment in the *Burch* case (p 153), where, as we have seen, the similarities between the two jurisdictions to set aside unconscionable bargains and to set aside transactions obtained by undue influence were highlighted:

> In either case it is necessary to show that the conscience of the party who seeks to uphold the transaction was affected by notice, actual or constructive, of the impropriety by which it was obtained by the intermediary ...

On the second question of whether the building society itself had acted unconscionably, the defendant's case centred on establishing the three requisite elements identified by Kay J in *Fry v Lane* (see above), namely: (1) a poor and ignorant man; (2) considerable undervalue/manifest disadvantage; and (3) lack of independent advice. So far as the last element was concerned, Ward LJ felt this was not so much an 'essential free-standing requirement' but more 'a powerful factor confirming the suspicion of nefarious dealing which the presence of advice would serve to dispel': *Dusangh*, p 235. Significantly, in this connection, Millett LJ, in *Burch*, also opined that 'the result does not depend mechanically on the presence or absence of legal advice' and, in particular, independent advice would not necessarily save a transaction which was so manifestly disadvantageous that no competent solicitor could have recommended it: *Burch*, p 156. Despite the fact, therefore, that it is a specific element in Kay J's formulation in *Fry v Lane*, the absence of independent advice falls to be treated only as a factor pointing towards the conclusion that a transaction is unconscionable. Conversely, the fact that the weaker party received such advice may assist the stronger party in showing that the transaction was fair, just and reasonable.

Moreover, mere inequality of bargaining power and transactional imbalance (that is, a disadvantageous transaction) were not enough by themselves to vitiate the transaction in the absence of unconscionable conduct. In this connection, it was apparent, on the facts in *Dusangh*, that the building society had not acted in any morally reprehensible way. Although it might have been commercially unwise for the society to put its trust in the defendant and his son, that was not to say that it was morally culpable for them to do so. (See, further, McMurtry, L, 'Unconscionability and undue influence: an interaction?' [2000] Conv 573.)

The governing elements, therefore, of the doctrine of unconscionable bargains may be summarised as follows:

(a) transactional imbalance (that is, the bargain itself must be oppressive);

(b) relational inequality (that is, the complainant was in a position of bargaining weakness); and

(c) unconscionable conduct (that is, the other party must have knowingly taken advantage of the complainant).

So far as transactional imbalance is concerned, the cases show that the complainant must have entered into a transaction which was substantively unfair, in that he received nothing or very little in return. In other words, the terms of the transaction are so unfair that they 'shock the conscience of the court': see *Boustany*, propositions 1–3. In *Burch*, for example, as we have seen, the crucial factor in the Court of Appeal's decision was the extreme substantive unfairness of the transaction which gave rise to 'grave suspicion' and cried 'aloud for an explanation': *Burch*, p 152, *per* Millett LJ.

The second element requires that the complainant be in some position of weakness (or 'special disadvantage') in relation to the other party: see *Boustany*, proposition 5. As we have seen, the phrase 'ignorant and poor' in this context has been redefined in the modern cases to mean someone who is not well educated and in a lower income group. Other 'disabling' characteristics would, no doubt, include, sickness, age, infirmity of the body or mind, drunkenness, illiteracy and 'lack of assistance or explanation where assistance or explanation is necessary': *Blomley v Ryan* (1956) 99 CLR 362, p 405, *per* Fullagar J. In *Alec Lobb Ltd v Total Oil (Great Britain) Ltd* [1983] 1 WLR 87, pp 94–95, Peter Millett QC (sitting as a deputy High Court judge) said that the doctrine was capable of applying 'if one party has been at a serious disadvantage to the other, whether through poverty, or ignorance, or lack of advice, or otherwise, so that circumstances existed of which unfair advantage could be taken'. It is apparent, for example, that inability to speak English, if taken advantage of, may come within the doctrine: *Barclays Bank plc v Schwartz* (1995) *The Times*, 2 August.

The third element of unconscionability, as we have seen, is also crucial to the granting of relief: see *Boustany*, propositions 1–5. Thus, in *Hart v O'Connor* [1985] AC 1000 (PC), the vendor, who was 83, entered into a contract for the sale of land to the defendant, a neighbouring farmer. The transaction was drawn up by the vendor's solicitor but, unknown to the defendant, the vendor was of unsound mind. The Privy Council, on appeal from the New Zealand Court of Appeal, held that, since the vendor's lack of sufficient mental capacity was not known to the defendant and there were no imputations against his conduct, the contract for sale was valid and could not be set aside as an unconscionable bargain. Lord Brightman identified two distinct meanings of 'unfairness' in the context of a contractual transaction. First, a contract may be unfair because of the unfair manner in which it is brought into existence. A contract induced by undue influence is unfair in this sense (that is, procedural unfairness). Alternatively, a contract may be described as unfair by reason of the fact that the terms of the contract are more favourable to one party than to the other (that is, contractual imbalance). According to his Lordship, both procedural unfairness and contractual imbalance were necessary to relieve a party from a transaction: *Hart v O'Connor*, p 1018 ('equity will not relieve a party from a contract on the ground only that there is contractual imbalance not amounting to unconscionable dealing'). However, he also intimated that contractual imbalance may be so extreme as to raise a presumption of procedural unfairness (for example, undue influence or some other form of victimisation). This is also acknowledged by Millett LJ, in the *Burch* case, where he suggested that, both in unconscionable bargain and undue influence cases, the court could 'infer the presence of impropriety from the terms of the transaction itself': *Burch*, p 153. (See, also, *Portman Building Society v Dusangh* [2000] 2 All ER (Comm) 221 (CA), p 235, where Ward LJ also refers to 'an evidential assumption of wrongdoing' if the transaction itself cries out for an explanation.)

8.3 DOES THE DOCTRINE APPLY TO GIFTS?

In Snell's *Principles of Equity*, 29th edn, 1991, London: Sweet & Maxwell (p 559), it is stated that the doctrine of unconscionable bargains '*a fortiori* ... must extend to the setting aside of gifts'.

An opposite view, however, was reached in *Langton v Langton* [1995] 2 FLR 890, where Mr AWH Charles QC (sitting as a deputy High Court judge) set aside a deed of gift procured by actual/presumed undue influence. It was not, therefore, strictly necessary for him to consider a further ground for setting aside the gift, namely, that it constituted an unconscionable bargain. The deputy judge, however, opined that, if the doctrine applied to gifts, it would mean that, in the case of all gifts by poor and ignorant persons without independent legal advice, the onus of proving that the gift was fair, just and reasonable would be placed on the recipient. That, in his view, would be a surprising result. Moreover, the formulation of the doctrine as expressed by Kay J, in *Fry v Lane* (1888) 40 Ch D 312, p 322, was limited to *purchases* of property and the description 'fair, just and reasonable' in that case was a phrase that applied to bargains and not gifts. In his judgment, the rationale behind the development of the doctrine of unconscionable bargains was to protect people who were in need of money from being taken advantage of by persons prepared to provide it for an exorbitant consideration. It did not, therefore, apply to gifts which was a different type of disposition and one where the donor was, by definition, not seeking a return.

As the deputy judge conceded, however, the doctrine has been applied to an unconscionable transaction which, although described and treated as a bargain, was in effect a gift: see *Cresswell v Potter* [1978] 1 WLR 244, p 259, *per* Megarry J ('what was done by the release was, in substance, that a gift was made by a wife who was being divorced to the husband who was divorcing her'). In *Langton* itself, the claimant had transferred his bungalow to his son and daughter-in-law by deed of gift. A non-exclusive licence to occupy the bungalow in favour of the claimant was entered into immediately after the gift and there was no doubt that it formed part of the overall transaction. However, none of the parties regarded the transfer of the property other than as a gift. In the deputy judge's view, therefore, the element of return introduced by the licence did not have the effect of converting the gift into a bargain, to which the doctrine of unconscionable dealing could apply: *Langton*, p 909.

The view taken in *Langton* does not accord with Australian authority. In *Wilton v Farnworth* (1948) 76 CLR 646 (High Court of Australia), the claimant was deaf, poorly educated and dull witted. His stepson persuaded him to sign various documents allowing the former to apply for letters of administration to the claimant wife's estate and releasing his interest therein to him. The court had no difficulty in setting aside the transaction as an unconscionable dealing. Rich J said (p 655):

> ... the jurisdiction of courts of equity is based upon unconscientious dealing. It has always been considered unconscientious to retain the advantage of a voluntary disposition of a large amount of property improvidently made by an alleged donor who did not understand the nature of the transaction and lacked information of material facts such as the nature and extent of the property particularly if made in favour of a donee possessing greater information who nevertheless withheld the facts.

Similarly, Latham CJ said (p 649):

> ... if a donee is the moving spirit in the transaction of gift, and the donor is of weak will or of poor mentality, a court of equity will set aside the gift unless it is shown that the donor understood the substance of what he was doing.

(See, also, *Louth v Diprose* (1993) 67 ALJR 95 (High Court of Australia), p 97, where Brennan J said: 'gifts obtained by unconscionable conduct and gifts obtained by undue influence are set aside by equity on substantially the same basis.') The better view, it is submitted, is that both gifts and bargains are subject to the doctrine of unconscionability: see, further, Capper, D, 'Unconscionable bargains and unconscionable gifts' [1996] Conv 308. Significantly, in Capper's view, gifts do not provide any distinction between undue influence and unconscionability. Indeed, it supports his premise, as we shall see later, that transactional imbalance provides merely an evidential function under both doctrines. In this connection, it has been held that the requirement of manifest disadvantage is not necessary for gifts: *Geffen v Goodman Estate* [1991] 2 SCR 353, p 378, *per* Wilson J. This must be right since otherwise it would be difficult to uphold gifts (which, by their very nature, are one-sided) under either doctrine.

8.4 COMMONWEALTH DEVELOPMENTS

8.4.1 Introduction

In the Commonwealth jurisdictions, the courts have tended to accept a more general doctrine of unconscionability. It will be convenient to examine briefly developments in Canada, Australia and New Zealand.

8.4.2 Canada

An early leading authority is *Morrison v Coast Finance Ltd* (1965) 55 DLR (2d) 710, which, interestingly, was cited by Lord Denning MR, in *Lloyds Bank Ltd v Bundy* [1974] 3 All ER 757 (CA), as illustrative of his proposition that the doctrine of unconscionable transactions extends to 'all cases where an unfair advantage has been gained by an unconscientious use of power by a stronger party against a weaker' (p 764). In *Morrison*, an elderly widow, with slender means, was persuaded by two men to mortgage her home and lend the proceeds to them so that they could repay a loan to the first defendant lender and buy two cars from the second defendant. The British Columbia Court of Appeal held that the transaction was unconscionable and granted relief. The case is significant in that it sets out the material ingredients for a successful claim to set aside a contract on the ground of unconscionability. The two vital elements were: (1) proof of inequality in the positions of the parties arising out of ignorance, need or distress of the weaker, leaving him (or her) in the power of the stronger party; and (2) proof of substantial unfairness of the bargain thus obtained by the stronger party. Once these elements were satisfied, a presumption of fraud arose which could only be rebutted by showing that the bargain as a whole was fair, just and reasonable with no advantage taken. In the course of his judgment, Davey JA said (p 713):

> The equitable principles relating to undue influence and relief against unconscionable bargains are closely related, but the doctrines are separate and distinct. The finding here against undue influence does not conclude the question whether the appellant is entitled to relief against an unconscionable transaction.

In his Honour's view, a plea of undue influence attacks 'the sufficiency of consent' whilst the doctrine of unconscionable bargains invokes 'relief against an unfair advantage gained by an unconscientious use of power by a stronger party against a weaker': *Morrison*, p 713. Despite this initial reluctance to assimilate the two doctrines under one umbrella of unconscionability, it is significant that, since the English decision in *Bundy*, the Canadian courts have adopted the broader formulation of 'inequality of bargaining power' enunciated by Lord Denning MR in that case as part of their law. In *McKenzie v Bank of Montreal* (1975) 55 DLR (3d) 641, for example, the Ontario High Court, applying *Bundy*, held that a bank, who had knowledge that the claimant had been acting under the undue influence of her partner, owed a duty of care to her to ensure that she appreciated and intended the consequences of the transaction. This meant providing the claimant with the necessary information and advice, or to see that she had obtained it. Since the bank had failed in that duty, the mortgage was set aside: see, also, *Buchanan v Canadian Imperial Bank of Commerce* (1979) 100 DLR (3d) 624 (British Columbia Supreme Court); and *Bertolo v Bank of Montreal* (1986) 33 DLR (4d) 610 (Ontario Court of Appeal). Indeed, some of the cases have gone further. Most notably, in *Harry v Kreutziger* (1978) 95 DLR (3d) 231, another decision of the British Columbia Court of Appeal, Lambert JA propounded a broader test of unconscionability based on 'community standards of commercial morality'. He said (p 241):

> In my opinion, questions as to whether use of power was unconscionable, an advantage unfair or very unfair, a consideration was grossly inadequate, or bargaining power was grievously impaired, to select words from both statements of principle, the *Morrison* case and the *Bundy* case, are really aspects of one single question. That single question is whether the transaction, seen as a whole, is sufficiently divergent from community standards of commercial morality that it should be rescinded. To my mind, the framing of the question in that way prevents the real issue from being obscured by an isolated consideration of a number of separate questions ...

In this case, the appellant, an elderly, inarticulate Indian with limited education, who was also partially deaf, agreed to sell his fishing boat for $4,500. In fact, the boat was worth $16,000, largely because of a fishing licence attached to it. The buyer, a man of greater business experience and with full knowledge of the true value of the boat, induced the sale by assuring the appellant that he could easily obtain another licence. Not surprisingly, the sale was set aside as an unconscionable bargain. Applying the test put forward by Lambert JA, the circumstances of the transaction revealed a 'marked departure' from community standards of commercial morality. Significantly, this test has been applied in several subsequent Canadian authorities: see, for example, *A&K Lick-a-Chick Franchises Ltd v Cordiv Enterprises Ltd* (1981) 119 DLR (3d) 440 (Nova Scotia Supreme Court). (For a full review of the cases, see Enman, SR, 'Doctrines of unconscionability in Canadian, English and Commonwealth contract law' (1987) 16 Anglo-Am LR 191.)

8.4.3 Australia

There are three landmark cases in the Australian jurisdiction which call for comment. The first is *Blomley v Ryan* (1956) 99 CLR 362 (High Court of Australia), where an uneducated farmer, 78 years old, who was mentally and physically weak, suffering from the effects of intoxication, conveyed his farm to the purchaser who knew of his disabilities and the inadequacy of the price. The transaction was held to be unconscionable and the contract was set aside. McTiernan J stated that the 'essence of the fraud' was that 'advantage was taken of weakness, ignorance and other disabilities ... and the contract was derived from such behaviour and it is an unfair bargain': *Blomley v Ryan*, p 385. In his view, the principle extended to 'all cases in which the parties to a contract have not met upon equal terms' (p 386). Fullagar J identified some of the circumstances adversely affecting a party which may induce the court to set aside the transaction. Among these, he listed, 'poverty or need of any kind, sickness, age, sex, infirmity of body or mind, drunkenness, illiteracy or lack of education, lack of assistance or explanation where assistance or explanation is necessary': *Blomley v Ryan*, p 405. In his view, the common characteristic was that they placed one party at a serious disadvantage to the other. He did not, however, consider it essential in all cases that the party at a disadvantage should suffer loss or detriment by the bargain.

The second notable case is *Commonwealth Bank of Australia v Amadio* (1983) 151 CLR 447 (High Court of Australia). In this case, two elderly migrants, who were unfamiliar with written English, were asked by their son to execute a mortgage in favour of a bank, over land which they owned, to secure the overdraft of a company which the son controlled. The son told his parents that the mortgage was to be limited to $50,000 and to be for six months only. The mortgage document, which the bank submitted for execution, also contained a guarantee which secured all amounts owing (or which might be owing) to the bank on the company's account. The parents executed the deed mistakenly believing that it was limited to $50,000 and to be for six months. The bank was aware that the parents had been misinformed about the contents of the mortgage. The majority of the High Court (Mason, Wilson and Deane JJ) held that the transaction should be set aside on the ground that the parents were under a special disability when they executed the deed, which was sufficiently apparent to the bank to make it unconscientious for it to be allowed to rely on it. Mason J concluded that the jurisdiction to set aside transactions as unconscionable arose 'whenever one party by reason of some condition or circumstance is placed at a special disadvantage vis à vis another and unfair or unconscientious advantage is then taken of the opportunity thereby created': *Amadio*, p 462. Thus, as under English law, three requirements were necessary to raise the equity:

(a) an inequality of bargaining power;

(b) an improvident arrangement; and

(c) an unconscientious taking of advantage of the party under a special disability.

Here, the parents were in a position of special disadvantage because they were mistaken as to the extent of their liability under the mortgage and also as to the financial circumstances of the son's company. Their age and background and their reliance on their son's misleading advice contributed to this situation. The bank, in turn, was held to know enough of these facts as to put it on inquiry as to whether, in fact, the parents did appreciate the nature of the transaction they were being asked to enter into. Given that the bank had sufficient knowledge, it was *prima facie* unconscientious for the bank to accept the parents' execution of the mortgage deed. This, in turn, placed the burden on the bank to show that the transaction was fair, just and reasonable in the circumstances. Clearly, one option for the bank was to have required the parents to seek independent advice. Alternatively, the bank itself could have given information about the nature and scope of the proposed loan transaction and the financial position of the son's company. As it had not done this, it was fixed with knowledge of the parents' equity and, hence, could not rely on the guarantee.

Both Mason and Deane JJ suggested that actual knowledge of facts from which the possibility of special disadvantage may reasonably be inferred would amount to 'wilful ignorance' capable of supporting the doctrine of unconscionable dealing. In the absence of wilful ignorance, however, no duty would have arisen on the bank to inquire about the possibility of special disadvantage. Unlike undue influence cases, therefore, constructive notice has no part to play in this context: *Amadio*, p 467, *per* Mason J. It is arguable, however, that the bank did have sufficient notice of a relationship of presumed undue influence between the son and his parents sufficient to put them on inquiry as to the parents' equity. Although undue influence was not pleaded on the facts, the case does bear some similarity to *Lancashire Loans Ltd v Black* [1934] 1 KB 380 (CA). Here, a daughter was held to be under the undue influence of her mother when she executed a charge in favour of moneylenders without independent advice. Since the moneylenders had notice of the facts which constituted the undue influence on the part of the mother, it was held that they were in no better position that the mother and that, therefore, the transaction had to be set aside. (See, also, *Bank of New South Wales v Rogers* (1941) 65 CLR 42 (High Court of Australia).)

Interestingly, Mason J considered (p 461) that, whilst there was 'some resemblance' between unconscionable conduct and undue influence, an important distinction was that:

> In the latter the will of the innocent party is not independent and voluntary because it is overborne. In the former, the will of the innocent party, even if independent and voluntary, is the result of the disadvantageous position in which he is placed and of the other party unconscientiously taking advantage of that position.

He acknowledged, however, that the two remedies were not mutually exclusive in the sense that only one of them could be available in a particular situation to the exclusion of the other. In his view (p 461):

> Relief on the ground of unconscionable conduct will be granted when unconscientious advantage is taken of an innocent party whose will is overborne so that it is not independent and voluntary, just as it will be granted when such advantage is taken of an innocent party who, though not deprived of an independent and voluntary will, is unable to make a worthwhile judgment as to what is in his best interest.

A similar conclusion was reached by Deane J, who considered the equitable principles relating to unconscionable dealing and undue influence as being 'closely related' but, nonetheless, 'distinct': *Amadio*, p 474. In his view, undue influence looks to the *quality* of the consent of the weaker party whereas unconscionable dealing looks to the *conduct* of the stronger party 'in attempting to enforce, or retain the benefit of, a dealing with a person under a special disability in circumstances where it is not consistent with equity or good conscience that he should do so': *Amadio*, p 474. These distinctions are, however, somewhat illusory. The doctrine of undue influence, it is submitted, does, in fact, involve the wrongdoer in taking unconscientious advantage of an innocent party who is in a disadvantageous situation: Phang, A, 'Undue influence methodology, sources and linkages' [1995] JBL 552, p 568, who writes that: 'under class 1 and class 2B undue influence, it may be stated that the innocent party is often manipulated into a situation of disadvantage.' And, as one Australian commentator has observed, relying on the factual similarities between the *Amadio* case and *National Westminster Bank plc v Morgan* [1985] 1 All ER 821 (HL):

> The parallels between presumed unconscionable conduct (contracting in the knowledge that the other party labours under a special disadvantage) and presumed undue influence (contracting in the knowledge that the other party reposes trust and confidence in one in the relevant sense) are significant. Both doctrines require sufficient awareness or perception on the part of the stronger party and, it is suggested, the tests for sufficient awareness should be the same in both cases. Both doctrines impose a similar duty: to ensure that the weaker party has formed an independent and informed judgment; this duty may be discharged by allowing the weaker party an opportunity to seek independent legal advice ... And, most importantly, both doctrines are designed to mitigate the risk of abuse by the stronger party of his position of special advantage. Abuse of a perceived position of special advantage is the thread that links these two equitable doctrines.

(See Hardingham, IJ, 'The High Court of Australia and unconscionable dealing' (1984) 4 OJLS 275, p 286.)

This, of course, reflects the view taken by Lord Denning MR in *Bundy* and his formulation of a general principle linking undue influence, unconscionable transactions (and other vitiating factors) under the 'single thread' of inequality of bargaining power: *Bundy*, p 765. In *Amadio*, the facts did not warrant any finding that the bank was in a confidential relationship with the parents since the latter had relied on their son, not the bank, to advise them on the nature of the loan transaction. Had, however, the bank 'crossed the line' into the area of confidentiality, then, clearly, issues relating to a presumed undue influence would have arisen for consideration: see, for example, *Bank of Montreal v Hancock* (1982) 137 DLR (3d) 648 (Ontario High Court of Justice).

In the third landmark case, the High Court of Australia sought to apply the concept of unconscionability to a situation where a surety wife does not understand the purpose and effect of the guarantee she signs and there is a failure by the bank to explain properly the transaction to her. In *National Australia Bank Ltd v Garcia* (1998) 194 CLR 395, the majority of the High Court, applying *Yerkey v Jones* (1939) 63 CLR 649, held that the lender had acted unconscionably in enforcing the guarantee against the wife because:

(a) she did not understand the purport and effect of the transaction;

(b) she was a volunteer because she did not obtain any benefit from the transaction;

(c) the lender was taken to have understood that, as a wife, she may have reposed trust and confidence in her husband in business matters and, therefore, to have understood that the husband may not have fully and accurately explained the effect of the transaction to her; and

(d) the lender took no steps to explain the purport and effect of the transaction to her or to ascertain whether it had been explained to her by a competent, independent and disinterested stranger.

The significance of this case is that the High Court rejected the *O'Brien* approach (grounded in the notion of notice) in favour of a (revived) wife's 'special equity' doctrine, which allowed her to set aside a guarantee on the grounds that she did not understand it and that its nature and effect had not been explained to her. This equity, however, was based, not on the status and abilities of married women, but rather the potential for abuse of trust within the marriage relationship. The element of notice, therefore, was only relevant in determining whether or not the lender knew, at the time of the guarantee, that the surety was married to the borrower. Strictly speaking, the basis for the court's intervention was not the equitable doctrine of unconscionable dealings, but a wider principle of equity preventing the unconscientious exercise of legal rights. In effect, the decision in *Garcia* imposes a strict (primary) liability on lenders to disclose full and accurate information to wives who act as sureties for their husband's debts. This liability, unlike the *O'Brien* formulation which is based on a lender's secondary liability arising on notice, does not depend on any finding of wrongdoing committed by the debtor husband. Indeed, the High Court in *Garcia* was mindful to point out that the case before it was not one where a husband had exercised undue influence over his wife. The Court also intimated that equity's special protection could extend to other relationships (for example, heterosexual or homosexual cohabitees): see, further, Bryan, M, 'Setting aside guarantees: reviving an old equity' [1999] LMCLQ 327; Brown, M, 'Suretyship and marriage: notice v unconscionability' (2000) RLR 152; Stone, E, 'Infants, lunatics and married women: equitable protection in *Garcia v National Australia Bank*' (1999) 62 MLR 604; and Finlay, A, 'Australian wives are special: *Yerkey v Jones* lives on' [1999] JBL 361.

It is important to stress, however, the different situations in which the *Amadio* and *Garcia* cases operate. In the former, it was held that it was unconscionable for a lender to enforce a guarantee obtained from a guarantor who is operating under a disability of which the lender has notice. In the latter, the unconscionability arises from the simple fact that the lender is aware of circumstances which indicate that the guarantor has failed to understand the transaction (that is, there is a relationship of trust and confidence between guarantor and borrower) and, nevertheless, failed to take steps to explain the transaction. As one commentator has put it: 'where *Amadio* requires some overreaching of the guarantor by the debtor, [*Garcia*] requires only defective comprehension ... and where *Amadio* requires knowledge of that overreaching on the part of the creditor, [*Garcia*] requires not even notice of the guarantor's defective comprehension': Chandler, S, 'Wives' guarantees of their husbands' debts' (1999) 115 LQR 1, p 3.

Finally, reference should also be made to *Louth v Diprose* (1993) 67 ALJR 95, where the majority of the High Court of Australia held that the respondent was entitled to recover a substantial gift of money which he had made to a woman (the appellant) with whom he had had a romantic relationship for several years. In fact, the respondent had been infatuated with the appellant and it was apparent that the latter had exploited his emotional dependence on her. When she needed a place to live, he bought a house for her and had it conveyed into her sole name. The judgment of Brennan J is of particular interest because his Honour sought to assimilate the court's jurisdiction to set aside gifts procured by unconscionable conduct with the 'similar' jurisdiction to set aside gifts procured by undue influence. In his view, both depended upon the effect of influence (presumed or actual), improperly brought to bear by one party to a relationship on the mind of the other whereby the other disposes of his property. This similarity 'gives to cases arising in the exercise of one jurisdiction an analogous character in considering cases involving the same points in the other jurisdiction': *Louth v Diprose*, p 98. The effect of his judgment is substantially to merge the concept of unconscionability with that of undue influence.

8.4.4 New Zealand

An early New Zealand case is *Harris v Richardson* [1930] NZLR 890 (CA), which concerned the sale of a life interest at a considerable undervalue by a bankrupt who had no experience in business matters without independent advice. The purchaser, on the other hand, was an experienced moneylender who was aware of the seller's struggling financial situation. The sale was set aside on the basis that 'the parties had not met on equal terms'.

Another landmark case is *Archer v Cutler* [1980] 1 NZLR 386 (Supreme Court of Auckland). Here, a contract for the sale of 10 acres of land was executed by the parties at the defendant's residence. Medical evidence later showed that the defendant was suffering from senile dementia. Although living alone, she was incapable of managing her own affairs and unable to keep proper appraisals of facts and conscious judgments on important matters. The claimant did not know of the defendant's impaired mental condition, nor of its effect on her ability to understand the bargain she had entered into. The claimant was also unaware that the agreed price of $17,000 represented a substantial undervalue for the land. The Supreme Court of Auckland held that the defence of unconscionable bargain was established. Although the claimant had no knowledge of the defendant's disability and he had not set out to take advantage of her, he was aware of her advanced years and some manifestations of her eccentricity. These factors, together with the defendant's lack of advice and her disadvantaged bargaining position, brought about by her unsoundness of mind, created such an inequality between the contracting parties as to render the bargain unconscionable. This was particularly so as the sale was at a significant undervalue. The decision clearly went further than the English and Australian authorities, which require that the stronger party actually take advantage of his position. As we saw earlier (para 8.2), in *Hart v O'Connor* [1985] AC 1000, the Privy Council (on appeal from the New Zealand Court of Appeal) held, overruling the *Archer* case, that a contract could not be set aside as an unconscionable bargain where the purchaser had acted completely innocently and was not guilty of any unconscionable conduct. Subsequent New Zealand cases have accepted this approach, albeit with some reluctance.

In *Nichols v Jessup (No 2)* [1986] 1 NZLR 237 (High Court of Auckland), the claimant sought specific performance of an agreement between himself and the defendant to grant mutual rights of way over their respective properties so as to improve the road access to the claimant's rear section. The High Court held, ostensibly applying the *Hart v O'Connor* decision, that because the claimant was aware of the defendant's weaknesses in regard to financial and property matters, including her lack of advice, and yet passively accepted the benefit of the transaction, which was manifestly one-sided, the agreement could properly be set aside as unconscionable. Pritchard J said (p 240):

> ... my reconsideration of this case in the light of [*O'Connor*] leads me to the conclusion that this agreement, although not originally extorted by an unconscientious exercise of power, should be set aside in exercise of the court's equitable jurisdiction on the ground that in all the circumstances it is not consistent with equity and good conscience that the plaintiff should enforce or retain the benefit of the transaction.

Significantly, as Pritchard J himself concedes, there was no evidence in this case to suggest that the claimant had consciously intended to take advantage of the defendant's ignorance when she was persuaded to agree to his proposal regarding the rights of way. In the absence of any moral fraud, therefore, the transaction should have been upheld: see, further, Bamforth, N, 'Unconscionability as a vitiating factor' [1995] LMCLQ 538.

In *Contractors Bonding Ltd v Snee* [1992] 2 NZLR 157, the Wellington Court of Appeal also applied the *Hart v O'Connor* ruling, holding that equity will only intervene to deprive parties of their contractual rights where they have unconscionably obtained benefits or have accepted benefits in unconscionable circumstances (that is, where they would be acting unconscientiously in receiving or retaining their bargain). In this case, the complainant was under a special disability at the time of contracting due to her mental incapacity resulting in a defective understanding of her affairs and of the transaction. That, however, in itself, was not enough to establish that the company was guilty of fraud. It had no knowledge of, and could not be expected to have any awareness of, her incapacity and, moreover, had no reason to believe that she was under the influence of her son. Moreover, the guarantee and mortgage over her house were standard commercial transactions with no unusual features which the company was required to disclose to the complainant. The transaction could not be characterised as improvident (amounting to contractual imbalance) nor was there any evidence of unfairness or overreaching on the part of the company. The result, therefore, was that the company could rely on its mortgage. Richardson J said (p 174) that 'the focus must be on the conduct of those alleged to have acted unconscionably' and 'an unconscionability inquiry involves an assessment of all the circumstances of the particular case'.

Interestingly, in *Walmsley v Christchurch City Council* [1990] 1 NZLR 199 (Christchurch High Court), Hardie Boys J opined that the concepts of undue influence and unconscionability were 'different concepts, although both are founded on fraud, in the sense of an unconscionable use of power'. In *Bowkett v Action Finance Ltd* [1992] 1 NZLR 449, also a decision of the Christchurch High Court, Tipping J set out the following circumstances which, in his view, would normally be present when a court finds an unconscionable bargain:

1 the weaker party is under a significant disability;

2 the stronger party knows or ought to know of that disability;

3 the stronger party has victimised the weaker in the sense of taking advantage of the weaker's disability, either by active extortion of the bargain, or passive acceptance of it in circumstances where it is contrary to conscience that the bargain should be accepted;

4 there is a marked inadequacy of consideration and the stronger party either knows or ought to know that to be so; and

5   there is some procedural impropriety either demonstrated or presumed
from the circumstances.

In Tipping J's view, not all elements need necessarily be shown, but elements
1–3 were crucial, as there could not be an unconscionable bargain without a
disability in the weaker party and knowledge and taking advantage thereof
by the stronger party: *Bowkett v Action Finance Ltd*, p 460. He also intimated
that absence of independent advice was a frequent feature of unconscionable
bargain cases. What was important was the 'cumulative weight of all relevant
points' in determining 'the ultimate question' as to whether the bargain could
properly be characterised as unconscionable so that equity should intervene.

8.5 AN UNDERLYING CONCEPT OF UNCONSCIONABILITY?

Undoubtedly, there is a close relationship between the principles relating to
undue influence and unconscionable bargains. Should the two be fused
within one all-embracing doctrine? Academic commentators differ on
whether this would be a useful process. One academic, in an influential
article, has argued for a merger of the two doctrines: Capper, D, 'Undue
influence and unconscionability: a rationalisation' (1998) 114 LQR 479. Other
writers have suggested that undue influence and unconscionability are
essentially separate and distinct concepts and favour preserving the
distinction between the two: Birks, P and Chin, NY, 'On the nature of undue
influence', in Beatson, J and Friedmann, D (eds), *Good Faith and Fault in
Contract Law*, 1995, Oxford: Clarendon.

According to Capper, the two doctrines share three common features,
namely:

(a) inequality in the bargaining positions of the parties (that is, relational
inequality);

(b) transactional imbalance; and

(c) unconscionable conduct on the part of the defendant.

So far as the requirement of relational inequality is concerned, this is present
in presumed undue influence cases, in so far as the complainant must prove
the existence of a relationship under which he (or she) generally reposed trust
and confidence in the wrongdoer. Such relationships, as we saw in Chapter 2,
are 'infinitely various' and do not warrant precise definition: *National
Westminster Bank plc v Morgan* [1985] 1 All ER 821 (HL), p 831, *per* Lord
Scarman. They are not necessarily fiduciary, but a vital element is trust and
confidence. Relational inequality is always present (by definition) in actual
undue influence cases, 'as the defendant would be unable otherwise to
exercise any such undue influence': Capper, p 500. The requirement is also to

be found in unconscionability cases in that the complainant must be shown to be suffering from some special disadvantage to warrant equity's intervention. The complainant's disabling circumstances, as we have seen, have been given a broad interpretation in the Commonwealth cases. Most notably, in *Blomley v Ryan* (1956) 99 CLR 362 (High Court of Australia) (p 405), Fullagar J listed, as examples, poverty, sickness, age, sex, infirmity, drunkenness, illiteracy and lack of education. In England, the reference to 'poor and ignorant' in *Fry v Lane* has also been broadened to include persons on low income and who are less highly educated. More generally, in *Multiservice Bookbinding Ltd v Marden* [1979] Ch 84, p 110, Browne-Wilkinson J stated that the categories of unconscionable bargains were not limited and that 'the court can and should intervene where a bargain has been procured by unfair means'. There is no reason to suppose, therefore, that the English courts would be any less reluctant to grant relief in an equally wide range of circumstances. Capper concludes that 'the kind of relational inequality sufficient to support a case of unconscionability is clearly very broad and there cannot be any difficulty in fitting cases of undue influence within it': Capper, p 486.

Turning to transactional imbalance, Capper concedes that this requirement does not feature in the actual undue influence category, which requires mere proof of actual coercion over the weaker party. His argument, however, is that transactional imbalance (that is, that the bargain itself must be oppressive) is not an essential requirement of any undue influence or unconscionability case (albeit invariably present), but simply 'powerful evidence in support of relational inequality and unconscionable conduct, which are the true invalidating grounds': Capper, p 486. On this point, he (like other commentators) doubts whether manifest disadvantage should be an essential feature of the presumed undue influence category. As we saw in Chapter 3, the better view is that manifest disadvantage should take the form of a purely evidential consideration when the wrongdoer is seeking to rebut the presumption of undue influence. In other words, there is no reason why a complainant should not rely on the doctrine even though the transaction itself is objectively reasonable. It will be recalled that, in Chapter 3 (para 3.6), the example was given of a solicitor who bought his client's house at a fair price. The requisite relationship of confidence would exist between the parties (that is, relational inequality) and there seems no reason why the presumption of undue influence should not arise, requiring the solicitor to show that the client had formed an independent and informed judgment. The mere fact that the price was fair would not be enough to rebut the presumption because 'there might be all sorts of reasons, apart from the price, why the client did not want to sell his house': *National Westminster Bank plc v Morgan* [1983] 3 All ER 85 (CA), *per* Dunn LJ. According to Capper, transactional imbalance is also not an essential precondition to a finding of unconscionability. Although many of the unconscionability cases do involve sales at an undervalue and other forms of contractual imbalance, this is not always the case. He cites, for example, the Australian case of *Blomley v Ryan*, referred to above, where the High Court of

Australia held that the decisive factors of unconscionability were the seller's mental weakness and the purchaser's unconscionable conduct. In that case, the property was sold for $25,000, its true value being not significantly more ($33,000). He also cites Deane J, in the *Amadio* case, who opined that, whilst most unconscionability cases involved inadequacy of consideration, this was not essential: *Amadio*, p 475. He concludes that 'if manifest disadvantage assumes the evidential role recommended for it in respect of presumed undue influence, then assimilation with actual undue influence and unconscionability becomes relatively easy': Capper, p 500.

Finally, so far as unconscionable conduct is concerned, this is, according to Capper, a requirement of both doctrines. It is clearly evident in actual undue influence cases and is an essential feature of the unconscionability cases. In his view, 'actual undue influence (without pressure) is only different from presumed undue influence in so far as what is presumed in the latter is affirmatively proved in the former': Capper, p 493. On this reasoning, therefore, both actual and presumed undue influence should be subsumed under a general doctrine of unconscionability. Although, in the presumed undue influence category, coercion and abuse by the defendant is less easy to discern, nevertheless, many of the cases on unconscionable dealing also concern little more than passive acceptance of benefits received under unconscionable circumstances. In *Hart v O'Connor* [1985] AC 1000 (PC), for example, Lord Brightman explained the meaning of unconscionable conduct in this context in this way (p 1024):

> ... it is victimisation, which can consist either of the active extortion of a benefit or the passive acceptance of a benefit in unconscionable circumstances.

Similarly, as we have seen, Richardson J, in *Contractors Bonding Ltd v Snee* [1992] 2 NZLR 157 (Wellington Court of Appeal), referring to *Hart v O'Connor*, stated that equity would intervene to deprive parties of their contractual rights where they have unconscionably obtained benefits or have accepted benefits in unconscionable circumstances: *Snee*, pp 173–75. Indeed, not all cases have involved 'clear and definite wrongdoing': Capper, p 494. As Capper explains (p 495):

> The *Fry v Lane* line of cases proceeds on the basis that where there is relational inequality and transactional imbalance, coupled with no independent advice for the plaintiff, either receipt of the benefit of the transaction is unconscionable in itself or the burden passes to the defendant to show that the transaction is fair, just and reasonable.

In his view, this evidential presumption, which arises in cases of extreme relational inequality and transactional imbalance, does not detract from the requirement of unconscionable conduct which, as we have seen, is essential in unconscionability cases. Indeed, this view was judicially endorsed recently by Ward LJ, in *Portman Building Society v Dusangh* [2000] 2 All ER (Comm) 221 (CA), p 235, where his Lordship spoke in terms of an 'evidential presumption of wrongdoing' in this context. Moreover, in Capper's view, there being no automatic presumption of unconscionable conduct in the unconscionability cases, there should equally be no automatic requirement of independent advice. This accords, of course, with the function of independent advice in undue influence doctrine. As Millett LJ observed in *Burch* (p 156), such advice is not always necessary nor always sufficient, since 'the result does not depend mechanically on the presence or absence of legal advice'. Significantly, his Lordship considered the role of the independent adviser to be 'not dissimilar' in both unconscionability and undue influence cases.

According to Capper, therefore, a new combined doctrine would work as follows (p 500):

> In essence the court would have to weigh up the three elements of relational inequality, transactional imbalance, and unconscionable conduct, and come to an overall judgment as to whether a particular transaction can stand. This would not, however, be a purely impressionistic exercise. Transactional imbalance would serve an evidentiary function, that is to say a sharp case of transactional imbalance would strengthen a case for relief founded primarily on relational inequality or unconscionable conduct, and the absence of any real imbalance would point the court away from the invalidity on either of these grounds. The principal grounds for relief would thus be relational inequality and unconscionable conduct. The more there was of one of these features, the less would be required of the other; and where one was not strongly in evidence transactional imbalance would be needed to bolster it. Where the parties to a transaction are on very unequal terms and the transaction is weighted strongly in favour of one party, unconscionable conduct can be inferred. Where the parties are on fairly equal terms and the defendant has clearly behaved unconscionably, the court could infer that the defendant's conduct has induced an unfair transaction if the transaction appears unbalanced.

This view is mirrored by another academic writer, Chen-Wishart, who argues that 'unconscionability should be recognised as the informing principle at the root of the *O'Brien* formulation which is, in turn, merely one application of the unconscionability jurisdiction': Chen-Wishart, M, 'The *O'Brien* principle and substantive unfairness' [1997] CLJ 60, p 62. She also suggests that both doctrines reflect same concerns and are subject to the same burden of proof. First, the requirement of 'special disability' in unconscionable dealing cases is reflected, under *O'Brien*, 'in the need to show that the surety's consent was tainted by the debtor's undue influence or misrepresentation'. Secondly, the requirement of an 'improvident transaction' corresponds with the *O'Brien* requirement that the transaction be manifestly disadvantageous (at least in the presumed undue influence category). Finally, the element of 'unconscientious advantage-taking' is mirrored in the need to show, under *O'Brien*, 'that the lender has constructive notice of the undue influence but obtains the benefit of the transaction without taking adequate steps to meet that suspected influence': Chen-Wishart, p 62. (See, also, Lehane, JRF, 'Undue influence, misrepresentation and third parties' (1994) 110 LQR 167, p 173.)

Birks and Chin, on the other hand, consider that there is a vital distinction between the undue influence and unconscionability cases. They regard undue influence as being 'plaintiff-sided' and concerned with the weakness of the claimant's consent owing to an excessive dependence upon the defendant, and unconscionability as being 'defendant-sided' and concerned with the defendant's exploitation of the claimant's vulnerability. In support of this contention, they draw attention to two features of the presumed undue influence cases. First, many of the presumed undue influence cases do not involve any conscious wrongdoing on the part of the defendant; on the contrary, the evidence shows merely a passive receipt of benefits arising from the transaction. Secondly, where the presumption of undue influence is raised, it is open to the defendant to rebut the presumption by showing that the complainant acted freely and with an independent will. This requirement, therefore, is directed at the issue of consent and is not concerned with any wrongdoing on the part of the defendant. Not all commentators agree with this analysis. Thus, Bigwood, for example, argues that undue influence is defendant/conduct-based in both its concerns and orientation: Bigwood, R, 'Undue influence: impaired consent or wicked exploitation?' (1996) 16 OJLS 503. In his view, both undue influence and unconscionable dealings concern a form of 'exploitation', although the source of the claimant's vulnerability is different in each case. Bigwood explains (p 514):

> The vulnerability in unconscionable dealings is not characteristically brought about through a special relation existing between the parties; typically it is on account of some social or transactional disabling condition unassociated (at least initially) with the defendant. In relational undue influence cases, however, the plaintiff is vulnerable precisely on account of a special antecedent relational condition (misplaced trust or reliance) relative to the defendant. And because this vulnerability is, or is presumed to be, so extreme in such cases, and the relation so worthy of society's protection, affirmative proof of 'exploitation' is not required in the same way as it is in unconscionable dealings cases.

In his view, however, despite these definitional differences between the two concepts, 'there is no logical reason' why the jurisdiction of unconscionable dealings could not include undue influence and also duress.

What is also overlooked in Birk and Chin's analysis, as we have already seen, is that the passive acceptance of benefits may itself be unconscionable in the circumstances of a particular case. As Capper points out, many of the unconscionability cases have this common feature and, therefore, there seems little reason why undue influence and unconscionability should not be assimilated. In his view (p 493):

... relational inequality is present in both and transactional imbalance should serve an evidentiary function. To maintain a distinction between the two based on a presumption raised by a relationship which nobody can define ... is to overwork that presumption.

His new doctrine would not be either specifically 'plaintiff-sided' or specifically 'defendant-sided' (as Birks and Chin maintain) because 'the stronger the plaintiff-sided factor the weaker the defendant-sided factor needs to be and vice versa, although a degree of unconscionable conduct would be present in all cases since the passive receipt of benefits flowing under a seriously unbalanced transaction where the plaintiff was clearly in an unequal relationship with the defendant would count as unconscionable conduct': Capper, p 500.

This unifying doctrine of unconscionability could also be extended to embrace the liability of a third party lender in circumstances where it has actual or constructive notice that the loan transaction is tainted with undue influence, misrepresentation or some other equitable wrong. Thus, in Australia, as we have seen, if a lender has the requisite degree of knowledge of an unconscionable transaction (for example, between a husband and wife), it will itself be treated as acting unconscionably in relying on the transaction. A good illustration is also to be found from the Canadian jurisdiction, in *Shoppers Trust Co v Dynamic Homes Ltd* (1993) 96 DLR (4d) 267 (Ontario Court). Here, the husband obtained a large loan from the claimant which was secured by a mortgage over the family home, which was owned solely by the wife. The husband had persuaded her to sign the documents at the offices of a solicitor who was acting for both the claimant and the husband. The wife was illiterate, had virtually no knowledge of her husband's business affairs and was fearful of her husband. There were also marital difficulties. The solicitor did not tell her that there was no legal requirement for her to sign, what the consequences of her signing would be, or that she should obtain independent advice. The Ontario Court held that there was a fiduciary relationship between the solicitor and the wife, which obliged the former to ensure that the wife fully understood the nature and consequences of her actions and to advise her to seek independent advice. The transaction was unconscionable because it was improvident (that is, the wife received no benefit under the mortgage) and also because the husband (and the solicitor) had taken advantage of their dominant position over the wife. Significantly also, it was unconscionable to permit the claimant (as lender) to take advantage of the mortgage in the absence of proper independent legal advice. As Capper points out, although such an approach still depends on notice (and thus is broadly similar to the test enunciated by the House of Lords in *Barclays Bank plc v O'Brien* [1993] 4 All ER 417), 'it focuses more directly upon the unconscionable conduct of the bank instead of the indirect test of notice of the undue influence of a third party': Capper, p 499.

There is no reason, of course, why the related doctrine of duress should not also feature in this assimilation process since it also embodies notions of relational inequality and unconscionable conduct associated with the doctrine of undue influence and unconscionable dealing. One serious objection, however, to any such process of amalgamation is the notion that this would lead to considerable uncertainty in our law. As one commentator has put it, 'the problem with this doctrine [of unconscionable dealings] is that it may prove as long as the Chancellor's foot and open up new vistas of litigation and uncertainty': Price, NS, 'Undue influence: *finis litium*?' (1999) 115 LQR 8, p 10. The uncertainty argument should not, however, be overstated. As with most other doctrines, a broader notion of unconscionability would inevitably lead to the laying down of more specific guidelines for determining its application. At the same time, there would be a more systematic approach to the development of the requisite principles which would avoid the current overlap and confusion arising from several related, but currently distinct doctrines. As Capper points out, a merged doctrine could actually lead to greater certainty because 'the courts might find it easier to develop clear and rational criteria for the resolution of these disputes': Capper, p 503. Phang has expressed himself in similar terms (p 571):

> If, indeed, this approach of amalgamation or consolidation is adopted, the many problems pertaining to linkages both amongst the various categories of undue influence as well as amongst the doctrines of duress, undue influence and unconscionability would vanish, and courts could set about the task of focusing their attention on bringing the new doctrine to legal maturity.

The point here is that, although the concept of unconscionability may be expressed in fairly broad terms, the courts would exercise the new jurisdiction according to well defined principles. This, as we have seen, is the approach taken in the Commonwealth jurisdictions, where the courts do not administer a general power to set aside transactions simply because, in the eyes of the judiciary, they appear to be harsh or unfair. On the contrary, far from acting in a wholly discretionary function, the courts have formulated specific tests for determining when a transaction should be set aside for unconscionability. There is no reason to suppose that a similar approach would not be adopted in this country.

8.6 CONCLUDING THOUGHTS

The law of undue influence is, clearly, not a 'world of neat and tidy rules'; on the contrary, an analysis of the modern case law reveals a highly technical and complex area of jurisprudence which is not always logical or consistent in its application.

SELECTION OF FORMS

The forms set out below (which are not intended to be exhaustive) are provided to assist the practitioner in the drafting of pleadings associated with undue influence claims. They should be treated merely as examples and not as standard precedents. The reader is referred to *Atkin's Court Forms*, 2nd edn, Vol 18(1), 2000 Issue, pp 417–20, 422–23, 433, 438–44; Vol 11(2), 1997 Issue, pp 291–92 and 295; and Vol 20, 1998 Issue, pp 239–43, for a further selection of useful forms in this area. These should now be read in the light of the guidance given by the House of Lords in *Royal Bank of Scotland v Etridge (No 2)* [2001] UKHL 44.

CONTENTS

PARTICULARS OF CLAIM

Mortgagee seeking possession of property, arrears and interest.

IN THE NONESUCH COUNTY COURT   Case No: NO7/01234

BETWEEN:

BOVINGTON BUILDING SOCIETY

Claimant

and

(1) HENRY SMITH
(2) SARAH SMITH

Defendants

PARTICULARS OF CLAIM

1   By a mortgage deed, dated 1 May 1998, and made between the Claimant of the one part and the Defendants of the other part, the freehold property known as 35 Luton Road, Bedford, Bedfordshire ('the property') was charged by the Defendants by way of legal mortgage in favour of the Claimant to secure the repayment to the Claimant of the sum of £100,000 together with interest as therein mentioned.

2   The mortgage was made in accordance with the covenants, conditions and stipulations contained in:

  (i)   the said mortgage deed;

  (ii)   the Claimant's Mortgage Offer, dated 2 April 1998; and

  (iii)   the Claimant's Mortgage Conditions (1998 Edition).

The Claimant will refer to these documents at the trial of this action for their full terms and effect.

3   By condition 7.1 of the said Mortgage Conditions, it is provided that s 103 of the Law of Property Act 1925[1] shall not apply to the mortgage and the statutory power of sale[2] shall be immediately exercisable by the Claimant in the event of, *inter alia*, the Defendants failing to pay any monthly payment or other payment due under the mortgage.

4   By condition 8.0 of the said Mortgage Conditions, it was provided that the Defendants pay in monthly instalments monies due under the mortgage.

5   By condition 8.1 of the said Mortgage Conditions, it was provided that monthly instalments due under the mortgage but not paid on the due date shall bear interest at the rate of interest payable under the mortgage for the time being.

6   The Defendants are in default of payment of the monthly instalments due under the mortgage.

PARTICULARS

The Defendants have failed to pay the monthly instalments due in January, February, March, April, May, June and July 2001.

7   The state of the account between the Claimant and the Defendants is as follows:

   (i)   The amount of the advance   £100,000

   (ii)   The amount of payments required to be made per month   £800

   (iii)   The amount of such instalments in arrears   £5,600

   (iv)   The amount remaining due under the mortgage   £90,000

   (v)   Current rate of interest at 6% per annum

   (vi)   Interest on the amount remaining due under the mortgage accruing at the rate of £14.79 per day

8   By a letter, dated 25 August 2001, the Claimant's Solicitors, Cartwrights, gave the Defendants seven days' notice within which to pay the said monthly instalments.

9   Notwithstanding the said letter, the Defendants have failed to pay the said monthly instalments or any part thereof.

---

1   This section regulates the mortgagee's exercise of its power of sale by requiring the service of a notice of payment of the mortgage money on the mortgagor. The power of sale is not exercisable until default has been made in payment for three months after service of the notice or some interest under the mortgage is in arrears and unpaid for two months after becoming due or there has been a breach of some other provision in the mortgage deed or in the 1925 Act.

2   See s 101(i) of the Law of Property Act 1925.

10 By reason of the matters aforesaid, the Claimant's statutory power of sale has become immediately exercisable and the Claimant is entitled to possession of the property.

11 The Claimant has not before the commencement of this action taken any proceedings against the Defendants in respect of the advance or interest due under the mortgage or in respect of the property.

12 The property consists of a dwelling-house within the meaning of s 21 of the County Courts Act 1984.

AND the Claimant claims:-

(1) payment of all monies due to the Claimant under the mortgage;

(2) in default of the parties agreeing the amount so due, all necessary accounts and enquiries;

(3) possession of the property;

(4) interest;

(5) further or other relief;

(6) costs.

Dated etc   TOM SMITH

STATEMENT OF TRUTH

I believe that the facts stated in these Particulars of Claim are true.

Signed ....

Full name: John Walters, Senior Accounts Manager, Bovington Building Society.

Address for receiving documents:

Cartwrights
23 Hosiery Lane
Luton
Bedfordshire
LX2 8QY
DX Luton 11

Solicitors for the Claimant.

DEFENCE AND COUNTERCLAIM

Wife alleging actual undue influence by husband. See *Bank of Credit and Commerce International SA v Aboody* [1992] 4 All ER 955 (CA). (It is likely that, in view of a wife's defence alleging undue influence, the mortgagee's claim for possession would be transferred to the High Court: see ss 41, 40(2), (3) and 42(2), (3) of the County Courts Act 1984. The matters which the court must have regard in deciding whether to order a transfer of proceedings are set out in r 30.3(2). In this connection, undue influence is the type of claim suitable for trial in the High Court.)

IN THE NONESUCH COUNTY COURT   Case No: NO7/01234

BETWEEN:

BOVINGTON BUILDING SOCIETY

Claimant

and

(1) HENRY SMITH
(2) SARAH SMITH

Defendants

DEFENCE AND COUNTERCLAIM OF THE SECOND DEFENDANT

DEFENCE

1   Paragraphs 1–9, 11 and 12 of the Particulars of Claim are admitted.

2   As to para 10 of the Particulars of Claim, it is denied that the statutory power of sale has become exercisable as alleged or otherwise as against

the Second Defendant. Further, it is denied that as against the Second Defendant, the Claimant is entitled to possession of the property, as alleged, or at all.

3   The Second Defendant avers that she was induced to enter into the mortgage transaction whilst acting under the actual undue influence of the First Defendant and that, therefore, she is not bound by the terms thereof.

4   Further, the Second Defendant avers that she entered into the mortgage transaction without knowing and/or appreciating the contents and true intention thereof.

PARTICULARS

(i)   The First and Second Defendants are, as the Claimant at all material times well knew, husband and wife having been married together since 20 January 1985.

(ii) Throughout the Defendants' marriage, the First Defendant has had the management and control of the Defendants' private finances and the Second Defendant has, at all material times, relied without question or inquiry upon the information given to her by the First Defendant as to financial matters generally and has deferred to the First Defendant's judgment in regard thereto without ever having had occasion prior to the matters giving rise to these proceedings to doubt or question the First Defendant's veracity or judgment in such matters.

(iii) The Second Defendant had, at all material times, placed complete faith, trust and confidence in the First Defendant and had never prior to the matters giving rise to these proceedings supposed nor had any reason to suppose that such faith, trust and confidence were not merited.

(iv) On 5 March 1998, the First Defendant applied for a mortgage with the Claimant in the sum of £100,000 to be secured on the matrimonial home of the First and Second Defendants, which was in their joint ownership.

(v) The purpose of the mortgage, which was known to the Claimant, was to provide capital to the First Defendant in his intended business venture as a restaurateur. The said purpose was expressed in the mortgage application form as completed in writing by the First Defendant and submitted to the Claimant.

(vi) The Claimant's mortgage offer, dated 2 April 1998, contained a written recommendation that the Second Defendant obtain independent legal advice as to the nature, terms and effect of the proposed mortgage transaction.

(vii) On 23 April 1998, the Second Defendant, accompanied by the First Defendant, attended the offices of Sturgeon and Co, a firm of solicitors, in order that the Second Defendant could be independently advised as to the nature, terms and effect of the proposed mortgage transaction ('the consultation').

(viii) A Mr Jones of the said solicitors' firm sought to advise the Second Defendant alone.

(ix) During the consultation, the First Defendant burst into the room, shouted at the Second Defendant and demanded she sign all relevant documents pertaining to the mortgage transaction. The Second Defendant did not read the said documents before signing them.

(x) At the time of the consultation and thereafter, the Second Defendant was placed under intimidatory and improper pressure by the First Defendant ('the undue influence').

5   The Second Defendant avers that the Claimant knew, at all material times, that the relationship between the First and Second Defendants was one of husband and wife. Accordingly, there was a clear and obvious risk that the First Defendant would exploit that relationship and exert undue influence upon the Second Defendant.

6   The Second Defendant avers that the said Mr Jones, in a letter dated 23 April 1998, informed the Claimant of the First Defendant's behaviour at the consultation with the Second Defendant. The Second Defendant will rely on this letter at trial for its full terms and effect.

7   By reason of the matters aforesaid, the Second Defendant avers that the Claimant had actual notice of the First Defendant's undue influence over the Second Defendant at the time the Second Defendant entered into the mortgage transaction.

8   The Claimant made no inquiries, or no sufficient inquiries, of the Second Defendant and took no steps, or no sufficient steps, to ensure that the Second Defendant understood the mortgage transaction or that the Second Defendant's consent thereto was free and informed.

9   Further, the Claimant made no attempt to meet the Second Defendant, whether separately from the First Defendant or at all, or to advise the Second Defendant as to the nature of the mortgage transaction.

10 In the premises, the Second Defendant is entitled to have the mortgage transaction set aside.

COUNTERCLAIM

11   Paragraphs 3–10 above are repeated herein.

AND the Second Defendant Counterclaims as against the Claimant:

(1)   an order that the mortgage transaction be set aside as between herself and the Claimant;

(2)   further or other relief;

(3)   costs.

Dated etc   HARRY JONES

STATEMENT OF TRUTH

I believe that the facts stated in this Defence and Counterclaim are true.

Signed…………………..

Full name: Sarah Smith

Address for receiving documents:

Goldstein, Roberts and Cohen
24 Turnpenny Road
London NE 27
DX London 56

Solicitors for the Second Defendant.

DEFENCE AND COUNTERCLAIM

Junior employee alleging presumed undue influence and unconscionable bargain and/or extortionate credit bargain under s 138 of the Consumer Credit Act 1974. See *Credit Lyonnais Bank Nederland NV v Burch* [1997] 1 All ER 144 (CA).

IN THE NONESUCH COUNTY COURT   Case No: NO/56789

BETWEEN:

BOLTON BANK LIMITED

Claimant

and

(1) JOHN JONES
(2) MARIA O'CONNOR

Defendants

DEFENCE AND COUNTERCLAIM OF THE SECOND DEFENDANT

DEFENCE

1   Paragraphs [   ] of the Particulars of Claim are admitted.

2   As to para [   ] of the Particulars of Claim, it is denied that the statutory power of sale has become exercisable as alleged, or otherwise, as against the Second Defendant. Further, it is denied that as against the Second Defendant, the Claimant is entitled to possession of the property, as alleged, or at all.

3   The Second Defendant avers that she was induced to enter into the charge whilst acting under the presumed undue influence of the First Defendant and that, therefore, she is not bound by the terms thereof.

4 Further, the Second Defendant avers that she entered into the charge without knowing and/or appreciating the contents and true intention thereof or the manifestly disadvantageous consequences of so doing.

PARTICULARS

(i) The Second Defendant, as the Claimant at all material times well knew, was the employee of the First Defendant in the position of a receptionist working at a sports club known as the Kingsley Sports Club and Health Spa ('the business'), which was owned and run by the First Defendant. The Second Defendant, to the knowledge of the Claimant, had no interest in the business save her salaried position as a receptionist.

(ii) As from January 1997, the First Defendant and Second Defendant became close friends and the relationship became one where the Second Defendant came to repose trust and confidence in the First Defendant.

(iii)In or around early February 1998, the First Defendant verbally requested the Second Defendant to provide £50,000 to refinance the business, and told the Second Defendant that he did not have the means to raise the said monies.

(iv)In or around late March 1998, the Second Defendant informed the First Defendant that she would charge her home ('the property') in the sum of £50,000 in order to provide the business with the capital required.

(v) The charge application form as completed in writing by the Second Defendant and submitted to the Claimant expressed the purpose of the loan to be in order to provide the First Defendant with the capital he required for his business.

(vi)The charge was to the Second Defendant's manifest disadvantage in that it was for the sole and exclusive benefit of the First Defendant.

5 The Second Defendant avers that the Claimant, at all material times, knew that the relationship between First and Second Defendants was one of employer and employee. Accordingly, there was a clear and obvious risk that the First Defendant would exploit that relationship and exert undue influence upon the Second Defendant.

6 By reason of the matters aforesaid, the Claimant was put on inquiry and on constructive notice of the possibility of undue influence, and of its exercise by the First Defendant on the Second Defendant.

7   The Claimant made no inquiries, or no sufficient inquiries, of the Second Defendant and took no steps, or no sufficient steps, to ensure that the Second Defendant understood the charge or that the Second Defendant's consent thereto was free and informed.

8   Further, the Claimant made no attempt to meet the Second Defendant, whether separately from the First Defendant or at all, or to advise the Second Defendant as to the nature of the proposed charge, or to recommend the Second Defendant to take independent legal advice.

9   Further or alternatively, the Second Defendant avers that the charge is an unconscionable bargain and not binding on her.

PARTICULARS

(i)   By Clause 8.5 of the Charge Conditions, the annual percentage rate of interest payable under the mortgage transaction is 58%.

(ii) By Clause 9.2 of the said Conditions, redemption within the period of the first four years of the term of the mortgage is prohibited.

(iii) The Second Defendant is a woman of modest means and inexperienced in financial or business matters.

(iv) The Second Defendant did not seek nor obtain any independent legal advice prior to entering into the charge.

10 The Second Defendant will aver that the First Defendant knowingly took advantage of her lack of financial and business experience in obtaining her consent to the charge and the Claimant acted unconscionably in accepting her consent thereto which was so heavily unbalanced.

11 Further or alternatively, the Second Defendant avers that the charge is, by virtue of its terms, an extortionate credit bargain within the meaning of s 138 of the Consumer Credit Act 1974.

PARTICULARS

The Second Defendant repeats sub-paras (i) and (ii) of the Particulars contained in para 9 hereof.

12 In the premises, the Second Defendant is entitled to have the charge set aside.

COUNTERCLAIM

13   Paragraphs 3–12 above are repeated herein.

AND the Second Defendant Counterclaims against the Claimant:

  (i)   an order that the charge be set aside as between herself and the Claimant;

 (ii)   further or other relief;

(iii)   costs.

Dated etc   HARRY JONES

STATEMENT OF TRUTH

I believe that the facts stated in this Defence and Counterclaim are true.

Signed...............

Full name: Maria O'Connor

Address for receiving documents:

Playgate and Co
Solicitors
35 Marble Road
London NW20
DX London 24

Solicitors for the Second Defendant.

DEFENCE AND COUNTERCLAIM

Cohabitee alleging presumed undue influence and/or misrepresentation by partner.

IN THE NONESUCH COUNTY COURT   Case No: NO/03456

BETWEEN:

FIRST CLASS BANK PLC

Claimant

and

(1) MICHAEL JONES
(2) AMANDA WATT

Defendants

DEFENCE AND COUNTERCLAIM OF THE SECOND DEFENDANT

DEFENCE

1   Paragraphs [   ] of the Particulars of Claim are admitted.
2   As to para [   ] of the Particulars of Claim, it is denied that the statutory power of sale has become exercisable as alleged, or otherwise, as against the Second Defendant. Further, it is denied that as against the Second Defendant, the Claimant is entitled to possession of the property, as alleged or at all.
3   Further, the Second Defendant avers that she was induced into the mortgage transaction whilst acting under the presumed undue influence and/or misrepresentation of the First Defendant and that, therefore, she is not bound by the terms thereof.
4   Further, the Second Defendant avers that she entered into the mortgage transaction without knowing or appreciating the contents and true

intention thereof and/or the manifestly disadvantageous consequences of so doing.

PARTICULARS

(i) The First and Second Defendants, as the Claimant at all material times well knew, were living together as if husband and wife and the Second Defendant reposed trust and confidence in the First Defendant and was content to leave all financial affairs concerning the property to the First Defendant.

(ii) On 12 March 1998, the First and Second Defendants applied for a mortgage with the Claimant to be secured on the property.

(iii) At all material times, the property was in the joint ownership of the First and Second Defendants.

(iv) The purpose of the mortgage, which was known to the Claimant, was to provide capital to the First Defendant in his intended business as a travel agent.

(v) The mortgage transaction was to the Second Defendant's manifest disadvantage in that it was for the First Defendant's sole and exclusive benefit.

5   Further or alternatively, the Second Defendant was induced to enter into the mortgage transaction by reason of and in reliance upon the material misrepresentations made to her by the First Defendant.

PARTICULARS

In or around April 1998, the First Defendant orally represented to the Second Defendant that the purpose of the mortgage transaction was to secure the advance of £100,000 whereas, in fact, the mortgage transaction was an all monies charge, unlimited in time and amount.

6   The Second Defendant avers that the Claimant, at all material times, knew that the relationship between the First and Second Defendants was one of the parties living together as if husband and wife. Accordingly, there was a clear and obvious risk that the First Defendant would exploit that relationship and exert undue influence upon the Second Defendant.

7   The Claimant's mortgage offer, dated 12 April 1998, contained a written recommendation by the Claimant that the Second Defendant obtain independent legal advice as to the nature, terms and effect of the proposed mortgage transaction.

8   Despite receiving and reading the said letter, the Second Defendant did not seek, nor obtain, any independent legal advice.

9   The Second Defendant avers that, at no time prior to the Second Defendant entering into the mortgage transaction, did the Claimant receive confirmation to the effect that the Second Defendant had received independent legal advice.

10 By reason of the matters aforesaid, the Claimant was put on inquiry and on constructive notice of the possibility of undue influence, and of its exercise, by the First Defendant on the Second Defendant in that:

    (1) The Claimant was, at all material times, aware of the relationship between the First and Second Defendant and was by that knowledge affected by notice of the risk that the Second Defendant might in exploitation of that relationship be subject to undue influence on the part of the First Defendant.

    (2) The Claimant was, at all material times, aware that the mortgage transaction was to the First Defendant's sole and exclusive benefit.

    (3) The Claimant failed to make reasonable or any inquiry and failed to take reasonable or any steps to satisfy itself that the Second Defendant entered into the mortgage transaction freely with full or requisite knowledge.

11 In the premises, the Second Defendant denies that she is indebted to the Claimant as alleged or at all and denies that the Claimant is entitled to enforce the mortgage transaction against the Second Defendant or is entitled as against the Second Defendant to the relief claimed or at all.

COUNTERCLAIM

12 Paragraphs 3–11 above are repeated herein.

AND the Second Defendant Counterclaims against the Claimant:

    (i) an order that the mortgage transaction be set aside as between herself and the Claimant;

    (ii) further or other relief;

    (iii) costs.

Dated etc   HARRY JONES

STATEMENT OF TRUTH

I believe that the facts stated in this Defence and Counterclaim are true.

Signed ……………………….

Full name: Amanda Watt

Address for receiving documents:

Crystal, Blake and Blake
Solicitors
London NE26
DX London 28

Solicitors for the Second Defendant.

REPLY

Mortgagee alleging delay and affirmation. See *Goldsworthy v Brickell* [1987] 1 Ch 378 (CA). (See Form 2, above.)

IN THE NONESUCH COUNTY COURT   Case No: NO/01234

BETWEEN:

BOVINGTON BUILDING SOCIETY

Claimant

and

(1) HENRY SMITH
(2) SARAH SMITH

Defendants

REPLY TO DEFENCE OF THE SECOND DEFENDANT

1   As to paras 3, 4 and 7 of the Defence and Counterclaim of the Second Defendant, if, which is denied, the Second Defendant was induced to enter into the mortgage transaction whilst acting under the actual undue influence of the First Defendant, the Claimant avers that the said transaction has been affirmed by the Second Defendant and ought not to be set aside by reason of the matters hereinafter set out.

PARTICULARS

(i) The Second Defendant was fully aware of the nature, terms and effect of the mortgage transaction by mid-May 1998, during which time, the Second Defendant had received verbal advice in relation to the mortgage transaction from her brother, Simon Lewis, an accountant.

(ii) With knowledge of the nature, terms and effect of the mortgage transaction, the Second Defendant remained content to make payment of the sums due under the mortgage to the Claimant.

2   Further, or alternatively, the Claimant avers that rescission should not be ordered because, from mid-May 1998, the Second Defendant was fully aware of the nature, terms and effect of the mortgage transaction and has unreasonably delayed in seeking an order for rescission.

Dated etc   TOM SMITH

STATEMENT OF TRUTH

I believe that the facts stated in this Reply to Defence of the Second Defendant are true.

Signed..........................

Full name: John Walters, Senior Accounts Manager, Bovington Building Society

Address for receiving documents:

Cartwrights
23 Hosiery Lane
Luton
Bedfordshire
LX2 8QY
DX Luton 11

Solicitors for the Claimant.

APPLICATION

Husband's trustee in bankruptcy seeking order for sale of property under s 14 of the Trusts of Land and Appointment of Trustees Act 1996.

IN THE NONESUCH COUNTY COURT   Case No: NO/02456

In Bankruptcy
Re Timothy Wood, a Bankrupt

The TRUSTEE IN BANKRUPTCY of the property
Of the above-named Bankrupt

Applicant

and

TIMOTHY WOOD

First Respondent

SAMANTHA WOOD

Second Respondent

LET Timothy Wood and Samantha Wood of 15 Church Street, Maidstone, Kent M12 B34, attend the Nonesuch County, 35 Court Road, Maidstone, Kent, before his Honour Judge Smythe on:

Date: 17 December 2001
Time: 10.30 am
Place: Nonesuch County Court

On the hearing of the application by William Boyce (the trustee in bankruptcy) for an order in the following terms:

1.   a declaration as to the respective interests of the First and Second Respondents in that freehold property ('the property') known as and situated at 15 Church Street, Maidstone, Kent M12 B34, registered in the joint names of Timothy Wood and Samantha Wood at HM Land Registry under Title Number WK12345;

2.   an order that the property be sold and that the First and Second Respondents and each of them do concur in such sale;

3.   an order that the conduct of such sale be given to the Applicant;

4.   an order that the First and Second Respondents and each of them should join with the Applicant and do all such things as may be necessary to procure the said sale of the property with vacant possession;

5.   an order that the First and Second Respondents and each of them do forthwith deliver up vacant possession of the property to the Applicant;

6.   an order that the net proceeds of sale of the property be divided and paid to the Applicant and to the Second Respondent in such shares as this Honourable Court shall think fit pursuant to the declaration contained in para 1 hereof;

7.   an order that the First and Second Respondents do pay the Applicant's costs of this Application;

8.   the grounds upon which the Applicant claims to be entitled to the order are:

The Applicant, being the trustee in bankruptcy of the First Respondent, wishes to realise the property through sale in order that the First Respondent's share of the property can be distributed amongst the creditors of the First Respondent.

The names and addresses of the persons upon whom it is intended to serve this application are:

(i)   Timothy Wood, 15 Church Street, Maidstone, Kent M12 B34

(ii)   Samantha Wood, 15 Church Street, Maidstone, Kent M12 B34

Signature............................

The Applicant's address for service is:

Booty and Dent
Accountants
12 Wiltshire Road
London SE8 1XY
DX

Bloom and Co
12 Casterbridge Road
London SE15 6TE

Solicitors for the Applicant
Dated..............2002

NOTE: If you do not attend the Court may make such order as it thinks fit.

ANSWER

Wife seeking postponement of sale on grounds of exceptional circumstances. See *Judd v Brown* [1998] 2 FLR 360; *Re Ravel* [1998] 2 FLR 718; and *Claughton v Charalamabous* [1999] 1 FLR 740.

IN THE NONESUCH COUNTY COURT   Case No: NO/02456

In Bankruptcy
Re Timothy Wood, a Bankrupt

The TRUSTEE IN BANKRUPTCY of the property
of the above-named Bankrupt

Applicant

and

TIMOTHY WOOD

First Respondent

SAMANTHA WOOD

Second Respondent

I, Samantha Wood of 15 Church Street, Maidstone, Kent M12 B34, the Second Respondent in this matter, in answer to the application of the Trustee in Bankruptcy of the First Respondent for an order for sale of the aforementioned property ('the property') say that:

1   The property is my family and matrimonial home and is owned jointly and equally by myself and my husband (the First Respondent).

2   I have lived in the property for seven years with the First Respondent and my three children; three girls, aged 3, 6 and 9.

3   The property is situated close to the primary school where the oldest two of my children are in attendance.

4   I work part time as a dental nurse. I am 38 years of age. Last year, I was diagnosed with lung cancer. I am currently undergoing a course of chemotherapy which is likely to continue for six months. It is likely that I will have to undergo major surgery within the next year. I have been told by my doctor that my chances of recovery will be damaged by stress if my home is sold. I believe that my health problems are unlikely to be resolved in the foreseeable future and I am very concerned about the emotional stress associated with an impending move if the property is sold.

5   In the light of the foregoing, I would ask this Honourable Court to refuse an order for the sale of the property, or alternatively, grant a stay of any order for sale of the property. An immediate sale of the property would cause exceptional hardship and inconvenience to myself and my family.

Dated etc   HENRY JONES

STATEMENT OF TRUTH

I believe the facts stated in this Answer are true.

Full name: SAMANTHA WOOD

                              Signature..........................

Address for receiving documents:

Schmidt and Co
Woodside House
Lonsdale Road
London SW6

DX London 14

Solicitors for the Second Respondent.

DECLARATION AS TO BENEFICIAL INTEREST OF BANKRUPT'S PROPERTY AND ORDER FOR SALE

IN THE NONESUCH COUNTY COURT   Case No: NO/02465

In Bankruptcy
Before his Honour Judge Wisdom
Re Timothy Wood, a Bankrupt

The TRUSTEE IN BANKRUPTCY of the property
of the above-named Bankrupt

Applicant

TIMOTHY WOOD

First Respondent

SAMANTHA WOOD

Second Respondent

Date: 17 December 2001

UPON THE APPLICATION of William Boyce (hereinafter called 'the Applicant')

AND UPON HEARING Counsel for the Applicant and Counsel for Samantha Wood (hereinafter called 'the Second Respondent')

AND UPON READING the documents recorded on the Court file

THIS COURT DECLARES that the Second Respondent is entitled to an equal beneficial interest in the freehold property ('the property') known as and situated at 15 Church Street, Maidstone, Kent M12 B34, registered in the joint names of the First and Second Respondents at HM Land Registry under Title Number WK12345, or the net proceeds thereof.

AND IT IS ORDERED:

1 that the property be sold at the expiration of three years from the date of this order;

2 that the conduct of the sale be committed to Bloom & Co, the Solicitors for the Applicant;

3 that [   ] be at liberty to bid for or become the purchaser of the property at the said sale;

4 that the proceeds of sale after payment thereout of what shall be due to any incumbrancers according to their priorities and of all proper costs, charges and expenses incurred in connection with the said sale be divided as to 50% to the Applicant and 50% to the Second Respondent; and

5 that the costs of the Applicant be determined by way of detailed assessment and be paid out of the bankrupt's estate.

AND the parties are to be at liberty to apply: (a) for further directions with regard to the said sale; and (b) generally.

INDEX